AlphaBrain

AlphaBrain

*How a Group of Iconoclasts
Are Using Cognitive Science
to Advance the Business
of Alpha Generation*

Stephen Duneier

WILEY

Published by John Wiley & Sons, Inc., Hoboken, New Jersey.
Published simultaneously in Canada.

For general information on our other products and services or for technical support, please contact our Customer Care Department within the United States at (800) 762-2974, outside the United States at (317) 572-3993, or fax (317) 572-4002.

Wiley publishes in a variety of print and electronic formats and by print-on-demand. Some material included with standard print versions of this book may not be included in e-books or in print-on-demand. If this book refers to media such as a CD or DVD that is not included in the version you purchased, you may download this material at http://booksupport.wiley.com. For more information about Wiley products, visit www.wiley.com.

Library of Congress Cataloging-in-Publication Data is Available

ISBN 978-1-119-33556-6 (Hardcover)
ISBN 978-1-119-33592-4 (ePDF)
ISBN 978-1-119-33591-7 (ePub)

Cover Design: Wiley
Cover Images: © aleksandarvelasevic / DigitalVision Vectors / Getty Images;
© a-r-t-i-s- / DigitalVision Vectors / Getty Images

Printed in the United States of America.
V10007139_122618

To my wife, Barbara, my daughter, Masie, and my son, Jackson, who will never stop helping me find my swing.

Contents

Preface

I began my career in finance in 1987 as a stockbroker at Drexel Burnham, back in the days of Michael Milken. I then traded exotic derivatives at Credit Suisse before there were standard pricing models. I ran currency option trading globally for Bank of America and emerging markets for AIG International. I spent 12 years as a global macro hedge fund portfolio manager, directly overseeing as much as $916 million in assets under management, and I founded and ran two hedge funds.

At about the same time I entered the industry, I began studying the cognitive sciences, particularly behavioral psychology and decision theory. So, as I was developing my own style, my own unique approach to investment and business management, I would apply everything I was learning about how the brain works, how we approach problems and make decisions to solve them.

As it turns out, when you do that, you wind up doing things very differently than most. But it wasn't just the approach that made me unique; it was the results it delivered that truly set me apart. For instance, in the first 12 months after I took over at Bank of America, we increased revenues by 70% without increasing costs at all. We did so on the back of a marginal adjustment to the way we made decisions as a group. In my first year running emerging markets for AIG International, we went from being the worst performing unit in the business to the best, as a result of a marginal adjustment to the way we approached problems. Over a 12-year career as a global macro hedge fund manager, I generated 20.3% average annualized returns spanning quiet markets, high-volatility periods, and chaotic moments, with a Sortino ratio that was twice my Sharpe.

When I took the helm at one hedge fund, we were on the brink of failure. We had let go all nonessential personnel, cut salaries to the bone, and hadn't raised a penny in assets since launch nor made a penny for our investors. Over the next 13 months, we increased assets under management 12-fold, from $100 million to $1.25 billion, beat our benchmark index by 2500 basis points net of fees, and every single portfolio manager had his career best year – all because of a few marginal adjustments to our decision-making process.

As happy as I have been with the results, anyone who has studied decision-making knows that what I've just listed are *outcomes*. We don't control outcomes. What we do control are all the tiny little decisions that we make along the way. Decisions that must be made rationally in order to improve the odds of achieving the outcomes we desire.

The majority of books on the subject of cognitive science focus on presenting evidence of our flaws. I don't want to discount the value of that evidence. It is essential material, for unless we accept that we are all susceptible to bias and other shortcomings that unconsciously lead to systematic errors in judgment, it is nearly impossible to overcome it. If you can't overcome it, you are as good as you will ever be.

AlphaBrain differs from the other books in that it applies these abstract, seemingly academic concepts to the industry of institutional investment management, but takes it one step further. Rather than simply make readers aware of our flaws, we will explore actual solutions to real world problems. Instead of reading yet another book on cognitive bias, then setting it down and going about your business in exactly the same way as you had been, you should expect to set the book down numerous times in order to contemplate your own actions as an institutional investor, and begin implementing real change. In order for that to happen, for you to experience a leap forward in the evolution of your decision-making, I must first convince you that you are as vulnerable to those mistakes as every other human being. The fact that you are likely very intelligent, well educated, experienced, and perhaps successful already, it makes my job that much more difficult.

I know from experience how difficult it is to read the works of Kahneman, Ariely, and Tversky, and see yourself as their flawed subjects, but until you do, the odds of you actually learning from it and experiencing that leap forward are drastically reduced. Let me share with you how I made the leap.

How a Mistake Made Me a Better Investor

Daniel Kahneman, one of the leading experts in cognitive psychology and author of some of the most widely read books on the subject, discusses the futility of teaching his findings in a section of *Thinking, Fast and Slow*, titled "Can Psychology Be Taught?" You'll have to read the book to learn why he came to "the uncomfortable conclusion that teaching psychology is mostly a waste of time," but I will share with you how I arrived at that same conclusion, as well as the mistake I made more than 20 years ago that enabled me to break through the barrier, shifting from a spectator to a practitioner.

One of the fundamental tenets of cognitive psychology is that we essentially have two systems at work in our brain. Kahneman calls them "System 1 and System 2," although Richard Thaler and Cass Sunstein refer to them as "Planner and Doer." What you call them isn't nearly as important as recognizing that there is a part of your cognition that is automated, intuitive, and quick to draw conclusions, whereas the other part is more deliberate, methodical, and intellectually demanding. When you read about these abstract characters, you may or may not agree that they relate to you, but you undoubtedly recognize their existence in others. Even if you do see these two distinct systems playing a role in your decision-making, it's unlikely you could do so in real time. Of course, with the benefit of hindsight, your task is made much simpler.

If your decision resulted in an unfavorable outcome, you are likely to attribute the decision to System 1 thinking, a temporary lapse in judgment, bad luck, or perhaps another person. If the result is positive, of course, we rarely seek an external source to apportion credit, least of all, luck.

In the moment, though, when we are gathering information, interpreting it, processing it, drawing conclusions from it or making decisions based upon it, it is almost impossible for us to recognize whether we are employing mental shortcuts that are likely to result in a systematic error in judgment or if we are objectively analyzing the situation, drawing upon our wealth of knowledge and experience to reach a thoughtful conclusion. I mean, how do you define an action as *dogmatic* versus *disciplined*, before the outcome is known? How do you differentiate between an impulsive decision and one based on educated intuition until after the result is experienced? The truth is, although the difference may appear glaringly obvious with the benefit of hindsight, it can only truly be objectively judged at the moment of inception. Those who have difficulty coming to terms with that subtle, yet significant difference likely have a great distance to cover before becoming practitioners of cognitive science themselves.

So, how was I able to make the leap from someone who had spent years simply studying the cognitive sciences to becoming a practitioner? I owe it all to my mother-in-law and a simple mistake I made on March 24, 1994. I know the exact date because it occurred in the hospital, one day after my first child was born. My mother-in-law asked if I'd like something for lunch and I gave her my order. Forty-five minutes later, she returned, handing me a sandwich and saying, "Here's your veal parmigiana hero." My hand automatically jerked away. "I didn't order a veal parmigiana hero," I stated emphatically. She insisted I had and we went back and forth before I finally introduced reason to the rhetoric.

I explained that while the veal parmigiana hero had been one of my favorite foods as a kid, after seeing a video years earlier which showed how calves are treated in order to make veal, I had made a conscious decision never to eat veal again – which is how I knew beyond the shadow of a doubt that I hadn't ordered a veal parmigiana hero this time. She apologized, I skipped lunch, and life went on.

A few months later my wife and I looked through pictures from the birth, as well as video we had taken around that time. That's when my life changed forever. It turns out that someone had been taking video in the room when I gave my lunch order. On the screen, I saw a person who looked just like me, and who sounded just like me say to my mother-in-law, "I'll have a veal parmigiana hero, please." It was like an out-of-body experience. I get chills to this day when I think about it. Immediately, my mind attempted to make sense of it all. *Someone dubbed over my voice. Someone doctored the tape. Someone went to a lot of trouble to make me look foolish.* The truth, of course, was a whole lot simpler, and there was no getting around it. In that moment when I had ordered the sandwich, my mind was engaged elsewhere, and that left System 1 or the "Doer" alone to hear the question, interpret it, process it, and answer it, all without me even being aware. You see, veal occupied a much greater portion of my memory than did eggplant. Avoiding veal was a conscious decision, but on that day my choice had been made unconsciously, even though I was wide awake and conversing. The result was a mistake, a poor decision, yet I had no idea I had made it and without the video evidence I would forever believe I was in the right and my mother-in-law had been at fault.

That was the last time I have ever felt 100% sure about anything that relied on my memory. It's also the moment when I truly understood what Kahneman, Thaler, Sunstein, and others meant in all those books, and rather than treating mistakes like these as remote possibilities, I came to see them as facts of life. If I was going to avoid them, I would have to make my vulnerability a fundamental part of my assumptions, and make the appropriate adjustments to my decision-making process.

Acknowledgments

My first debt in life goes to my loving parents, Fred and Shelly Duneier. The book's dedication records my boundless love for my wife, son, and daughter. I will forever be grateful to my sister, Michelle Duneier Donner, and her husband, Craig Donner; my sister, Allison Duneier Cohen, and her husband, Todd Cohen.

I am also filled with appreciation for my sister and brother-in-law, Jackie Ripps Fodiman and Robert Fodiman; my brother-in-law, Richie Ripps; my late mother-in-law, Ginny Ripps; and my father-in-law, Marvin Ripps, and his wife, Gloria Ripps. My nieces and nephews deserve special thanks: Matt, Caitlin, and Garrett Donner; Kendall and Devon Cohen; Sydney, Ray, and Morgan Fodiman.

In each stage of my life I was fortunate to have acquired a true friend: Eric Wesch, Matt Haudenschield, Anders Faergemann, Lynda Kestenbaum, and Warren & Melissa Matthews.

For his expertise, thank you to my cousin Mitchell Duneier. In bringing this book to life against all odds, I thank my esteemed colleague, Jake Vincent. The book could not have been completed without his brilliance. Christina Verigan of John Wiley & Sons encouraged me to pursue this project. Her extraordinary support, wise advice, and editorial touch were indispensable. She was the greatest editor I could ever hope for.

Finally, I wish to thank my fiber arts community, my Bija Advisors clients and subscribers, my faculty colleagues at UCSB, and my students over many years for taking the red pill with me.

About the Author

For nearly 30 years, Stephen Duneier has applied cognitive science to investment and business management. The result has been the turnaround of numerous institutional trading businesses, career best returns for experienced portfolio managers who have adopted his methods, the development of a $1.25 billion hedge fund, and 20.3% average annualized returns as a global macro portfolio manager. A visiting professor of decision analysis and behavioral investing in the College of Engineering at the University of California, Santa Barbara, Duneier holds an MBA from New York University's Stern School of Business.

Through Bija Advisors' coaching, workshops, and publications, he helps the world's most successful and experienced institutional investors improve performance by applying proven, proprietary decision-making methods to their own processes.

Duneier was formerly global head of currency option trading at Bank of America, managing director in charge of emerging markets at AIG International, and founding partner of award winning hedge funds.

Duneier's artwork has been featured in international publications and on television programs around the world. It is represented by the renowned gallery, Sullivan Goss, and has earned him more than

60,000 followers across social media, as well as a Guinness world record. As Commissioner of the League of Professional Educators, Duneier is using cognitive science to alter the landscape of American K–12 education.

As a speaker, he has delivered informative and inspirational talks to audiences around the world for more than 20 years on topics including how cognitive science can improve performance and the keys to living a more deliberate life.

Duneier is originally from Long Island, New York, and has lived with his wife, Barbara, and their two children in London and Santa Barbara.

A study of one hundred incorrect diagnoses found that inadequate medical knowledge was the reason for error in only four instances. The doctors didn't stumble because of their ignorance of clinical facts; rather, they missed diagnoses because they fell into cognitive traps. Such errors produce a distressingly high rate of misdiagnosis.

—Jerome Groopman, MD, *author of* How Doctors Think

Yep. Inside each and every one of us is one true authentic swing. Somethin' we was born with. Somethin' that's ours and ours alone. Somethin' that can't be taught to ya or learned. Somethin' that's got to be remembered. Over time the world can rob us of that swing. It gets buried inside us.

—The Legend of Bagger Vance

Part I

Decision Analysis

Chapter 1

Marginal Improvement, Significant Impact

Decision-Making as a Skill

What we do as human beings is make decisions. Whether we are investment managers, athletes, parents, or students, the one true commonality we share is the decision itself. Regardless of the implications, who is making the decision or the field in which it is being made, the decision-making process always has the same basic components and should always follow the same path.

Decision-making is a skill. In fact, I would argue it is *the* skill that we humans possess. However, it is rarely understood to be the underlying source of all other more readily identifiable skills. Instead, we look at a tennis player and think, he is skilled at swinging a racquet or chasing down balls. We look at a politician and think, she is particularly adept at negotiating or salesmanship. We think of successful fund managers and attribute their success to their ability to identify patterns or steel their nerves under pressure. In reality, steeling your nerves is a decision, a skill that can be taught and learned. Swinging a racquet properly

3

and influencing others are decisions as well. They can be taught and learned. They can be practiced and improved via the decision-making process. When you truly grasp this concept, and are able to properly frame everything by the decision, to view the world through the lens of the decision-making process, you come to realize that in order to truly excel at anything in life, both personally and professionally, you must focus on the decision as a problem to be solved.

A professional athlete cannot simply turn off the decision-making process when they aren't on the playing field. To make optimal decisions at the baseline, they must make the right nutritional decisions, practice decisions, footwork decisions, rest decisions, investment decisions, coaching decisions, and so on, even when they are nowhere near the court. To be world-class tennis stars, they must analyze their decisions, refine them, gather data on them, and approach them deliberately. It is a 24/7 job to reach and maintain their positions as among the greatest players of all time. Same goes for surgeons, actors, and yes, investors.

Becoming a world-class decision maker isn't a 9-to-5 job, it is a lifestyle. It requires not just practice, but repeated, deliberate practice. The kind that requires the employment of cognitive strain, a concept we will return to over and over again throughout this book. It is challenging. It requires sacrifice and a significant investment of time and effort. *AlphaBrain* is fundamentally a book about how to improve your decision-making as it applies to institutional investing, but the concepts and the science behind it are applicable to any one of the millions of decisions made on a daily basis by every single one of us in every aspect of our lives.

Spectators in Our Own Decisions

Far more often than any of us would like to believe, we are mere spectators in the decisions we make, even in decisions of great consequence. If we are spectators in the decisions we make, it means we are bystanders, as opposed to the active participants we perceive ourselves to be, in the investments we make, the businesses we run, and even the lives we lead.

I know what you are thinking. You're smart, highly educated, experienced, and very successful. What I am saying doesn't apply to you. As it happens, not only don't those qualities keep us from being spectators or grant us immunity from the problems it can cause, but they often make us even more vulnerable. I understand it may be a difficult pill to swallow, so let's consider a study that might help prove the point.

Professors Brian Wansink and Junyong Kim conducted an experiment among north Philadelphia's moviegoers. To half the participants, they provided a free large bucket of popcorn while the other half received a very large bucket. Half of each group were provided fresh delicious-tasting popcorn. The other half received 14-day-old stale popcorn which participants later rated a 2 out of 10.

If we are rational decision-makers there are only two primary reasons for us to consume food: we eat to be satiaed and/or because it tastes good. Therefore, if we are active participants in the decisions we make, the size of the portion should not affect how much we eat but the perceived taste should. As it happens, those who received the fresh, delicious tasting popcorn in a very large bucket ate just over 40% more than those who received it in the smaller container. On the other hand, those who were provided with popcorn that they themselves described as "terrible" and "disgusting" in a very large bucket, consumed just under 40% more than those who ate it from the smaller one.

Dr. Wansink has conducted numerous experiments of a similar nature, the most famous one involving bottomless bowls of soup, always delivering similar results. Regardless of the fact that we are awake and aware when faced with choices, very often we don't actively participate in the decisions we make.

Perhaps you are thinking that the poor snacking habits of moviegoers falls short of proving that we are spectators in decisions of great consequence. After all, we go to the movies to escape the real world, so perhaps it's only natural that we would leave our rational decision-maker hat at home for those couple of hours. Before you summarily dismiss studies regarding eating habits of any kind though, consider this. Excess weight and obesity play a role in roughly 80% of all American deaths and disabilities.

In any event, let's turn our attention to a rather well-known study involving the entire adult populations of some of the most advanced and highly educated countries in the world as it relates to a decision most would perceive to be of great consequence. Johnson gathered data regarding countrywide organ-donor participation rates across a number of major Western European countries. In Denmark he found that just 4% of the country's adult population had elected to donate their organs upon death. Meanwhile, right across the bay in Sweden, the participation rate was 86%. Fourteen percent of the citizens of the United Kingdom had volunteered their body parts while just across the English Channel nearly 100% of the French had done so. Perhaps most surprisingly, while only 12% of the German population was willing to donate their internal organs, Austria, a country that shares a language and so many cultural aspects with Germany, and separated only by an imaginary line on the ground, had a participation rate of roughly 100%.

The question that must be asked is, how could the overwhelming majority of the populations in countries that enjoy so many cultural similarities and are geographically connected arrive at polar opposite conclusions regarding a decision of such great consequence? The answer is really quite simple, and yet astonishing. They all approach decisions in exactly the same way. Sounds counterintuitive, right? After all, every individual is considering the same set of relevant factors and has the same two options from which to choose, so how can it be that they could all consider those factors in the same way and yet arrive at polar opposite conclusions?

As it turns out, the countries with low participation rates run "opt-in" programs. In those countries, if you do not take action (i.e., make a decision), you will not be an organ donor. On the other hand, those with very high participation rates run "opt-out" programs, meaning if you do not take action you *will* be an organ donor. In other words, the common bond shared by the great majority of these predominantly educated decision-makers in some of the most advanced nations on earth is that the overwhelming majority of them are little more than spectators in at least some of their own decisions, even decisions of great consequence.

Of course, if you were to stop an average Austrian on the streets of Vienna, show them these statistics and ask, "Why is it that Austrians are so giving, so selfless?" You can be sure they would tell you about their culture of kindness and compassion. What is very unlikely is that they would tell you the answer is simply that the majority of Austrians don't participate in their own decisions but instead let others choose for them. And yet, that is the reality.

This is significant because if we aren't actively participating in decisions such as how much popcorn we eat or whether to donate our organs, yet these decisions are being made, then someone else must be making them for us. In effect, we are outsourcing some our most important decisions to people and institutions we haven't vetted, typically without even realizing it. For many of your most important decisions, regardless of whether you realize it or not, you aren't the decision-maker. In the case of the free popcorn, the most influential person in the decision-making process isn't the moviegoer, but rather it is the person who decides the size of the bucket. For the hundreds of millions of adults around the world who are or are not organ donors, the most influential person in the decision was not the potential donor, but the person who framed the question as opt-in or opt-out. Consider that for a moment. The difference between hundreds of millions of lives being saved versus lost is affected by individuals who no one knows, no one voted into office, and no one vetted for their qualifications and beliefs. In fact, it's very likely even they don't appreciate the power they wield. After all, everyone is free to make their own choice. The question maker's only input is to ask, "If you would like to be an organ donor, check here" versus "If you would not like to be an organ donor, check here."

When studies like these brought to light just how little decision-makers participate in their own choices, it was a game changer. Whereas in the past, corporations and government entities would attempt to educate workers on things like the value of saving for retirement and rainy days, it became apparent there is a much more effective and efficient way to get people to make decisions in their own best interest while still allowing them to exercise free will. Simply reframe the question when they enroll in savings plans. Rather than asking if they'd like to participate in a savings plan, the default is to deduct the maximum amount from their paycheck each month. If they would like to opt out, they must check a box. That seemingly inconsequential adjustment can be the difference between an entire population needing a government-funded social safety net or not.

What we've discovered as a result of decades of research in the cognitive sciences is that humans make decisions in fairly predictable ways, where even the smartest, most educated, experienced, and successful among us are unconsciously affected by things that have the potential to produce systematic errors in our judgment. Marketers are well aware of this and have been capitalizing on it for generations. Now that policymakers have become aware of this tendency as well, attempts are being made to influence the decisions of their constituents to help them make decisions that are in their own best interest simply by reframing the way decision problems are presented to them. It is a concept known as, *decision architecture*. A powerful, yet simple approach to nudging decision makers in the right direction without impeding their free will. We will return to this idea of decision architecture time and again throughout AlphaBrain, for it is one of the most powerful tools for overcoming decision-related mistakes, and as such, it is fundamental to the approach presented in this book. Be forewarned though, it will be applied differently than you've seen it before.

Marginal Improvement and Its Outcomes

Novak Djokovic spent years as the number one ranked men's tennis player in the world, but that wasn't always the case. Back in 2004, when he first turned professional, he was ranked 680th. In fact, in his first two years he didn't come close to breaking into the top 100. At the time, he averaged $250,000 per year in prize money and lost more matches than he won. It wasn't until the end of his third year that he skyrocketed up the ranks to finish third in the world. For the next four years, he held that spot, earning an average of $5 million in prize money per year and winning an impressive 79% of the matches in which he competed.

Truth is, his number-three ranking belied an undeniable truth that was apparent to everyone, except perhaps Novak himself. Although Djokovic was ranked just one notch below Switzerland's Roger

Table 1.1 Novak Djokovic's overall performance, 2004–2016

	2004–2005	2006–2010	2011–2016
Rank	100+	3	1
Annual Prize Money	$300,000	$5 million	$14 million
Matches Won (%)	49%	79%	90%

Federer and Spain's Rafael Nadal, his game had more in common with 30th-ranked Radek Stepanek than the superstars at the top. As each tournament approached, commentators, writers, and even the fans spoke of the field as though it were comprised of Federer, Nadal, and then everyone else. Over and over again, Djokovic was snubbed, and he wore the hurt on his sleeves. In press conferences and on-court interviews he came across as arrogant and disrespectful of his opponents and everyone else involved with the game, including the fans. The more he demanded respect, the less he garnered. Novak's character, maturity, and mental strength were questioned with every loss and outburst.

Four years later, everything changed. He leapfrogged the superstars to attain the top ranking and remained there for years to come. In addition to tripling the prize money he earns each year, Djokovic now wins an astounding 90% of all the matches that he plays (Table 1.1). Not surprisingly, that chip on his shoulder disappeared along with the losses. Novak is now a fan and establishment favorite. When all is said and done he will likely be remembered as one of the greatest to ever play the game.

What is most interesting about all of his incredibly impressive statistics – the ones that everyone quotes and that we use to define Novak Djokovic as a future hall of famer – is that he doesn't directly control any of them since they are outcomes rather than inputs. If he has a tough match, he wouldn't go home and say to his coach, "I'd like to work on winning more matches." His coach, in turn, wouldn't respond by suggesting that instead he should work on winning more prize money.

Although we cannot control them, the decisions we make affect the probability that one outcome will occur relative to all other possibilities.

The better our decisions, the more likely we are to achieve the outcome we desire. Due to the continuous and compounding nature of all the millions of decisions we face on a regular basis, even a marginal improvement in the decision-making process itself can have a huge impact on our results.

Novak Djokovich's career provides evidence of the power of marginal adjustments. We can quantify and track his ability to make better decisions as his career progressed by looking at the percentage of points that he has won, because in tennis the typical point involves just slightly more than one decision. Therefore, we can think of his points-won percentage as his *decision success rate*. Back when Djokovic was winning 49% of the matches in which he participated, he was winning 49% of the points he played. In order to win 79% of his matches, he had to improve his decision success rate to just 52%. Then, to attain the number-one ranking, to earn an average of $14 million per year in prize money alone, and to win a dominating 90% of his matches, he had to raise his decision success rate to a surprisingly mundane, 55% (Table 1.2).

As you just read about Novak's progress and how he improved his game, perhaps you find it difficult to connect the gains to decisions rather than physical actions. After all, tennis is a physical endeavor. To get better, you might expect that Djokovich worked on his serve, maybe adding more spin or racquet speed making it harder for his opponents to return it. Some might speculate that he practiced sprinting drills in order to improve foot speed so that he could run down more of the difficult shots. He may have worked with a yoga instructor on improving his flexibility, allowing him to stretch further and expand his reach, thereby increasing his ability to defend more of the court.

Table 1.2   Novak Djokovic's performance, 2004–2016, including points won

	2004–2005	2006–2010	2011–2016
Rank	100+	3	1
Annual Prize Money	$300,000	$5 million	$14 million
Matches Won (%)	49%	79%	90%
Points Won (%)	49%	52%	55%

These are all excellent ways to improve one's tennis game, and it's very possible Djokovich worked on some or even all of them. Although we may think of each of these improvements as physical actions, they are also decisions. He must decide that he wants to play the game of tennis, win more matches, reduce the odds of his opponent returning his serve, reduce the odds of him being aced or not being able to reach a passing shot. Each objective, known in decision analysis as an *outcome,* is a problem he seeks to solve. The action, physical or otherwise, is the solution he chooses to solve that problem. Each aspect — from defining the outcome, to understanding what factors affect our ability to achieve it, and finally, choosing the action that gives us the best odds of doing so — is an integral part of the decision-making process. (We'll do a deeper dive into this shortly.)

In Novak's case, if he had decided that he wanted his opponents to miss more of his serves he may have increased the spin and/or racquet speed. He may have chosen that as a course of action because it would be more difficult for his opponent to hit a ball that changes direction sharply and even erratically, especially when they have less time to react. It's a perfectly logical decision, and precisely the type of approach that springs to mind anytime we contemplate how to improve results. If you want to improve results, you must get better by raising the level of your game. Swing *quicker*, spin *more*, run *faster*, jump *higher*. It seems so obvious that is what we need to do in order to achieve better outcomes. There is, however, an easier, more powerful, and indeed more rational approach.

Marginally Speaking

The start of a new year is that moment when many of us vow to improve by making some adjustment to our behavior that will make us happier, prouder, wealthier. Although it's tempting to set grand pronouncements of the radical changes we will implement in the coming year, there are two reasons that may not be the correct approach. Marginal change is not only more powerful than you might think; as shown by Novak Djokovic, it is also far more likely to be implemented. Exercising more is one of the most common New Year's resolutions. When many of us set this goal, it's likely with an alcoholic drink (or turkey leg) in hand. Exercising for just 30 minutes a day three times a week sounds easily achievable, but it's not. Otherwise, it wouldn't be the most commonly unresolved resolution.

In reality, how we spend the majority of our time is nearly set in stone. What differentiates one year from the next is what happens on the margin. It is there in those moments that we define our lives: the year we lost weight, bought a new home, markets crashed, kids went off to college. As big as these events are, they all exist on the margin of our lives, where everyday, we eat, work, sleep, watch TV, and relieve our bowels in an almost rhythmic pattern. It is the marginal stuff, the things we don't do regularly, that require effort and attention. It makes us uncomfortable, and it challenges and rewards us far more than what happens in the bulk of our time.

According to the US Department of Agriculture (USDA), the average man with a sedentary lifestyle should take in about 2,300 calories per day. The reason is that the average sedentary man burns approximately 2,300 calories each day. The sum total of mundane activities such as sleeping, eating, brushing your teeth, and watching TV requires the energy provided by 2,300 calories. On the other hand, for the average active man, the USDA suggests taking in 2,700 calories per day. Yes, the difference between living a sedentary lifestyle and an active one requires just 400 extra calories a day, or roughly what you will consume in a large cup of Coca-Cola.

My point is that the bulk of what we consume and burn is prede-termined, unalterable. Diets and exercise regimes exist on the margin. In the scheme of things, they are little more than minor adjustments to our daily routines, but the impact can be life changing. One less glass of wine at dinner. Small fries rather than large. Whole grain pasta instead of refined. Seemingly tiny adjustments that can produce dramatic results, yet generate enough friction in the moment to keep us from doing what is in our own best interest longer term.

The same applies to how we perform at work, no matter what the job is, but let's look at the portfolio manager (PM) as an example. The role involves just three fundamental aspects: developing a view, deciding how to express it, and when. For most PMs, the majority of what they do is also fairly set in stone. They acquire information in the same way, utilize the same instruments, invest in the same assets, and use the same indicators to determine timing that they have used for years. Truth be told, much of the accumulation of information used to derive views happens with very little thought, being predetermined by geography, firm, and industry. So, as it is with diet and exercise, adjustments and improvements at work occur at the margin.

When I took over the investment process at a hedge fund years ago, it was my job to turn PMs who had excellent sell-side pedigrees, but very little success on the buy-side, into positive performers. Although it was expected that I would make sweeping changes, I understood that after 25 years in the business, they were, for the most part, who they would always be. Like a good fitness trainer, my job was to understand their deeply entrenched habits and suggest the marginal behavioral adjustments that could unleash dramatic improvement.

Over the next 13 months, thanks to one seemingly minor tweak, namely forcing the PMs to formally answer the simple question, "Why?" whenever they made a decision, resulted in all of them achieving the best buy-side performance of their careers by a very wide margin and the firm outperforming its benchmark index by 2500 basis points. I didn't change how the portfolio managers gathered information. I didn't have them use different instruments, invest in different asset classes, discover new technical indicators, or tighten up their stop-losses. I simply had them become more aware of their own actions, challenging them to recognize when their decisions were inconsistent with their own beliefs.

Truth is, no matter how good the trainer, how beautiful the gym, or powerful the juicer, the great majority of people fail to stick with even marginal adjustments. The same goes for PMs, but the question is, why?

It is at the margins where vast potential exists, but it is also where you are challenged, feel uncomfortable, unnatural even, and that can be exhausting. If it wasn't, it wouldn't be on the margin; it would be a fundamental part of who you are.

What makes an exercise routine effective is resistance. Without it, you don't get stronger or more fit. You must get your heart pumping, the lactic acid flowing, and the oxygen churning. As they say, "No pain, no gain." Well, the same goes for your mental well-being. You need to challenge how you think, read publications that fire up neurons, and create new connections in the brain by questioning your beliefs. Not just those about the US dollar, but about the type of information you should be gathering and even how you spend your time.

The Power of Avoiding Mistakes

Since 2000 Bill Belichick has been far and away the most successful head coach in the NFL. Having won slightly more than 80% of their 200 regular season games since then, his team the New England Patriots is head and shoulders above the competition. At the time of writing, they are the reigning Super Bowl champs for a record fifth time under his leadership and have won 24 playoff games. The results speak for themselves, but when compared to the other 31 coaches in the league they are simply astounding (Figure 1.1).

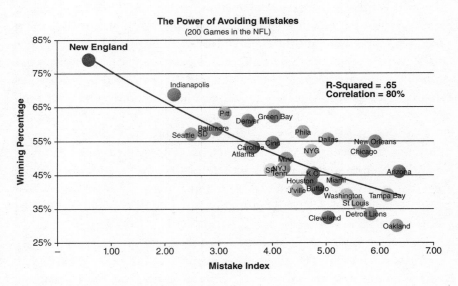

Figure 1.1   The Power of Avoiding Mistakes

In fact, his record is so spectacular that many have accused him of cheating, seeing no other way to explain his incredible success. The reason even the experts are at such a loss for an explanation is that none of the usual explanations apply. Although Belichick has exceptional players on his roster, they rarely come to him as stars. He has something of a knack for turning unsung players into superstars who are then poached for their "outlier" skills. Yet time and again, those same players fade back to mediocrity when traded to other teams. The only true constant has been quarterback Tom Brady, a sixth-round pick from the 2000 draft when 198 players, including six quarterbacks, were selected ahead of him. Indeed, Brady is regarded by most as a superstar, but unlike all the other role players in Belichick's regime who have garnered that kind of praise while on his roster, Brady never left, so whether he would be such a success with another team is up for debate. There is actually one other semiconstant for Belichick's Patriots, though. They've always had one of the league's best place kickers. Initially, it was Adam Vinatieri and since 2006, Stephen Gostkowski. Two of the greatest to ever play the position. The fact that these are the only two constants is actually very significant. More on that in a moment.

In the absence of a clear explanation for why Belichick has been so successful, the experts have resorted to creating narratives that appeal to deep-seated beliefs. Truth is, if they really want to understand the secret of his success, all they need to do is listen to what he says in every pre and postgame interview. Although the press describes him as evasive, the reality is, the faulty communication lies in the experts' inability to see past their own flawed, unsubstantiated bias. Coach Belichick's answers to questions like, "How did you prepare your team for your opponent's explosive offense or dominating defense?" is repeated so often it has become a slogan used on T-shirts and billboards. The answer goes something like this. "We didn't prepare for them. We prepared ourselves. If all 11 players on offense, 11 on defense, and 11 on special teams simply do their job, we have a good chance to win."

Since it's not sexy nor does it sound scientific, and because it's assumed that everyone needs to do their job in order for a team to win, commentators simultaneously complain about and mock his evasiveness. Although it may sound like a stock answer, he's actually giving away his secret. Not everyone has ignored his mantra, though. Two of the top four playoff contenders in the 2016 college football playoffs were coached by Belichick disciples, Nick Saban's University of Alabama and Kirk Ferentz's University of Iowa. Listen to their press conferences and you'll hear an eerily similar message.

I'll be honest, they are my favorite press conferences, because they speak my language, as well as that of the only other coach to lead four teams to Super Bowl victories, Chuck Noll of the Pittsburgh Steelers. His mantra delivered the same message. "Before you can win a game, you first have to not lose it." Whether you use Noll's words or Belichick's, "Do your job," the message is the same: don't make mistakes. Although that may sound obvious, surprisingly few experts in fields that involve elements of luck and skill (like ours), truly grasp just how different the approach is from the norm. Watch any football game with this mantra in mind, and you'll see the game in a whole new light. You will discover that in almost every game, the outcome is determined by one team making fewer mistakes than the other. Don't take my word for it though. The data makes the strongest argument.

In order to create a "mistake index," I selected the one statistic from each of the three aspects of the game (offense, defense, and special teams) that best represents a mistake in its purest form. It turns out there is a phenomenal correlation between a team's mistake index and their winning percentage over time. Truth be told, because of the natural competitive edge created with ball possession, the predictive power is nearly identical if we limit the inputs to two simple statistics—offensive giveaways and field goal conversions. In other words, if the player on offense who touches the ball most frequently can avoid handing it over to the opponent and the player responsible for converting a field goal/extra point attempt into points can do so with great frequency, you are likely to wind up with a far better record than your opponents. See how Brady and Gostkowski fit in now?

Think about Tom Brady and what adjectives are most commonly attached to his name. It's not "explosive," "powerful," or even "creative," but rather "calm" and "unflappable." In looking for someone to manage his offense, Belichick doesn't seek out the scrambler or the guy who can thread the needle. First and foremost, he wants someone who won't relinquish the competitive edge they have when simply possessing the

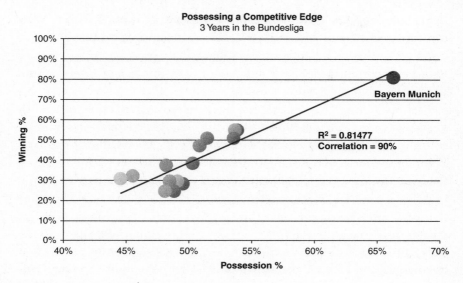

Figure 1.2   Possessing a Competitive Edge

ball. That is Brady's strength. Combined with Stephen Gostkowski's 88% field goal percentage, Belichick's team provides a formidable foe for any opponent.

As it turns out, Belichick, Noll, Saban, and Ferentz aren't the only ones to discover the power of avoiding the mistake of relinquishing a competitive advantage to the opponent. Since taking the helm in 2013, Bayern Munich's coach, Pep Guardiola, has zeroed in on the very same aspect of his game (Figure 1.2). Although his mantra has been adjusted to fit soccer, the message is exactly the same. Above all else, he drills into his players that ball possession is of the utmost importance. While in possession of the ball his team is more likely to score and less likely to incur a penalty than its opponent. In other words, as it is for American football, simply possessing the ball creates a competitive edge. Therefore, it should only be relinquished when attempting a high probability shot on goal. By pushing time of possession to extreme levels, opponents have a greater tendency to become frustrated, making them more emotional, thereby leading to more mistakes. Those mistakes generate penalty kicks and breakaway opportunities for Pep's squad, both of which lead to high probability shots on goal.

None of this is rocket science. In fact, it's all fairly obvious. Why then don't all coaches and athletes focus on reducing mistakes? Much of it can be explained by cognitive bias and incentives.

Commentators, highlight reels, and the most often quoted statistics all tend to focus on the upside outlier. If an athlete wants to increase his pay, he need only create a narrative that appeals to our cognitive bias for extreme events. A single, spectacular one-handed catch shown repeatedly on ESPN's Sports Center and retweeted a few million times will override the mundanity of a hundred dropped passes over the course of a season. Just ask Odell Beckham Jr. or, if you're a basketball fan, Jeremy Lin. Simply scoring a goal won't set you apart from your peers, but just one well-placed bicycle kick might. A low probability missed shot (so long as it isn't taken in the final seconds of a big game) will fade into the background of a team sport with numerous players, all of whom share in the blame for a loss. However, one spectacular shot, and by spectacular I mean a low-probability shot that required more luck than skill, will be attributed to the shooter and much of the success laid at her feet. As a result of this skewed risk/reward attribution, much of which we owe to a cognitive shortcoming, athletes expend less effort trying to tilt the odds of success in favor of them and their teams over time by reducing mistakes, and instead concentrate on threading the needle, swinging for the fences, and unleashing the bone jarring hit in the hopes of being noticed.

There's another reason we focus on creating the memorable play, even at the expense of winning more games. We have a natural predilection for stories that help us make sense of the world in which we exist, even if those stories run in direct opposition to reality. It's more appealing to look at Belichick's phenomenal win/loss record and concoct a spectacular story of deceit and chicanery than to accept that he has crushed his competition by simply reducing mistakes. The same goes for athletes like Novak Djokovic competing in individual sports. When we are presented with the statistics that show just how dominant he is, we create a narrative of extraordinary dominance over his opponents. He was ranked number one in the world from 2011 to 2016, amassed nearly $17 million in prize money in 2016 alone, and wins roughly 90% of the matches he plays. Given those statistics, who in their right mind would expect him to lose to anyone, let alone a young upstart? In explaining such dominance, we go to great lengths to create a story of almost super-human ability, but the reality is quite different. In achieving everything just described, he still wins just 55% of all the points he plays. That's a mere 3% better than when he was ranked third and earned one-third the prize money. Even more interesting, when he was ranked 680th in the world and earning less than $100,000 per year, he was winning 49% of the points he played. As it turns out, the difference between good, great, and once-in-a-generation is smaller than we think. Novak isn't superhuman. He simply makes slightly fewer mistakes than every one of his competitors.

No matter what it is you want to become better at, it can only be achieved by reducing mistakes. Consider the simple objective of running faster, for example. In order to run faster you must actually run less slowly. The question then is, what is it that tends to reduce our running speed? Perhaps we become fatigued or run out of breath quickly. If we simply run more often, this speed impediment will gradually affect us less quickly and less frequently. Ever wonder what someone coaching an athlete like Usain Bolt, the fastest man to ever compete in the 100 meter dash could possibly offer, day in and day out? The answer is, suggestions for making fewer mistakes. If you move your elbow out to the side even a millimeter, it forces an adjustment in another part of your body to keep you simultaneously upright and moving forward. So, if you keep the elbow flowing in the correct direction, it makes you faster. Reduce friction between your legs, between your skin and the air. Reduce your weight. Reduce your need to breath harder. Gains are all a function of the reduction of mistakes. When one runs faster than anyone else, we define them as "superhuman." To be superhuman is to be free of the mistakes common to most human beings attempting the same feat.

So what does this have to do with investing? Everything. Making money in our business comes down to two things; having a portfolio with more winners than losers and/or bigger winners than losers. As it is with most coaches and athletes, investment managers tend to focus on the latter, and that has a great impact on every aspect of their game, from the risk management techniques employed to the rise in popularity of momentum trading. In placing greater focus and importance on skewed returns per trade, much like athletes, we tend to sacrifice the winners to losers ratio. So, if we want to know how to break away from the pack, we should tear a page out of the playbook of those who have already done it, focusing more on making fewer mistakes by relinquishing that competitive edge only when a high probability shot on goal is available. Simply stated, it's easier to improve our winners to losers ratio by avoiding mediocre trades than it is to win the lottery, a few times per year.

The same principle applies to all athletics, as well as politics, medicine, policymaking, business, and investment management. Name any goal, dream, or aspiration of yours, personal or professional, from losing weight to clearing your bucket list, from generating better investment returns to identifying higher quality managers, and you have defined an outcome that you desire. Improve your decision-making even marginally, and your odds of realizing that outcome go up dramatically, as it has for Djokovic, Belichick, and Guardiola. The way to improve your decision-making is by reducing mistakes. It sounds simple enough, but as anyone who has ever tried to lose weight, improve their golf game by even a couple of strokes, or consistently beat the S&P knows, it is not.

Chapter 2

Blinded by Bias

Mistakes and Markets

Artificial intelligence and machine learning is suddenly all the rage, and for good reason. It is the future of this, and most every other industry. If you've been paying attention to the evolution of technology over the past 2.6 million years, you knew it was coming. Wherever human beings have shouldered the bulk of the effort, we have always sought to replace humans with technology that could do the job better, faster, more efficiently and – since the invention of capital – cheaper. It began with the most basic, brute force physical tasks and has progressively involved more nuanced, cognitive processes. Along the way, the progress has been exponential, not linear. Through AI and machine learning, technology is now attempting to improve on how we make decisions, and truth is, it won't require much effort. Not because technology represents some sort of miracle, but because we do such a poor job of it.

More than 60 years of research in the cognitive sciences provides an abundance of evidence proving that humans are prone to mistakes at every stage of the decision-making process. From defining the problem to be solved, to researching and predicting the relevant external factors that will likely affect our ability to achieve them, as well as assessing and implementing the actions we should take in order to improve our chances of realizing those objectives, we are vulnerable to systematic errors in judgment. Luckily, technology can help us overcome our short-comings, but it will not come without a price, and like the hunters, gatherers, cotton pickers, and factory workers who came before us, we who make a living in finance will be called on to pay it – and, likely, sooner than we think.

To conceptualize how this will work, let's simplify all financial markets down to the game of poker. As it is with all others, there are two elements at work in the game – skill and luck. No player can purposefully capitalize on luck, leaving skill to separate the good players from the bad. In the good old days of the game, skilled players extracted value by bluffing and reading the actions of the other players. Experienced players identified basic behavior patterns ("tells") exhibited by less accomplished opponents and sought to take advantage of them. In other words, they were capitalizing on the mistakes of their opponents.

Then the "geeks" got involved, playing poker after work for hours, before convening at local bars to dissect the action until dawn. Over time, they had distilled the game down to what it is, a game of chance where the odds can be calculated and updated every step of the way. With the probability of every possible outcome being calculable, every decision along the way could be scripted according to a set of predetermined rules, a copy of which is available for free on many Internet sites. When the number crunchers began appearing at the big tournaments, they paid less attention to the other players than to the probabilities. Very quickly, the old style of play and those who practiced it, were confined to the opening rounds of the major poker tournaments, essentially serving to bankroll an ever-increasing purse for the number crunchers.

As good as they are, however, the new breed of poker players is still human. No matter how much they value the power of probabili-ties, occasionally they succumb to ego, emotion, fear, greed, and other mistake-inducing issues, not to mention the limited processing power of the human brain. In other words, as much as this new breed has improved on the old approach by reducing the number of mistakes they make, in the end they remain human. And by human, I mean flawed.

In order to remove the potential for these flaws to occur, one of the six players at a poker table decides to bankroll his Cray supercomputer. He programs it to make decisions based on the probabilities of the game, while also incorporating information it gathers in real-time regarding facial ticks, posture, body heat, heart rate, chemical levels, and other physical embodiments of stress and excitement, while analyzing their correlation to betting behavior and the cards those players are holding relative to all the others. You can imagine the advantage the computer has over the rest of the players, but let's take a moment to truly understand what that advantage really is.

The computer has a competitive advantage, not because it does things better than the other players, but because it does them with fewer mistakes. Its edge requires that there are players at the table who are making decisions in a way that is different from how they should be made, whereas simultaneously Cray makes them as they should be. After seeing the game's pot gravitating toward Cray and away from the humans, one of the other players decides to bankroll his own supercomputer, leaving two computers and four humans at the table. The gains for the computers are limited to what the humans have left, meaning the potential for Cray 1 has just been reduced, because future earnings will be split between it and Cray 2.

Eventually, all the players choose to step out of the game, and instead replace themselves with Cray supercomputers of their own. At that moment, every player (computer) is making decisions based solely on the probabilities. No more "reads" of the players are possible. The outcome is now exclusively a function of chance. Skill plays no role whatsoever. Think about that for a moment. When the humans were removed from the game, so too were mistakes. Without the mistakes, skill no longer plays a role. The game is reduced to purely one of chance or luck, like betting on the roll of fair dice. In other words, in order for one player to have a competitive advantage attributable to skill, at least one of the other players must be making mistakes. That mistake is what makes skill possible. Take away the mistake, and all that is left is luck.

Imagine for a moment, one of the players who bankrolls a Cray decides that he can improve on the computer's performance by overriding it when he senses an opportunity that the computer isn't programmed to capitalize on, or perhaps turns it off for a bit when the machine is in the midst of a bad run. Although either of these decisions may appeal to our intuition (because we have been taught to take action like this), they are a weakness. We might rationalize the action by saying this is a combination of "art" and science, but when we do, what we are really saying is that this is a combination of decisions driven by unfounded beliefs rather than those supported by evidence.

This applies to markets as much as it does to a poker game. What skilled managers are capitalizing on are the mistakes of others. Remove humans from the markets and you remove the ability to create a competitive edge. Skill ceases to exist. If our goal is to make fewer mistakes, the objective is to make human intelligence behave more like artificial intelligence. To do so, we must focus on process.

Blind to Our Blindness

A wealthy woman was walking through an upscale part of town carrying a purse containing a great deal of cash when suddenly a man came up behind her, grabbed the purse, and took off with it. Luckily, she was able to get a good look at him and provided the police with a detailed description. The perpetrator was a man between 20 and 30 years old, just over 6 feet tall, with red hair and a pronounced limp. A man standing across the street witnessed the crime and provided the exact same description to another police officer, thereby corroborating the evidence.

A few hours later, police officers witnessed a man matching all these characteristics coming out of an electronics store carrying a large television. When they discovered that he had paid cash for the TV, they arrested him. During the trial, the prosecution called a statistician to the stand and asked, "Sir, can you tell us what the probability is of someone matching all the characteristics of the perpetrator?" The expert witness responded, "Yes, it's rather simple. You take the probability of someone in this city matching each of the characteristics, and then multiply them all by each other. In this case, it results in a vanishingly small probability of 0.0002%."

Given that this was all the evidence available in this case, it was understandable that jurors found the defendant guilty. Unfortunately, given the evidence provided, there is a 95% chance that an innocent man was imprisoned as a result.

The mistake made by these jurors is one that has been made hundreds, and possibly thousands of times over the past three decades in cases where DNA was the only evidence presented. The phenomenon is now recognized as "Prosecutors' Fallacy," and it occurs when jurors, and even defense attorneys, replace the question they are meant to answer, with one framed by the prosecutor. Here is how it works.

As it relates to the case of the stolen purse, the jury is tasked with answering, "What is the probability the defendant is innocent, given that he matches all the characteristics?" Instead, the prosecutor asks the statistician, "What is the probability of matching all the characteristics, given that a person is innocent?" The two questions sound, if not identical, then so close in meaning that arguing otherwise would seem pedantic. And that is exactly what the prosecution intends.

How could the appropriate question be answered correctly? It would require just a few more questions being asked, prior to drawing a conclusion. How many people live in this city? 10 million. How many of them match all the characteristics? $10,000,000 \times 0.0002\% = 20$. Of those 20, how many are guilty? Just one. How many of them are innocent? 19 of the 20, or 95%. Therefore, the answer to the question posed to this and all other juries, "Given the evidence, what is the probability the defendant is innocent?" is 95%.

It's a simple mistake, but one that has resulted in people actually being put to death. Unfortunately, it isn't the only mistake on display in this case.

Knowing that there is just a 5% chance that the defendant is guilty given the evidence provided, most people would render a verdict of innocence. But what if the probability of guilt weren't nearly as low? At what point, would you decide to send the man to prison? 50% probability he is guilty? 80%? 90%? In other words, how certain of his guilt would you need to be before rendering a guilty verdict?

Now let's suppose, instead of being on trial for purse snatching, you are judging whether he is guilty of murder, and if he is, he will be put

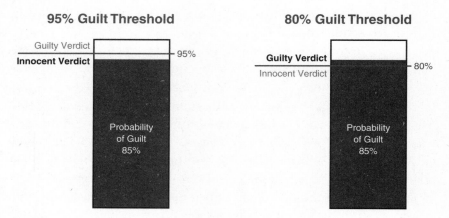

Figure 2.1   Guilt threshold influence on verdict.
SOURCE: Bija Advisors.

to death. Knowing that you are determining the fate of this man's life, would you perhaps raise the threshold? What if the murder occurred in the small town in which both you and the defendant live? Would the possibility of letting a murderer go free to kill again, with the next victim potentially being one of your family members or friends, lead you to lower the threshold? What if the victim's family were sitting in the courtroom sobbing and pleading for closure, would you lower the threshold again? What if the defendant were your mother, your child, or you? Would you want to raise the threshold for judging guilt to per-haps 100% certainty? In each of these scenarios, the probability of the defendant's guilt is unchanged. Indeed, your opinion about whether he is guilty is also unaltered. Instead, the only thing that is changing is the level at which you determine that a defendant should be judged "guilty" and pay for the crime, rather than "innocent" and return home (Figure 2.1).

In order for a fair trial to occur, the jury must not only properly calculate the odds of guilt based on the evidence provided, but they must also apply the same threshold to all of their verdicts. As you've witnessed, unless that threshold is set prior to knowing the facts of the case, there is an excellent chance that the threshold will be adjusted as they come to light. What this means is that there are two separate and distinct types of mistakes jurors are vulnerable to making. One relates to properly calculating the odds of guilt, while the other has to do with consistently setting the bar for a guilty verdict.

What if instead of presenting the evidence to jurors, we were to enter it into a computer that would then run a simple algorithm to accurately ascertain the probability of guilt? That probability could then be compared to a threshold that had been agreed upon through a popular vote, and consistently applied in all cases. In those cases where the defendant is judged guilty, a standard sentence would be consistently applied according to the rule of law. In other words, remove the potential for all human error and bias from the system, by removing humans from the process. No more jurors. No more judges.

Would you be in favor of such a change? If not, why not?

An overwhelming number of people to whom I have posed this question to over the years has answered with an emphatic, "No." The question is, why would you not want to remove the potential for bias to creep into such an important decision? Could it be that you feel the bias would likely work in your favor if you were to find yourself on trial? Perhaps you believe that if you simply had an opportunity to explain yourself, to appeal to a human being's compassion, they would see that you aren't a bad person and therefore make concessions in your case. Fair enough (pun intended).

It's only natural that you would feel this way. We humans are optimists by nature. That is why we tend to underperform our expectations, launch businesses at such an extraordinary rate in spite of the overwhelming odds against success, and why projects typically come in late and over budget. It's this optimism bias and an unrealistic belief in our decision-making prowess that makes so many distrustful of self-driving cars and hesitant to turn over investment decisions to the machines, let alone a systematic decision-making process. The fear is related to the possibility that the machine could break down or make a mistake. Instead, we want the ability to override the machine, to step in and make an adjustment if we feel it isn't properly assessing the situation. Perhaps it is misinterpreting or even ignoring some nuanced information. Because the machine doesn't have the ability to make a snap judgment on the fly, it's thought to be inferior to the more flexible, creative human brain.

In the Rubik's Cube in Figure 2.2, we are interested in accurately assessing the color of the center pieces. If you are like most, you see the top center piece as a solid brown, while the center piece on the side facing you is a rather bright orange. No deliberation is required, no uncertainty exists. After all, we can see it with our own eyes, the ultimate arbiter of reality. In court cases, nothing trumps the power of an unbiased eyewitness account. Unless we can see something for ourselves, there will always remain a seed of doubt. Unfortunately, even if our eyes see things correctly, our brain doesn't always do a great job of processing the information delivered by them. What's worse is that we are often blind to our own blindness. And such is the case with this Rubik's Cube.

The reality is, those two squares are exactly the same color, represented by the exact same hexadecimal code. When I remove everything else from the image, your brain is able to "see" the squares as the brown squares they truly are (Figure 2.3). Even now that you have been

Figure 2.2   Rubik's Cube.
SOURCE: Image by Dr. R. Beau Lotto.

Figure 2.3   The brown and orange squares.
SOURCE: Image by Dr. R. Beau Lotto.

educated, well aware of the shortcoming of your brain's ability to properly process the information, when you look back at the original image, you still cannot see them as they truly exist. Go ahead and try. You can't make the adjustment. You can't reprogram your brain to process the information correctly. Unfortunately, regardless of the fact that we are smart and educated, we remain flawed.

However, if I were to employ a simple technology like Photoshop's eyedropper, I would know with great certainty that those two squares are the exact same hue, as evidenced by the hexadecimal code #905822 (Figure 2.4).

It provides an excellent example for how technology can help us improve our decision-making. Unfortunately, it's rare for us to do so. You see, in order to make the decision to ignore what our own eyes tell us, to override our own intuition and assessment of the world, we must first recognize that we are doing it wrong. We must believe that we are making a mistake that requires fixing.

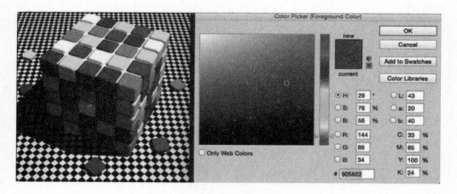

Figure 2.4   Hexadecimal code of the two squares.

In the case of the Rubik's Cube, you are probably so certain that you are correctly identifying the tile colors as brown and orange, that even now you are questioning whether I am playing a trick on you. Perhaps I replaced the orange tile with a brown one when I dimmed the rest of the image. Even seeing the Photoshop demonstration, there remains a seed of doubt.

The reality is, visual illusions are little more than parlor tricks. They are interesting, we snicker at them and share them, but it is extremely rare for us to accept that these types of things happen to us dozens of times a day, even when we are facing decisions of great consequence. The only true way to avoid mistakes like these is to accept that we are as vulnerable as everyone else, to identify those moments when we are particularly likely to falter and make preparations ahead of time to either overcome them or, at a minimum, reduce their impact. Only when we accept our blindness can we truly see.

Minimizing Effort

At Raboud University in the Netherlands, researchers discovered something interesting about the human brain as it relates to visual information. It turns out that we see not just with our eyes, but with the brain as well. In Figure 2.5, no triangle exists, but it is implied by

Figure 2.5   What the brain sees.

the placement of the three Pac-Man shapes relative to each other. Prior to the recent findings, it was believed that the brain simply filtered the information that came in through the eyes, but now we've come to realize that it actually interprets it. That was the big news, but it was the ancillary finding that I think is far more fascinating, and relevant to our job of interpreting what we see in markets.

It turns out that the group of three Pac-Man shapes triggers less brain activity than the one all by itself, because triangles and circles are far more prevalent in the world than Pac-Man shapes. The single Pac-Man shape is unexpected and therefore requires more processing by our brain. In other words, if something appears easy to explain, even if it's simply due to familiarity, less brain activity is needed to process that information, compared to when something is unexpected or difficult to account for. That is the cognitive ease our brains seek to achieve, and as we will discover, it is what leads to so many of the mistakes that we make in our decisions and keeps us from achieving so many of our goals.

Chapter 3

Rational Decisions

The Science of Decision-Making

Decision theory is the field of study focused on decision-making. Those who work in the field tend to concentrate their efforts in one of the two main disciplines, normative and descriptive. *Normative decision theory* is the study of how we should make decisions. It makes heavy use of statistical analysis and requires an understanding of probabilities. Normative decisions are made objectively, without emotion and can be repeated by following a systematic pattern of behavior. The goal is a rational decision.

A decision is considered *rational* when the decision maker does what is most reasonable given all the relevant information available at the time the decision is made. Rational decisions are what we aspire to achieve. They are optimal. On the other hand, a decision is considered *right* if the outcome is at least as good as all other possible outcomes. In other words, it is considered right, because the actual outcome was successful. Importantly, rational decisions are not necessarily the same as right decisions, and the decision that winds up being right may not have been rational. The key difference between the two is that a decision can be deemed rational versus irrational at the moment it is made, whereas the assessment about whether it was right or wrong can only be made with the benefit of hindsight.

Take the example of two teens, Brian and James, both of whom attended a late-night party where alcohol was consumed. Brian elected to get a ride home from a friend who had been drinking heavily. James chose to ride with a friend who hadn't had a single drink. Brian made it home without incident, whereas James was paralyzed when a distracted driver ran a red light. It's clear to anyone reading this that James had made the rational choice, whereas Brian made the right one. I know it's hard to accept that the correct term to use for Brian's choice is *right,* but according to the definition, it is.

There is no controversy in a situation like this. James made the correct choice even though it worked out poorly. Even knowing the outcomes, you would still say that James made the rational decision whereas Brian had been foolish. Unfortunately, few decisions are as cut and dried as this. More often than not, we are not accurate historians of decisions, but rather revisionists. Once the outcome is known, the initial expectations are erased forever. Decisions that were once deemed rational are recategorized as suboptimal simply because they didn't turn out to be right. Information that led us astray is discounted, whereas that which corroborates the outcome is elevated in value, and the "mistakes" are now glaringly obvious.

It isn't intentional; it's just what our brains do to help us make sense of a complex world. However, in the case of James and Brian, it's simply impossible to retrospectively convince ourselves that Brian decided well and James poorly, so we make sense of it in one of three ways. We question whether the sober teen was in fact sober, assume there is more to the story, or assign it to a higher power. When it comes to the decisions we make as investors, however, more often than not, we play the role of revisionist historians, and that doesn't come without consequences.

The technical term for what I've described is hindsight or outcome bias. It's when you change your assessment of whether a decision was rational simply because you know the outcome. Here's where it gets tricky. You gather copious amounts of historical data, speak to numerous experts, listen to opposing viewpoints, and develop a rational strategy given all the relevant information. Your boss (or investors) agrees that your analysis is sound and your expectations are reasonable. That's not to say that they don't see how it could potentially go wrong or that they are unwilling to express those concerns in the moment. Of course, there are always risks, and you've properly considered them. In light of the risks and rewards, given their appropriate weightings, you all agree the investment is warranted.

Unfortunately, you aren't judged by whether your decisions are rational. Your decisions, your investments, your portfolio, your fund, and potentially even your own self-worth are more often judged by whether they were right. In other words, your decisions are judged by the outcome, not the process, and that can be dangerous for a number of reasons.

The table in Figure 3.1 was posted on LinkedIn. No caption was attached. No mention of the fact that it was based on only three data points, nor the decision-making that led to the results. But that's what we do. If a decision turns out to be right, it must have been due to solid decision-making, and vice versa.

Well, if Brian, the teenager who rode home with a drunk driver were a fund manager, he'd have been among the top performers, whereas James would have been in the bottom. The thing is, correct (or right) decisions can only be judged with the benefit of hindsight, but investors have to make investments and allocate to managers prior to the results being known. Therefore, as investors, we must somehow make the distinction between returns that were generated by (1) rational decisions as part of a consistent decision-making process, (2) a selection of rational decisions that are part of an inconsistent decision-making process, or (3) simply irrational decisions that happened to work out well.

Just because Brian wound up getting home safely doesn't mean that we should have expected it, nor does it mean that we should expect the same result going forward. However, since his poor decision wasn't punished, we should expect that he will likely employ that same decision-making process in the future. Given that likelihood, Brian isn't someone I would expect to survive very long.

As it relates to investment management, there are two distinct difficulties in conducting a proper assessment, and this applies not just to the allocator, but to the traders and portfolio managers themselves. First, once you see the result, it's nearly impossible to unsee it. When the outlier event that you had acknowledged beforehand actually comes

Top & Bottom 20 Funds of 2016

Top

Investment Funds	Return	Date
TULIP TREND FUND, LTD - A	16.75	25 Mar 16
ARCTIC BLUE CAPITAL 3X	15.91	29 Feb 16
PASSPORT SPECIAL OPPORTUNITIES FUND LTD CLASS AA	14.49	29 Feb 16
SABA CAPITAL OFFSHORE FUND LTD	11.60	24 Mar 16
RENAISSANCE INSTITUTIONAL EQUITIES LP (B)	10.88	25 Mar 16
CONQUEST MACRO FUND, LTD (COMP)	10.00	30 Mar 16
DORSET ENERGY FUND, LTD - CLASS A	9.74	25 Mar 16
FORT GLOBAL DIVERSIFIED	9.56	25 Mar 16
ORTUS AGGRESSIVE FUND (CAYMAN) LTD	9.44	29 Feb 16
ROY G. NIEDERHOFFER DIVERSIFIED OFFSHORE FUND	9.28	30 Mar 16
RUSSIAN PROSPERITY FUND - A	9.27	24 Mar 16
MERCHANT COMMODITY FUND (THE) - COMPOSITE	9.27	25 Mar 16
ALTIS GLOBAL TREND PORTFOLIO	9.07	29 Feb 16
CRABEL FUND SPC LTD CLASS A	8.29	25 Mar 16
TWO SIGMA COMPASS CAYMAN FUND	7.92	29 Feb 16
QMS DIVERSIFIED GLOBAL MACRO	7.80	29 Feb 16
CANTAB CAPITAL PARTNERS QUANTITATIVE FUND (THE) - USD ARISTARCHUS	7.49	25 Mar 16
MILLBURN DIVERSIFIED PROGRAM	7.38	30 Mar 16
TEWKSBURY INVESTMENT FUND, LTD - B	7.23	24 Mar 16
RENAISSANCE INSTITUTIONAL DIVERSIFIED ALPHA FUND INTL. LP.A	6.86	25 Mar 16

Bottom

Investment Funds	Return	Date
WELLINGTON MANAGEMENT INV BERMUDA LTD BAY POND A/1 NI	−24.28	29 Feb 16
SFP VALUE REALIZATION FUND	−23.30	24 Mar 16
PERSHING SQUARE INTL LTD	−20.98	22 Mar 16
OKUMUS OPPORTUNISTIC VALUE FUND, LTD CLASS A	−20.61	29 Feb 16
CCI MICRO HEALTHCARE PARTNERS LTD	−19.87	29 Feb 16
LOREM IPSUM MASTER FUND LP	−19.23	29 Feb 16
LANSDOWNE GLOBAL FINANCIALS FUND LTD. -N-USD	−19.14	18 Mar 16
SR GLOBAL FUND H - JAPAN (Real Perf)	−18.92	28 Mar 16
JENOP GLOBAL HEALTHCARE FUND LTD SERIES A	−18.72	18 Mar 16
ALTAI CAPITAL PARTNERS OFFSHORE, LTD	−17.51	29 Feb 16
AMAZON MARKET NEUTRAL FUND CLASS A USD	−17.25	25 Mar 16
CAPEVIEW AZRI 2X FUND	−16.44	24 Mar 16
PERCEPTIVE LIFE SCIENCES OFFSH FUND, LTD	−15.66	24 Mar 16
GLENVIEW CAPITAL PARTNERS (CAYMAN), LTD	−15.27	29 Feb 16
LANSDOWNE EUROPEAN EQUITY FD, LTD - A (EUR)	−15.24	25 Mar 16
TRISHIELD SPECIAL SITUATIONS FUND LLC	−14.36	29 Feb 16
TELLIGENT GREATER CHINA FUND	−13.88	29 Feb 16
TOSCA CLASS A - USD	−13.71	29 Feb 16
SEER CAPITAL PARTNERS OFFSHORE FUND LTD	−13.23	29 Feb 16
VISIUM INSTITUTIONAL PARTNERS FUND LTD	−13.21	24 Mar 16

Figure 3.1 Lots of data from a small sample.

true, the immediate response is, "I knew it!" However, the truth is, you didn't *know* it. You simply considered it to be a possibility, but with the benefit of hindsight, that outlier possibility appears to have been all but inevitable, not just to the outsider judging them, but to the decision-makers themselves. The same goes for decisions that work out well. When the stock markets rally, investors often ask, "Why should I invest with a hedge fund and pay 2/20, when I could get that kind of return just being long the S&P?" That comment, as well as the inability to acknowledge that when a hedge fund manager goes long equities the resulting returns are alpha both serve as evidence of hindsight bias. I'll expand on this shortly.

The only true way to overcome this bias when assessing a manager, or your own trades, is to keep records of the decision-making process, complete with all the evidence gathered, the probabilities assigned to different outcomes, the drivers for those probabilities, and the triggers for meeting/missing those expectations. In so doing, a trader who has a cold streak or who misses an opportunity they had once considered, can maintain a state of equanimity. That in turn improves the odds that they will continue to make decisions that are probabilistic in nature, rather than emotionally driven by P&L. It also provides evidence of rational decisions being made as part of a consistent decision-making process. That's important because it means it is repeatable.

Here's the problem with having decisions judged by the outcome. If my boss and I agree that I am making a rational decision by investing in XYZ and it doesn't work out, but he maintains his opinion of me based on the fact that my decision was rational, then I will continue to make decisions in the same manner. If, however, in light of the outcome he changes his opinion of me, then he has just injected uncertainty into my decision-making process – an uncertainty that cannot be resolved. That tends to lead to a more bureaucratic and risk-averse approach. I will explain why this is the case later.

Going back to our teens, how would either of them adjust their behavior if Brian, having arrived home safely, is rewarded by his parents for making the right decision, whereas James is punished for having been in an accident? Of course it sounds silly, but how is it different from what is done by allocators and traders every day?

The truth is that rational decisions provide the best odds of success *over time*. If I want to lose weight, I will reduce the number of calories I take in and increase the number of calories I burn. In doing so, I improve the odds that I will lose weight. Does it mean I will lose weight every day, every week, or even every month? No. Is it possible I can gain weight at some point along the way? Yes. Should I change my approach in those moments? Of course not.

There are kids who drive drunk without incidence for a time. There are people who chew tobacco for many years without any problems. There are those who can eat whatever they want without gaining weight while they're young. There are investment managers who make irrational decisions or lack a consistent investment process of any kind, yet generate positive returns for a while. However, none of these represent good bets over time.

Right is not the same as rational. Rational decisions simply improve our odds of being right. If rational decision-making is repeated in a consistent manner often enough, you should expect to be more successful than someone who does not. Is it guaranteed? No, but we are in the business of playing the odds. It's true, past results do not necessarily guarantee future performance. However, rational decision-making is certainly more predictive of success than those that have simply been right for a time. There will be times when we will be right and times when we will be wrong. All we really control is whether we are being rational. The question is, how can we tell if we're being rational?

Swing Analysis for Portfolio Managers

In 2013 the Seattle Seahawks lost in the divisional-round of the playoffs. In the press conference that followed, Russell Wilson, the team's quarterback and leader on the field, talked repeatedly about how he was looking forward to analyzing the game tapes. Now that may not sound odd to you, perhaps because you've heard that sort of thing so often, or maybe because it just makes sense. Take a second to think about it for a moment, though. At his fingertips, Russell has every stat imaginable readily available to him, including the final score, pass completions,

completions by receiver, batted passes, yards per catch, yards after the catch, and on and on. There isn't any statistic you can think of that he can't access at a moment's notice. Why then would he take the time to review game film?

When a reporter asked exactly that, here was Russell's answer.

I like to watch my footwork more than anything and see, you know, am I getting the ball out on time? Are my reads correct? Am I reading it the way I wanna read it in terms of the progressions? I think for me, when I'm getting my depth and my drops, and I'm making the right protection calls, and I'm getting back in my drops and just trusting the right read, it's pretty hard to stop. I think that's what shows on the film. I just basically play the game over again in my head. I watch all the down and distances, and look at the situations again, and just play the game again.

Russell went on to lead the Seahawks to a stunning defeat of the Denver Broncos and quarterback Peyton Manning in the Super Bowl the very next season. Denver quarterback's coach, Greg Knapp, spoke about his conversation with Peyton Manning after the game. "I told him the day after the game we were going to watch it when he came back, not right then, but the first day he was back, and we were going to watch it *without the emotion* of what just happened."

Opening the wounds of the Super Bowl was only the first step of a complete deconstruction of the previous season – a pass-by-pass analysis by Manning of Manning. For one of the most meticulous minds in the game, it was the beginning of weeks and months spent breaking down not just opposing defenses but himself.

Manning judged his decisions, footwork, and throwing motion one pass at a time. He did so not from the overconfident perspective of one of the greatest to ever play the game, but rather as someone eager to uncover and learn from his own mistakes.

Manning put himself under the microscope.

"If you ever feel like that's not important – like, 'Hey, I don't need to watch last season; I know what we did; I know what I did wrong' – no, you don't know," Manning said. "You need to watch it. Watch the bad plays. It's not fun to watch bad plays, to sit there and say, 'That's a bad decision' and 'That's a really bad decision' and 'Horrible read.' … No matter how old you are, you need to go into that prepared to be constructively criticized and learn how to grow out of the mistakes every year."

The value of video analysis in sports isn't really in question. Odds are if you've taken a golf lesson in the past five years that video analysis of your swing was probably a big part of it. In fact, golf instructors say most clients expect, and often demand it. The same goes for baseball players, tennis players, runners, and even swimmers.

Years ago, it dawned on me that I, too, could benefit from a similar process, wherein I reviewed not just my P&L and trade statistics, but an objective break down of every play, every progression, and every read; my play calling and footwork. In other words, rather than reviewing the outcomes, I would review the process itself. But how? We can't film the thought process that leads to a trade. We don't record our thoughts when we change our minds midway through the life of a trade. It isn't possible to see whether it was a bad view, poor structuring, or pressure from management at a moment of psychological vulnerability that caused a position to falter. Or is it?

By chronicling every trade, including why it is on, what the expectations are for every factor I see influencing it (and me) over time, what my plan of action is, reasons it's unlikely to work out in the end, and updating it all as the trade progresses, I am effectively creating game film that can be reviewed and critiqued, objectively and without emotion. Particularly when I'm experiencing a period of poor performance, I can remain unbiased, to continue seeing things clearly so that I don't compound a bad turn of events with bad decisions. Whereas many are likely to ease up on the critical analysis when they're doing well, it is equally important to recognize when good luck is raining down on you, to remain alert, disciplined, and yes, unbiased in that very vulnerable moment.

One of the other benefits of video analysis in the sporting world is identifying tendencies that are likely to result in injury over time. Without a thorough analysis of those potentially damaging tendencies, athletes, particularly those with a strong work ethic, who tirelessly practice their swing, over and over again, are at great risk. The same could be said for professional investors. What tendencies do you have that, in times of stress, you spend more time on that may actually put you at greater risk?

Asking the Right Questions

Richard Cantrell is a 48-year-old institutional investment manager. His teenage daughter, Jessica, is going to a concert with her friends tonight. They are a large group so will be traveling in two cars, one driven by 19-year-old Todd and the other by his 16-year-old brother, Bobby. Naturally, Richard is concerned about his daughter's safety, so he wants to be sure she will be in the car with the better driver. Luckily, the other kids are being dropped off at Richard's house and the whole group will leave from there, giving him an opportunity to have a conversation with the brothers before she leaves.

Todd is home from college for the weekend. He's a freshman studying finance at Richard's alma mater and even joined his old fraternity. He's driving a five-year-old Volvo that looks like it just came off the showroom floor. His younger brother, Bobby, isn't sure which college he wants to attend. At the moment he's more concerned about his new Ford Mustang, which is going to the body shop tomorrow for repairs. Apparently, "some old lady" wasn't paying attention when she backed out of her parking spot and clipped the back corner of his car. Neither of the boys has received a traffic violation, or at least neither was willing to admit it to Richard. They are both clean cut, well spoken and would never think of drinking and driving. If it came to it, which "it most certainly will not," they would call their father to pick them all up rather than drive while intoxicated.

Based on the information gleaned during his investigation, with whom would you have wanted your daughter to ride?

Well, Todd is older, making him a more experienced driver, not to mention he drives a car commonly associated with safety, which also happens to be in pristine condition. He is following the same life path as Richard, so naturally he assumes Todd is likely to approach other decisions in a way that is consistent with his own as well. Although it's possible young Bobby is telling the truth about the old lady, Richard has yet to meet a teenager who ever thought anything was their fault, so he treats Bobby's story with a grain of salt. Plus, Mustangs are muscle cars and we all know what type of driver is attracted to that kind of power. Richard is the analytical type. He doesn't like to rush to judgment, but given the information available he would rather be safe than sorry, so despite her protests, he insists that his daughter ride with Todd, or not at all. She promised to abide by his wish.

Jessica kept her promise, but never made it home. On the way back from the concert, Todd ran a red light. An 18-wheeler plowed into the passenger side of the Mustang, killing all four occupants. Todd's blood alcohol level was nearly twice the legal limit.

Richard consoled himself with the knowledge that he had done all he could to keep his daughter safe. Given the information available, he had made the right decision. The problem is, Richard had fallen prey to numerous cognitive biases, which, despite his best intentions and experience, undermined the entire decision-making process and led to a fatal error. Let's analyze Richard's assessment to see what I mean.

Roughly 50,000 students from all walks of life currently attend Richard's alma mater, and hundreds of thousands more attend schools that are nearly identical to it. In the years since Richard's graduation, millions have passed through that institution and others like it. To assume Todd approached decisions in a similar way to Richard solely because of the institution he attended is farfetched, no matter how much it appeals to his, and our, intuition. Todd was home for vacation from school where his battered Camaro was parked that night. His parents, knowing James' poor driving record, insisted that he drive their Volvo while he was home. That didn't sit well with James and so after "one or two beers" at the concert, he pressured his younger brother to swap cars for the ride home.

While Todd was sincere when he told Richard that he wouldn't drive while intoxicated, unfortunately, Todd had a different definition of what it meant to be intoxicated. He truly believed he was "okay to drive." In fact, like Richard, Todd also believed he was a better driver as a result of his three years behind the wheel (see Figure 3.2). His overconfidence resulted in a more cavalier attitude toward the driving experience. So, unlike his younger brother who was still a cautious driver, James liked to

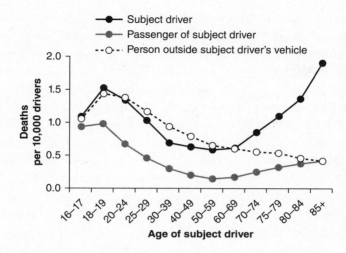

Figure 3.2 Age as related to fatal auto accidents.

drive with the music turned up loud and didn't think twice about other potential distractions caused by his passengers. Todd truly believed he was a good, responsible driver who was prepared for any situation. After all, he'd been driving successfully for three years without a single fatality or even fender bender (that he considered to be his fault), and he was responsible because he always demanded that his passengers wear their seatbelts.

The decision-making processes of both Todd and Richard are representative of the process so pervasive in our industry, complete with all the usual cognitive biases, including framing, representativeness, the halo effect, and availability. Consider the following.

Frank Swanson is the Chief Investment Officer of a large endowment. He is a stickler for details. Before he will consider investing in a particular hedge fund, the fund must pass a screening process based on a checklist of items that, over the course of many decades, have become generally accepted characteristics of the most successful investment managers. In addition, he relies on the intuition honed over his 25 years in the business. If something just doesn't feel right to him, he will pass. It's a process that has served him well, as evidenced by the fact that he now oversees $45 billion in diversified assets.

Today, Frank and his team are meeting with the leaders of two young hedge funds. The first, started by the former global head of foreign-exchange and interest-rate trading at a marquee investment firm where he had a reputation for making a lot of money, launched with $500 million in assets under management (AUM); $50 million of it came from his own pocket. With three years under their belt, they haven't knocked it out of the park, nor have they blown up. Like most established firms, they've experienced a few good runs with the occasional rough patch, but nothing that should raise alarm bells. They have 15 analysts, an economist who used to work at the Federal Reserve and another from the Bank of England, plus 10 portfolio managers with experience in a wide range of asset classes. They employ tight speed bumps to ensure no single portfolio manager can "do too much damage," and in any case, the majority of risk is taken by the chief investment officer (CIO). They use the most revered law firm, accountants, auditors, and fund administrators to handle their administrative and operational needs, and employ the most trusted risk-management software, which is overseen by an independent risk officer. The firm subscribes to the best-known independent research and has direct access to thought leaders throughout the industry.

A man who had been a portfolio manager at three different hedge funds over the past 10 years runs the other fund being assessed today. All three had failed for three different reasons, none of which appeared to be tied to his actions. Although he had produced excellent returns, his Sharpe ratio was barely above 1.0. Although he had run several very profitable institutional trading businesses prior to moving to the buy-side, they were all within second-tier banks and insurance companies, so he isn't well known throughout the industry. The firms who handle their legal, accounting, auditing, and administrative work are also well known and reputable. The CIO doesn't believe in outsourcing research, trade structuring, or execution, so he doesn't have any analysts, nor do they subscribe to outside research either. All ideas are internally generated by scouring economic and market data in the same manner that produced his top-tier track record, and goes a long way to explain why his returns are so uncorrelated to every major index. His fund currently has just $20 million in AUM, mostly from friends and family, but he has previously managed upward of $1 billion in his independent portfolios.

Based on the information gleaned during Frank's investigation, with whom would you have invested?

If you are being honest, the clear winner is the first fund. Purely from a marketing and fundraising perspective, simply coming out of a prestigious firm, such as Goldman Sachs or Morgan Stanley, provides a distinct competitive advantage. That credibility translates into commitments from other credible institutions, which creates a credibility cascade, resulting in the $500 million launch. With such a base, other large institutions with both minimum investment and maximum proportion rules in place can participate. Being familiar with the allocator "checklist," the first manager catered to them all. Truth be told, he believed in the value of the checklist, too, which is why he didn't hesitate to pull together so many analysts, economists, and advisors.

As for the second fund manager, while he may have a more transparent and superior track record, qualifying his accomplishments requires more work. He suffers from something akin to guilt by association. Although it is clear that he was not responsible for the downfall of the firms at which he had been employed, simply being associated with them created a mental hurdle that had to be overcome, precisely the opposite of what the other manager had working in his favor, at least on the surface. In reality, they were both affected by what is known as the *availability cascade*.

It is a phenomenon in which one bit of information creates a baseline expectation and each additional bit serves to reinforce that expectation. Our ears perk up to new information that supports the original narrative, while contradictory evidence goes unnoticed. Every step of the way, the story seems to unfold, becoming more powerful and seemingly more obvious, regardless of the predictive value of the data, or even whether it is valid.

Mistakes in Common

Truth is, in both Richard (the dad deciding which car to have his daughter ride in) and Frank's (The CIO deciding how to allocate assets) analyses, there wasn't any information provided that was of any predictive value. Every bit was meant to trigger bias in you, the reader, by appealing to our deep-seated beliefs. Even the description of Frank conveyed little information of real value, yet it likely generated serious bias within the reader's mind.

The both analyses were perfunctory at best. In neither case was any inquiry made regarding the decision-making process of any of the participants. How did Todd arrive at his decision to attend Richard's alma mater? Why did the first manager employ tight speed bumps? How did the second manager deliver such uncorrelated returns so consistently? How does Todd define intoxication in that moment? Would one beer qualify? Why did he select the Volvo? How much did the first manager's group at his old employer make in the five years before he took over relative to what it made under his guidance? How about the three years since? Why would you (not) employ analysts? Questions that should have been asked were ignored, and in the absence of those answers, the missing pieces were filled in with bias.

When you understand how decisions should be made in order to generate better results over time, you have a better understanding of the questions that should be asked in order to better predict the performance of drivers, traders, portfolio managers, CIOs, and allocators. To do so requires fighting our natural inclination to achieve cognitive ease by relying on gut feel and intuition, in favor of inviting cognitive strain by asking questions that require deep reflection and investigation. Truth be told, the correlation between alpha generation and the information being used to make investment and allocation decisions by the majority of decision makers in this industry is highly speculative at best. Simply working at a highly regarded, very profitable investment firm is no more predictive of the ability to generate alpha as a hedge fund manager than attending your alma mater can predict a teenager's ability to deliver your daughter home safely. More on this shortly.

Descriptive versus Prescriptive Decision Theory

The second of the two dominant disciplines in the study of decision-making is descriptive decision theory. Whereas normative decision theorists study how we *should* make decisions, descriptive decision theorists study how we *actually* make them. For the past several decades, a growing number of researchers have been focusing their efforts in this area. Some of them, like Daniel Kahneman, have developed something of a cult following for their work, and rightly so. What they've discovered is that far more often than any of us would like to believe we make decisions in a way that differs from how we *should* be making them.

I am involved in a third, less-traveled discipline within the field, known as *prescriptive decision theory*. Here, we attempt to help decision-makers close the gap between how they actually make decisions and how they should. In order to do so, we must first understand what it is that exists in that gap. Simply stated, what exists between how a decision is made and how it should be is a *mistake* (Figure 3.3). Remove the mistake and you have a decision made in the manner in which it should be.

The question we should be asking then is, why do we make decision-related mistakes, and is there a common theme among them? The answer has a lot to do with the sheer volume of decisions that we face on a regular basis. It simply isn't possible to thoughtfully collect data, then properly process and assess it in order to select the most appropriate action for every one of the million plus decisions we face each and every day. In case you think that figure represents an exaggeration, consider how your day begins.

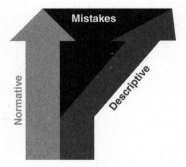

Figure 3.3   Mistakes exist between how a decision is made and how it should be made.

The alarm goes off. Before you open your eyes, you choose whether to hit snooze. Then you repeat the decision a few minutes later. At some point, you decide to get out of bed. Then, should you relieve your bowel? In the toilet? Sitting or standing? Lift the seat? Flush when you're through? Lower the seat? Wash your hands? Hot water, cold, or some combination thereof? How much soap? Rinse? Brush teeth? Hold it in left hand or right? Put toothpaste on the bristles only, or across your knuckles? For how long should you brush? How long on each tooth? Leave the water running while brushing? Rinse? Shower? Breakfast? You get the point. Before you have even removed the sleepers from your eyes, you have already faced and made hundreds of decisions. Effectively, hundreds of decisions made before you are even awake. Choices that affect the rest of your day and your long-term health, for all intents and purposes, made routinely without you being involved as an active participant. Instead, you make many of these decisions through a combination of habits, intuition, and gut feel. They are mental shortcuts, or what cognitive scientists call heuristics, used to make so many of our more *automated* decisions.

Most scientists would agree, employing heuristics is absolutely necessary. Our brains just don't possess the processing power, nor do we have the time to apply a proper decision analysis to every choice we face. For the majority of these routine tasks, making decisions by employing heuristics works just fine. Theoretically, heuristics allow us to be more efficient decision-makers, freeing us to focus our attention and employ cognitive strain where the consequences are significant. Unfortunately, heuristics are so readily available and require so little effort to employ that we tend to rely on them far more often than we should even when the consequences are as significant as life and death. It is in the moments when we should be employing cognitive strain, but fall back on heuristics, that we make the majority of our mistakes. Although heuristics are necessary for us to function on a daily basis, when they are employed in situations that require a more thorough analysis, we become vulnerable to unconscious influences that have a tendency to produce systematic errors in judgment.

Chapter 4

Decision Analysis

We Are All Students of the Same Game

Students in my Decision Analysis class have to create one decision log per week. The assignment requires that they analyze an actual decision they have faced or are currently facing. The decisions they choose to analyze include whether they should break up with their girlfriend or boyfriend, where they should go for spring break, what job to accept and how much to spend on their weddings. Initially I provide very little guidance, so they do their best to produce an analysis that they believe will show me they are methodical and deliberate in their approach. Even when it is clear that they simply chose the path of least resistance, they will attempt to generate a narrative that explains their approach as rational and thoughtful.

Much to their chagrin, I actually provide very little advice as it specifically relates to the assignment throughout the entire semester. At least that's what many of them believe. Truth is, the entire course, including reading material, case studies, and lectures is about the process of decision-making. We cover statistical concepts such as probabilities and Bayes Theorem, mistakes some very smart people have made in applying these concepts, the components of a decision, and real-world examples for applying it all to actual business and policy decisions. Students are also exposed to esoteric terms used to describe proper process and systematic errors. I purposely provide little guidance for the decision logs so that I can ascertain whether they are making the connection between the material they are studying and the concurrent decisions they are facing.

Before going further, let me be clear. These students are some of the smartest, most driven individuals among their contemporaries around the world. They finished high school with highly competitive GPAs and standardized test scores, are graduating seniors or graduate engineering students at one of the finest engineering programs on Earth (UCSB's College of Engineering has more Nobel Laureates on the faculty than any other). Despite these qualifications, it typically takes many weeks before they are able to make the direct connection between the material and their own actions. Regardless of how long it takes for it to click that these aren't merely theories we are covering and that this course isn't simply about memorizing a collection of terms they'll never use again, the progression toward that realization follows a very consistent pattern.

Stage 1: Autopilot

In this phase students follow the protocol that's served them well for their entire academic careers. Very little thought is put in. Instead, they rely on their intuition to produce just another in a long line of documents meant to satisfy yet one more course requirement.

Stage 2: Cognitive Ease

Even though they are incorporating the proper terminology into the log, they aren't actually applying the ideas. In other words, they are attempting to satisfy what they believe I want to see by effectively delivering the same decision analysis, except this time they've swapped out layman's terminology in favor of the more technical terms. Nothing really about their approach to decision-making has changed except for how they describe the process. It is a superficial adjustment – no real substantive progress has been made.

Stage 3: Stress

After a number of logs have been submitted – all of which have likely received grades well below what they're used to – the stress sets in. They worry about the final course grade based on the current trajectory. Office hours become more crowded and pleas for extra credit opportunities flood in. My response is the same every time. Spend less time worrying about grades and more effort applying what you are learning to your own decisions. Invite cognitive strain. Dig deeper, ask tougher questions and replace leaps of faith with statistical analysis. This is the phase that can act like quicksand, even for many of the top students. They will dig in their heels, working harder to argue their case rather than applying the concepts. They will complain, beg me to just tell them what I want so they can deliver it, pass blame and claim too little time available before finally dropping their defenses. Hopefully, it happens before the semester comes to an end, but when it does ... fireworks!

Stage 4: Cognitive Strain

This is the phase that keeps me coming back for more each semester. When students drop their defenses, when they stop fighting cognitive strain and instead invite it, that's when the magic happens. They begin seeing the whole world through new, high-powered lenses. Some have described it as similar to that moment in *The Matrix* when Neo (Keanu Reeves) takes the red pill. Although the benefits are amazing, they require hard work to achieve, and that is perhaps one of the best lessons they will learn. Thankfully, most of them seem to realize it. The evidence can be found in their course feedback:

> "Taking this class has changed my life! I learned the importance of questioning everything. It helped me quit smoking, deal with rejection, among other serious negative outcomes and more than that, it allowed me to open my mind to possibilities. This is the most rewarding class I have taken, but demands you putting in work. Please utilize this with an open mind and do not be very sticky to what you believe in."

Author's Note: The red pill – as opposed to the blue pill – is swallowed by Neo when offered a choice by Morpheus in the movie's famous scene. Taking the red pill is perceived as Neo's desire to see undoctored truth (things as they really are).

"If I could I would take this course every term. What you learn here is something to be used every day. It is difficult to master the subject, but you will feel the difference in your life if you make the effort."

"Incredibly challenging course, but I enjoyed every single class. Duneier is the GOAT."

"If taken advantage of and if you delve yourself into applying concepts of this class to real life, very valuable stuff! Thank you!"

"I learned a lot that I believe will have a measurable impact on my life."

"Best course ever! Very challenging and practical course. By far the most interesting class I've taken with a noticeable change in personal decision-making."

"The most interesting/insightful course I have taken in college. Extremely practical and applicable to real-world apps. Course is challenging and encourages students to think."

I share this with you, because the stages are very similar to what I've discovered in working with clients. We all want to avoid cognitive strain. Our brains are phenomenal at convincing us that we are invoking it even when we are simply using more technical terms or codifying a poor process so that it appears more systematic and rational. Thanks to technology we can gather all kinds of data, run all kinds of analysis, but if we don't ask the right questions at the right moments, we risk turning sporadic mistakes into systematic flaws.

These days, I am interviewed regularly about the rise of artificial intelligence and machine learning in the world of finance. Here's the thing about the ease with which we can gather data and run massive analytical programs, not to mention the ability to effectively outsource optimization to machines that can think and process far faster than we could ever hope. Optimization requires that you properly define the outcome you desire, and that is what I've discovered is so often ignored by decision-makers at the university and CIO level.

As an example, when my students submit a decision log about where they should go for spring break, they will typically present three potential destinations from which they must choose. Often, the choices are something along the lines of Acapulco, Las Vegas, or New York City. Three terrific options for your typical spring breaker! The problem is, they don't have much in common. The fact that they are the options being considered tells me that very little work has been done as it relates to properly defining what it is they hope to achieve, what the important factors are, and how they will choose from among them. In other words, what gives them pleasure? What are the key factors by which they will judge the trip a success or failure?

They will express frustration in quantifying the difference in utility gained by lying around a pool as scantily clad, beautiful people circulate around them and enjoying a beer at a trendy restaurant in SoHo. They have difficulty comparing a $5 margarita on the beach to a "free" cocktail served at the blackjack table. Instead, they choose to imagine a moment of peak pleasure in each location and compare the utility gained in each of those scenarios as judged in the moment of contemplation. If they happen to be sitting in the hot sun, struggling with the humidity as they are weighing their options, it's likely a trip to humid Acapulco will be less desirable than a visit to bone dry Las Vegas, and so on.

You can see how quickly all these considerations become burdensome, and perhaps unnecessarily so. That's when we say things like, "we could think about this forever, but ultimately, we just need to make a decision. After all, all three are phenomenal options and I'm sure I'll enjoy any of them." That's when the brain's desire to maintain cognitive ease has officially won.

The same goes for investing. It seems like such a simple process. Find a machine that can generate the best returns and allocate to it. Oh, if only it were that simple. You see, the best a machine can do is improve the accuracy of our predictions, and it does so by gathering more information and considering more factors in its analysis. Given that most in this industry do little more than the bare bones minimum in this area, it's easy to see how depending on machines for this part of the job will yield great improvement. Still, producing more accurate odds of success is only a small piece of the decision-making and investment process. An investor must define *and understand* their risk tolerance. A machine doesn't guarantee results, it simply optimizes its predictions of the future based on how the investor defines his objectives. Therein lies the potential conflict. A machine is programed to play the odds, it doesn't care if it wins or loses whereas the investor (programmer) clearly does.

Just as students should take the time to understand what they enjoy, what their monetary constraints are (beyond simply, "How much is in my bank account today") and what aspects of each of their options can affect their ability to achieve the outcome they desire, so, too, should investors consider what it is they desire, before choosing between a systematic, long-short equity fund, a 30-year US Treasury, and an equity index ETF.

Decision Analysis

We use the term *decision* without batting an eye, yet when I ask a classroom of graduate students enrolled in my course called Decision Analysis, "What is a decision?" you could hear a pin drop. Some might say, it's a choice that you make, but that's only a small component of it. A decision is the combination of a problem you want to solve, the data you collect to understand it, the analysis you conduct to find the optimal solution, as well as the action you choose in order to achieve the result you desire. All combined these steps form a decision.

I find it easiest to visualize a decision by breaking it down into its three key components: acts, states, and outcomes. The *outcome,* as stated earlier, is essentially the problem you are trying to solve. As an example, say you want to lose 10 pounds ahead of next month's high school reunion. A loss of 10 pounds is the outcome you desire and the problem you want to solve. You could choose to cut out all carbs, run 10 miles a day, or eat a box of jelly donuts twice a week. Each of these *acts* represents a potential solution to the problem at hand. Yes, eating jelly donuts is a possible solution, albeit one that is very unlikely to result in the desired outcome. The reason it probably won't get you where you want to be, has to do with what we call *states*. These are the factors that affect our ability to convert an act into the outcome we seek to achieve. We can't control them, but we must account for them if we are to have any hope of succeeding. The fact that our bodies convert sugar into fat, exercise burns more calories than sitting still, and jelly donuts are calorie-dense is simply how these things work. They are *states* of the world. If we hope to choose the act that provides the best odds of us losing 10 pounds ahead of our reunion we'd be wise to factor them in.

It's tempting to view the world so simplistically. I want to lose 10 pounds, so I'll work out every day until the reunion. After all, it's not rocket science. Working out burns calories. If I burn more than I consume, I will lose weight. Everyone knows that, therefore no data needs to be collected. No analysis is required. Problem solved.

This is how we typically make decisions. Through a combination of common knowledge, logic, and intuition, we make assumptions about the states and use them as the foundation for additional assumptions, before eventually leaping to conclusions about the most appropriate act. Every step of the way, we attempt to achieve and maintain a state of cognitive ease (i.e., avoid cognitive strain). In other words, we do our best to avoid thinking deeply. It's not our fault though. The human body is an efficiency-maximizing machine. Consider the evidence.

If you take in precisely the same number of calories and follow the exact same fitness routine when you are 50 as you did when you were 20, you will gain weight. The reason is, as we age, our bodies become more efficient at utilizing calories. Therefore, we don't need to consume as many of them in order to complete a particular task, which was certainly helpful for aging hunter-gatherers thousands of years ago. As their ability to find food slowed so too did their need to consume it. There's another aspect to efficiency maximization that relates to productivity.

Heuristics

Recall those images of the predator species such as lions, lounging lazily in the shade of a lone acacia tree in the Serengeti. Lionesses, the ones who do the majority of hunting for the pride, can sleep up to 18 hours a day, whereas their male counterparts often do so even longer. When they aren't sleeping, they move methodically, conserving as much energy as possible, until an opportunity for a high-probability kill presents itself, and then they go all out. Running at full speed, bringing down beasts two or three times their size, then tearing the flesh from bone is physically demanding work, requiring a tremendous number of calories to execute. After a big meal they can sleep a full 24 hours before waking up again. Cheetahs, the fastest land animals, are even more efficient. If the kill doesn't happen quickly, it will give up the chase, otherwise it risks exhausting its store of calories before it can replenish them, leading to death by starvation. So, while predator animals might appear lazy, they're actually being efficient with the limited amount of energy they have at their disposal.

Although very few of us still hunt for our survival, the technology that has made food so plentiful evolved at a much more rapid pace than have our bodies. As a result, we remain hard-wired to conserve calories which is not quite so advantageous in an age when calorie-dense foods are so readily accessible, in microwavable, bite-sized pieces. Hence the increase in extra chins, love handles, and the plethora of health issues that accompany them.

As it happens, we are just as efficient when it comes to cognitive activity, and the effects are similarly destructive, even if they aren't visible to the naked eye. Throughout our lives, we are constantly accumulating information, with the great majority of it being gathered indiscriminately. Meaning we don't deliberately seek it, nor do we really investigate it. More accurately, we rub up against it. Unless that information is challenged at the moment we come into contact with it, it becomes part of our beliefs, regardless of its validity. Once stored in our mental database, it is difficult for us to recall its specific origins, which puts information sourced from academic journals on equal footing with those derived from, say, the plot of a novel, a movie trailer, or even a satirical article. This is significant, because all new information that we gather is assessed according to that which came before it. You can see how this might lead to problems if we were to base our decisions on such a flawed database. As they say, "Garbage in, garbage out." Unfortunately, that is exactly what we do.

In order to achieve and maintain a state of cognitive ease, we employ heuristics, a fancy term for mental shortcuts, such as intuition and gut feel. Rather than questioning the validity of our beliefs, we assume they are based on solid evidence, the result of thoughtful research and analysis over the course of our lives. Its reliability is therefore unassailable, at least in our view. That confidence extends from information gathering to the intuitive analysis of the data it produces. We may, for instance, recall a decision from our past that, at least on the surface, appears very similar in nature to the one we are facing today. As far as we remember, that one worked out well, so without having to invest much mental energy, we can draw the conclusion that the same act chosen back then would be the most appropriate this time around as well. Do that enough times and you will develop a rule of thumb, allowing for even less mental effort and speedier decisions the next time around. In effect, the mistake is being codified, like an athlete who practices incorrectly, over and over again. The more highly educated, more experienced, and especially the more successful we believe ourselves to be, the more confident we will be in our intuition, which, in turn, encourages us to rely on it even more often. That is how we become more mentally "efficient" as we get older.

The Biggest Mistake in Decision-Making

Making good decisions is a skill like any other. Sure, you can be taught the fundamentals, even some of the key mistakes that the majority of people make. After reading all the books, taking courses, starting the journals, and even employing a coach, there will remain a wide dispersion in the abilities among decision-makers. In other words, decision-making isn't a binary endeavor, where either you've read the books and are an expert, or you haven't and you're not. There are degrees of expertise and excellence, as there are for all skills.

To improve our decision-making skills, we must take what we as a species have learned about ourselves through decades of research and incorporate it into our process. Then, not only must we practice it consistently, but gather data and make additional marginal adjustments along the way in order to build upon our strengths, and either diminish our weaknesses or reduce their impact on the results. It sounds simple but it's not. It turns out there's one incredibly powerful impediment standing in our way: Ourselves.

It's difficult to compare decision-making as a skill in its own right against other endeavors such as swinging a tennis racquet or running a business, because when you distill everything and anything down to its simplest form, you are left with the decision. Investing, golfing, lifestyle management, even plumbing are nothing more than an amalgamation of millions of decisions, grouped together by common factors. At their root, they are all the same business – the business of decision-making. Focus on and improve the decision-making process, and you will improve your results in any field you choose.

All decisions, whether we're talking about the decision to put the toilet seat down after using it or to cut our losses on a fund manager, are comprised of the same components – outcome, states, and acts. The decision-making process should follow the same pattern, in the same order, whether the decisions being made involve investments, calling a play in the NFL, or launching the space shuttle. The more we know with certainty, the higher the probability the optimal action can be taken. Therefore, evidence should trump beliefs in order to better inform the decision, no matter how strongly those beliefs appeal to our intuition or how many others around us agree with what our gut suggests.

Since I began teaching and coaching others to improve their own decision-making process, I've discovered a key mistake in the approach of nearly everyone with whom I've ever worked. It is a flaw that I have yet to read about in a single textbook or best seller on the subject. Even after weeks of discussing it with clients and lecturing on it with students, it often remains an issue, and perhaps the greatest hurdle to their improvement. This mistake reduces creativity, leads to square pegs being forced into round holes, and endless cycles of firefighting. What I am about to describe is not the *only* mistake commonly on display in human decision-making, but because it is the very first step in a proper decision-making process, it affects everything that comes after it. From that moment on, no matter how consistent, evidence-based, and proactive our decision-making process may be, our choices will very likely be suboptimal.

If you want to improve your decision-making, this is where I recommend you begin focusing your effort, but be forewarned, the solution is so deceptively simple, even after I bring it to your attention and emphasize its importance, it is still very challenging to incorporate. Sure, you'll give a nod to it and maybe even feign an attempt to satisfy the task, but most have difficulty getting their minds to employ the cognitive strain necessary to truly, definitively, and properly attend to it.

What I am talking about is beginning the decision-making process by answering the very simple question, "What is the problem you are attempting to solve?" Yes, *before* you begin considering the advantages of one act versus another, weighing the pros and cons, or running a cost/benefit analysis, you must first very specifically define the true problem you are attempting to solve, the outcome you desire, and the criteria by which you will assess your decision. That is the very first step in normative (proper) decision-making, no matter what decision problem you face.

If that seems obvious to you, yet you didn't take issue with how I worded the opening sentence four paragraphs ago, there is a disconnect. "All decisions, whether we're talking about the decision to put the toilet seat down after using it or to cut our losses on that fund manager" is how the sentence started, and immediately it sets you up to skip step number 1. You see, whether you should cut your losses on an investment manager isn't the decision problem. Cut or don't cut, are simply two possible acts from which to choose in order to solve a specific problem. They are options typically produced as a result of our employing heuristics, meaning mental shortcuts like gut feel and intuition. We then "analyze the decision" by further employing heuristics rather than a systematic, disciplined and consistent approach.

Think about it. The question about whether you should drop a manager is very likely to be triggered by an event that evoked an emotion, be it a loss, a recent conversation, or comment from a third party. Emotion is a factor we'd rather not have influencing our decision-making. Let's pretend though that emotion wasn't a factor. Even then, simply jumping to the question about whether you should drop the fund manager will most likely follow a path derived by the instinctive response to the question. In other words, whatever characteristic you first recall as it relates to this manager, will have a powerful influence on the entire analysis, regardless of the weighting it should hold based on the evidence.

Fact is, when your decision-making process begins with "should I or shouldn't I," you have already stacked the odds of an optimal decision heavily against yourself, and thrown the door wide open to the type of predictable irrationality you've read about in all those books and articles.

At that point, cognitive bias isn't just a potential factor that you need to consider, it is an integral part of your process, indistinguishable from any other aspect of your process.

A client I coach provided a terrific example of this during one of his sessions. He described how difficult the end-of-year employee reviews had been. He had all the employee information, feedback from senior management, and data, yet he struggled to conduct what he would consider a "valid" assessment. The reason is that the *Outcome* component of the decision, as it relates to the original hiring of that employee, had never been properly defined, including the criteria by which that decision would be assessed. So, there he sat with all the information you would think necessary to properly assess the decision, yet he had no rational way of assessing the *act* chosen to solve the original decision problem. That left open the very likely possibility that his assessment wouldn't match that of the employee's version, and possibly, the assessment of every other manager. Therefore, rather than conducting a proper assessment that optimally would leave no gap whatsoever between the firm's assessment and the employee's, he was left to craft a narrative. Not an evidence-based decision analysis but, instead, just a coherent story. In the past, that would have satisfied my client, and possibly the employee too, but since working with us, he now thinks about his decisions differently. In that moment, it begged the very simple, yet overlooked questions, "What is the purpose of the assessment itself? What is the firm trying to accomplish with the act, and are we actually achieving that outcome, or are we simply spinning our wheels and wasting time?"

As I said earlier, fixing this mistake is difficult, and it isn't the only common one that we make on a regular basis, but if you are looking for that one marginal adjustment that can radically improve your decision-making and positively impact your performance, this is where you should start. Be forewarned though, this is a skill and it takes time to develop. I can practically guarantee that simply reading about it here won't change your behavior. It requires a feedback loop. It requires a particular type of coaching, but even the best coach cannot help if you are unwilling to change. The exercises that are required in order to overcome this costly mistake are frustrating, aggravating, and often counterintuitive. My students hate me during this phase, and so do many of my clients. It is the defining phase in our relationship. From that moment it goes one of two ways. Either I never hear from them again, or they become die-hard believers for life. Again, it is that moment in the Matrix when Neo takes the red pill, when everything he's ever believed – down to the way he perceives and interacts with the world around him – changes forever. In the film, his body convulses, he vomits, and falls unconscious. Is it the end of his journey? Quite the contrary! It is a necessary step in order for his journey to begin.

Why is it so difficult to fix? We have been programmed to approach decisions from the wrong end of the process because we have become so accustomed to relying on heuristics (mental shortcuts). Cognitive ease is a habit, a function of our inherent desire to maximize efficiency. Yes, it served us well when we had to conserve calories between meals, but in today's world it can be a true impediment to optimal decision making (and happiness). It's a hassle to properly define decision problems. It requires that you silence the voices in your head, and those around you, that are constantly pushing you to take action before proper analysis and prioritize with incomplete information. How do we prioritize? We focus our attention on putting out fires, but also on those things that just happen to come into our view. It takes serious effort to concentrate your attention on the bigger picture, to contemplate deeper meaning and objectives. It's far easier to just "get this out of the way" and *then* get to that other stuff. Problem is, we rarely get to the other stuff. So, decision after decision, we skip steps one and two, choosing instead to get right to the heart of the matter, step number 3. Choosing between the acts that immediately come to mind, without ever truly understanding what it is the act is intended to achieve or what factors need to be accounted for.

I recently spent an afternoon with a coaching client and his team. My questions were designed to specifically and completely define steps 1 and 2, but every response was about jumping straight to step 3. Keep in mind that there are only three fundamental steps in every decision. If steps one and two are completed correctly, step 3 hardly requires any effort whatsoever. New, outside-the-box ideas immediately spring to mind, and the optimal alternative act is blatantly obvious to everyone in the room. However, if you insist on skipping the first two steps, step three can be debated for hours with little or no progress. As it was for the client who was attempting to do a proper assessment of his employees, it is nearly impossible to arrive at a normative decision that, if challenged, can be settled definitively. Instead, they are resolved with, "Let's just agree to disagree."

A version of that is what most portfolio managers experience every moment after they initiate a position. If the objectives and states aren't properly defined prior to entry, the choice between alternative acts of "continue to hold" or "unwind" will provide a never-ending quandary, fueling doubt until the trigger is pulled and, very likely, even longer. However, if steps 1 and 2 are properly managed, that final step regarding the unwind requires almost no effort whatsoever. Much more on this as we progress.

Chapter 5

How to Solve Any Problem

T he majority of students who take my course are concentrating their studies in engineering, psychology, or economics. Typically, very few of them consider themselves artists. At the start of a semester, I ask my new students whether they can draw a copy of a photo of Brad Pitt – I mean a near-flawless replica of the photo. The overwhelming majority responds with a resounding "No." Some claim they don't possess the artistic gene, whereas others concede that with enough training, they probably could do it.

The truth is, I can teach just about anyone to draw a near perfect replica of this photo in a matter of seconds. It doesn't require a particular genetic gift or the development of a physical skill. The problem isn't one of artistry, but of decision- making.

For so long, we have defined creativity as an ability to devise something representative, perhaps even functional, out of abstraction. Thinking creatively, or creative problem solving is often described as thinking "outside the box," which in itself is an abstract concept. It begs the questions, what is the box, who made it, and how?

The answer is, the box is actually a frame, constructed by you as a function of all the information you've gathered leading up to this moment, and how you went about gathering it. In observing how others behave, solve problems, and gather their own data, you build the foundation of your framework. The way it is delivered to you, complete with the biases possessed by the people who have conveyed it, affects the frame through which all new information is considered and problems are approached. Therefore, there is no one box but, rather, a unique box assembled by each and every one of us for ourselves. You can't think outside your own box, only the box of someone else. In order for me to teach you how to draw a perfect replica of Brad's image, I don't need to teach you a new physical skill. Instead, I must reframe the problem for you. By doing that, your frame expands, allowing you to solve it for yourself.

Take a look at Figure 5.1. When I ask my students, "Can you create a near perfect replica of *this* image, in which each box contains a solid pigment?" with great confidence, they giggle and answer emphatically, "Yes, of course!"

Well, this second image is a portion of Mr. Pitt's eyeball, as seen when the original photo is viewed at 30x zoom. It is arguably the most difficult part of the photo to replicate. If you believe with great confidence that

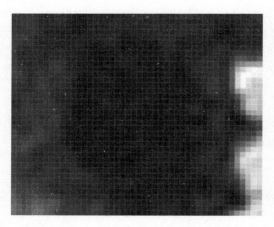

Figure 5.1   A portion of Brad Pitt's eyeball at 30x zoom.

you can replicate the most difficult part of the photo, it must follow that you can do the same for all the other segments. Therefore, you must be able to replicate the photo in its entirety.

The same goes for any problem you face, whether it is how to lose weight, gather more assets, or generate better returns. Simply by reframing the problem, new solutions − often obvious ones − will suddenly appear, seemingly out of thin air. In that moment, your frame expands. With this new solution lying firmly within the bounds of your new frame, and certainly well within your skillset, it becomes impossible to understand how you missed such an apparent solution.

Truth be told, in showing you how to create this image of Brad Pitt, I've actually given you the skill necessary to become a world-class artist. I suspect you're thinking, "that's not real art, and it certainly wouldn't make me a world class artist," but you'd be wrong. Chuck Close, one of the highest-earning artists in the world for many decades, creates his art using this very technique. Recently, he's taken it in a slightly different direction, but the principles are the same.

Close Enough

What you see in Figure 5.2 is a poorly lit photo of a Chuck Close painting. For those unfamiliar with his work, here is what British art historian, Tim Marlow, had to say about this American artist. "[Close is] a kind of lone figure in contemporary art − no one else is doing what he is doing. He's a painter's painter, but his reputation is still growing. I'd put him among the top 10 most important American artists since abstract expressionism, no question." Of course, Close's paintings aren't everyone's cup of tea, but he is a giant in contemporary art, having had major retrospectives at the most prestigious museums in the world, and his paintings consistently fetch many millions of dollars at auction.

It may not be apparent from Figure 5.2, but Chuck Close is a portraiture artist, beginning as a photorealist before moving into more abstract work. He has created massive portraits composed of dots made with a pencil eraser dipped in charcoal, some using torn pieces of paper in different shades of gray and still others using nothing but his

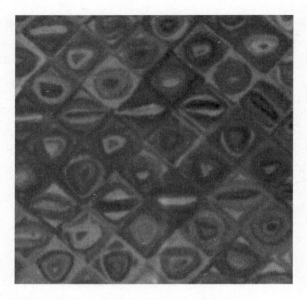

Figure 5.2   Close-up of Chuck Close painting.

fingerprint and an inkpad. In the photo shown in Figure 5.2, he uses pixels filled with colorful, amoeba-like shapes to generate a beautiful self-portrait.

Don't see it? That's because I cut out the rest of the image. I truncated your frame of reference and selected only what I wanted you to see in order to tell you a specific story. If I had shown you the entire painting, you might have missed all the intricate details of this section, including the interplay of lively colors and childlike shapes. I could have selected a similarly sized section of any one of his many paintings that employs this style to create a portrait. With only that section, you would see beauty, color, and artistry, but you could never see depth or how that section contributes to and is affected by those surrounding it.

If I provided you with each individual section of every Close creation in which he employed this technique, you could hold your own in an intelligent, in-depth conversation about the intricacies of Close's paintings with any expert on his work. However, you would know so little about the paintings themselves. You'd be hard pressed to recognize whether it is of a man, a woman, or even a person at all. In discussing the fine details, you might sound intelligent, even to someone who knows the big picture, and would likely believe it yourself, but the truth is you'd know very little about the subject.

Storm of the Century

In January 2015, Anderson Cooper began the night's episode of *360* by telling his viewers that we could look forward to a special two-hour edition of the show that would bring us all the latest on the Storm of the Century. The first 27 minutes featured live reports from around the northeast where reporters spoke of 30-foot waves, erosion of the shoreline, hurricane force winds, and snow drifts that forced the closure of schools and transportation systems. Anderson brought in an expert, a CNN weatherman, who went to great lengths to explain why they would never cry wolf about such a storm, because then no one would listen to them in the future. They went on and on about the catastrophic consequences and the intelligent decision-making by governors and mayors in the region to deal with them proactively.

Over the course of 27 minutes, one of the most viewed news outlets in the world ignored every other story it had been presenting as "vital" information just hours earlier. It was as though nothing mattered except the weather in the northeast. They showed us just one small portion of the entire canvas of what was newsworthy, and we were glued to the screens. For hours, it dominated social media and phone conversations. Millions adjusted their schedules, canceled meetings, and moved cars off the streets. Everything else in the world took a back seat.

The truth is, the weather wasn't the only newsworthy story that night, any more than bedbugs, ISIS, the Brexit vote, or Trump's election were when the entire world was hyperfocused on them for a time. Ultimately, they are all just tiny sections of a much bigger painting. They all are essential to the big picture, but must be understood within the context of the whole to be of value.

We See What We Are Shown

Visual illusions are terrific metaphors for the cognitive illusions we fall prey to all the time. The problem is, we have so much faith in our ability to gather the right information, accurately assess it, and make proper decisions based upon it all, that even in the face of opposing evidence, we tend to trust our gut over the facts. Sure, we see the mistakes being made by others, and, occasionally, we may even see how we ourselves may have been vulnerable to it in the past, but in the moment it is occurring, we are blind to our blindness.

In Figure 5.3, there are 12 black dots that you can easily see one, two or even three at a time. However, it's nearly impossible to see all 12 simultaneously. There is much speculation and study surrounding why this is the case. As it relates to the topic at hand though, I'm less concerned with why, and more interested in the fact that we are blind to three-quarters of the relevant information that is staring us right in the face. We are fully cognizant of the existence of all 12 black dots, and can see to all the edges of the image (the big picture), but can't process it all simultaneously.

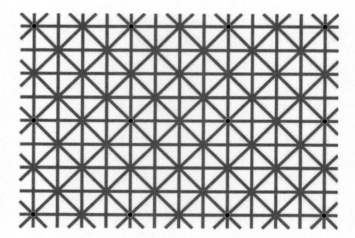

Figure 5.3 Twelve black dots on a dark-gray grid.
SOURCE: J. Ninio and K.A. Stevens, "Variations on the Hermann Grid: An Extinction Illusion," *Perception* (2000). Reproduced with permission of SAGE.

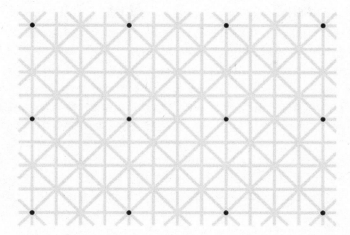

Figure 5.4   Twelve black dots on a light-gray grid
SOURCE: J. Ninio and K.A. Stevens, "Variations on the Hermann Grid: An
Extinction Illusion," *Perception* (2000). Reproduced with permission of
SAGE.

However, if I make one minor adjustment to the image (Figure 5.4),
dimming the gray lines that connect the dots, suddenly it all comes into
focus. In other words, if I reduce the irrelevant information, what we in
the business of investment management call the noise, suddenly what is
relevant becomes blatantly obvious.

Going back to the Rubik's cube example from Chapter 2, when
asked what color the two center pieces are, we instantly ignore all the
extraneous information. Well, that's what we believe happens at least.
The reality is, as this example shows, once information is processed by
our brains, it becomes incredibly difficult to ignore it. Not until the
irrelevant information is deemphasized can we see the environment as it
actually exists.

In 1999, the CIA declassified articles written for the agency between
1955 and 1992. One of them was an article written by Richards Heuer
called "Do You Really Need More Information?" In it, Heuer describes
a study wherein they asked horseracing handicappers to rank the importance of 88 handicapping factors, such as the weight of the jockeys, age
of the horses, and footing of the track. They then provided the handicappers with the data related to the five they ranked as most important,

and asked them to handicap races. Then they were given the data related to their top 10 factors, the top 20 factors, and finally, the top 40 factors in order to handicap races.

Surprisingly, as they added more information, their accuracy actually began to decline. Although that alone is informative, the real value of this study and the many that followed was in discovering that the confidence of the handicappers grew as more data was made available to them. In fact, by the time they had all 40 top factors at their fingertips, their confidence was twice what it had been with just the top five. In other words, there is empirical evidence of a negative correlation between the accuracy of predictions and the confidence predictors have in them.

This can have a big impact on our returns. Since we tend to size our positions relative to the confidence we have in them, we are likely to overweight positions merely as a result of the availability of unnecessary information.

In his book *The Psychology of Intelligence Analysis*, Heuer explains that "experienced analysts have an imperfect understanding of what information they actually use in making judgments. They are unaware of the extent to which their judgments are determined by a few dominant factors, rather than by the systematic integration of all available information. Analysts use much less available information than they think they do." He found the same held true for doctors diagnosing illnesses, as well as experts in other professions, too.

In the end, he concluded that "individuals overestimate the importance we attribute to factors that have only a minor impact on our judgment, and underestimate the extent to which our decisions are based on a very few major variables."

In his book *Fooled by Randomness,* Nassim Taleb shares his take on the subject when he writes, "It takes a huge investment in introspection to learn that the thirty or more hours spent 'studying' the news last month neither had any predictive ability during your activities of that month nor did it impact your current knowledge of the world."

Thirty-two years earlier, Amos Tversky and Daniel Kahneman first published their findings on the matter in an article entitled, "Judgement under Uncertainty" in *Science*. They explained that in order to make decisions when the outcome is uncertain, we rely on our beliefs to assign probabilities to each of the potential outcomes. What they discovered is that very often the heuristics, or mental shortcuts we employ lead to biased expectations that can result in "severe and systematic errors."

They describe a phenomenon known as judgment by representativeness through a series of examples and experiments, one of which is particularly applicable to Taleb's point. In it they tell subjects that a group consists of 70 engineers and 30 lawyers. Without providing any additional information, they asked the subjects what the probability is that a particular individual selected from that group is an engineer. Participants correctly judged it to be 70%.

They then provided the following personality sketch of the individual in question.

"Dick is a 30-year-old man. He is married with no children. A man of high ability and high motivation, he promises to be quite successful in his field. He is well liked by his colleagues."

The description was meant to convey no information relevant to the question. Therefore, when asked again what the probability is of him being an engineer, the answer should have remained 70%. However, the subjects now judged the probability to be 50% after reading what was essentially worthless information.

"Evidently, people respond differently when given no evidence and when given worthless evidence. When no specific evidence is given, prior probabilities are properly utilized; when worthless evidence is given, prior probabilities are ignored."

Armed with the evidence that even perfectly innocuous information can have a detrimental impact on our ability to make rational decisions, it should make us question the real value of all the news and research being packaged for our consumption, but let's take it one step further.

Imagine for a moment that I am the publisher of a global macro research newsletter. I understand that the global macro landscape moves at a rather slow pace, with the release of new information that has the power to alter the medium to long-term trajectory of markets, economies, and policy – the type that truly qualifies as "signal," occurring just a few times a year. However, there are very few clients who would subscribe to a weekly newsletter wherein the majority of them consisted solely of the sentence, "Same views as last week. Nothing of significance has changed." To stay in business, I have to find interesting topics to write about and make a compelling argument for why they are both significant and relevant to the reader. The same goes for every newscast, newspaper, and magazine. When nothing of significance is occurring, they must still produce content, and convince readers that it is of great importance to their investments, businesses, and lives. It is then left to us to make a distinction between the signal and noise among all the content. (As we've seen, we do a very poor job of it.) In essence, the very thing for which we go to these content providers – a way to make a distinction between signal and noise – is actually made worse by relying on them.

So how do we use all this to improve our results? It is clear that we as decision-makers must make a concerted effort to first correctly identify what the key factors are and then work to actively avoid overexposure to any additional factors. In fact, any time and effort we expend to suppress our natural urge to gather more data and read more research, may actually contribute more to our bottom line than giving in to it. Yes, I'm suggesting that gathering smaller quantities of higher quality information is actually better than large quantities of unvetted narratives.

Stay Home, See the World

When I first started trading emerging markets it was firmly believed that locals had a distinct competitive advantage over the rest of us. Those who worked at major institutions with a strong network with local presence were feared. Guys like me didn't have a chance. It was, and for many it is still believed, that you must visit the countries in which you invest. We did the road trips, meeting with central bankers, government officials, and local business leaders. I took notes on who we met, where we went, and what we learned. I also tracked my performance in the days, weeks, and months that followed. What I discovered was a distinct lack of correlation between the trips and my performance. On those trips, I was actively seeking confirmation of the views I held before the trip. If I was bullish before, I would be even more bullish when I returned, and vice versa. In other words, I learned for myself exactly what Heuer had discovered decades earlier.

Yes, I sounded important when I sent around my notes, showing all the high-profile executives and policymakers with whom I had met. My analysis gained credibility by association, but the reality was, it didn't do a thing for my bottom line, and as a trader, only the bottom line matters. So for more than two decades now I have had a strict rule not to visit those countries in which I am actively involved. The trips were a waste of time and energy that surprisingly had no impact on my trading results, they were no more than a distraction. As the research has proven, by seeking confirmation of our views and inevitably finding it, confidence in our expectations increases and so too will its proportional weight in our portfolios and returns. The reality is, no matter how many meetings I have, companies I meet with, factories I visit, or behaviors I observe, they will always represent just a sliver of the whole picture. How representative that sliver is of the whole is impossible to know, and without that information, it is potentially more harmful than helpful.

I know it is difficult to believe that traveling less, gathering less data, and reading less research can actually improve your returns. It goes against everything we believe. Our brains utilize heuristics, or shortcuts, more commonly than we'd like to think, and they are dependent upon the deeply engrained beliefs we hold. When information is presented that challenges those beliefs, we experience cognitive dissonance, which is best described as a feeling of great unease when we hold two conflicting views. In order to rid ourselves of that uncomfortable feeling, we are driven to resolve it, typically by ignoring evidence in favor of the new argument and seeking what confirms the more deeply engrained belief. It's how we maintain inner peace, and it is why, even after reading this and other books on the subject, it is still very difficult to stop reading research, newspapers, and magazines, watching the news, going to industry conferences, and meeting with experts, something I forced myself to do more than 20 years ago.

ABQs of Research (Always Be Questioning)

I came across an article titled "The Fascinating Story Behind Why So Many Nail Technicians Are Vietnamese" on my Facebook newsfeed today. It was shared from a Yahoo feed, which was fed by an article on TakePart.com. In the article, the writer mentions that 80% of nail technicians in Southern California are Vietnamese and they account for 51% of the total across the United States. She then goes on to quote a number of other statistics such as the size of the nail industry ($8 billion), the GDP of Vietnam ($12 billion) and how important it is to these US-based technicians to send a sizable proportion of their income back home. It's such a feel-good, fun, and truly fascinating narrative – including a famous celebrity and grand historical context – it's hard not to want to share it with others. In other words, it's highly likely this story would spread like wildfire. (I mentioned the story to my wife and she informed me she had read about it last week in *People* magazine.)

However, being aware that we are susceptible to availability bias, the part of my brain responsible for critical thinking is immediately awakened. As entertaining as it is, the entire story hinges on one important fact. The majority of nail technicians in America, and particularly in Southern California, are of Vietnamese descent, and by a very wide margin. Take that away and suddenly its significance is dramatically reduced. So naturally I did some digging. Since neither the Yahoo version, nor the original TakePart post included a source, I had to search the web. I came across the same story on blog after blog and numerous well-established media sites, but only one, NPR, referenced the source. Turns out, the source was a poll taken by Nails Magazine, which was kind enough to share the results and methodology online, in a very colorful pdf. Finally, I had the info necessary to confirm what I'd read, and could feel confident that it was factual, and therefore worthy of being forwarded. Actually, it didn't. According to the *Nails Big Book 2014–2015,* one of the key sources for the most important statistic in the article is described as follows: "We surveyed the readers of VietSALON, our Vietnamese language publication for salon professionals."

I don't know how much it biased the results to have a Vietnamese language publication for salon professionals as the primary contributor to the polling, but I believe it is significant enough to make a rational reader skeptical of the findings. Now, I know what you're thinking. Who cares? It's just a silly story. In a world filled with far more important problems, can't you just let us enjoy a fun one?

Imagine LeBron James chooses a diet of Twinkies and soda combined with a regimen of couch sitting in the off-season. His coach chides him, complaining that he won't be able to compete when the season begins again. LeBron, one of the best players in the league year after year, consoles his coach by saying, "Relax, it's not like I'm going to do this when the season starts. When I'm on the court, I'll be in tip-top shape, as always."

Our brains are muscles that require exercise, just as much as any other muscle, but it is the most important one for our chosen professions. Unless you want to be susceptible to the availability bias, availability cascade, or any of the other potentially damaging cognitive biases in your investment process, you must train yourself to think critically at all times. Unfortunately, you cannot simply turn it on when it's important and off when it isn't. Critical thinking requires serious mental effort at all times, making it a way of life.

Working Smarter, Not Harder

Recently, one of the best investors in the world, someone who has had entire book chapters dedicated to understanding his process, asked a very thoughtful question related to the Vietnamese nail salon story. "Given that today we are flooded with information and stories, how do you cut through the information noise and figure out which stories to spend time approaching analytically? How do you force rank all the things that you could think about today so that you get the best 'bang for your buck' from exerting this effort?" (I believe the fact that he still asks these questions has a lot to do with why he is so good at this.). My advice, as mentioned above, is to stop reading all of these stories, and here's why.

Cognitive science is essentially the study of how we gather, process, draw conclusions from and ultimately use information to make decisions. It's important to note, our brains take in information at an extraordinary pace. We see it, read it, hear it, feel it and taste it, and as soon as we come into contact with it our brains automatically go to work integrating it with everything that came before, in an effort to maintain a clear, consistent and cohesive picture of the world in which we live.

The problem is our brains can't thoughtfully process all that data at such a rapid rate. Neither can we set any of it aside until we have the time to give it our undivided attention. It is an automated response that we cannot turn off. The evolutionary solution we've developed is known as heuristics or mental shortcuts which most of the time they work just fine. That's what cognitive scientists tell us at least, but it's a bit misleading. It is true – most data can and should be handled by employing heuristics. We don't need to contemplate why the light is red; we simply need to stop. The identification of a tree as a source of shade when we're hot and water as something that can satisfy our thirst should be left to our automated system, and incoming data like that does in fact make up the majority of information we receive and process. However, we should not take that to mean that our automated systems do a similarly satisfactory job with processing information we depend upon to make decisions of real consequence. You see, what cognitive scientists also agree on is that more often than we'd like to believe, heuristics result in systematic errors in judgement, otherwise known as bias, and worst of all, we are almost always oblivious to when they are occurring or what triggered them.

Our best defense is to recognize when we will be most vulnerable and take action to defend ourselves at those moments. This requires being proactive. It means you must first acknowledge a future moment as one of vulnerability, and one that you are unlikely to recognize as such at the moment it is occurring.

Unfortunately, much of the information we gather is processed by our automated system, which Kahneman and Tversky call System 1. Fundamentally, System 1 seeks cognitive ease. It doesn't contemplate questions like "How," "Why," or "Is that accurate" when it is processing incoming data. It simply picks out what it wants, what feels right. It seeks confirmation of the world order as you have already firmly established it. It perks up when it identifies something as familiar and gives it priority. What are things that will feel familiar to you? Things you heard first. What you read last. Things you've heard repeatedly. Information delivered via sources that have established themselves in your mind as trusted sources will be treated as familiar-by-proxy, thereby being attributed a higher level of importance and value. To be honest, System 1 isn't very discriminating. The right word grouping and even carefully selected color hues can evoke a sense of familiarity, thereby keeping System 2, the more skeptical, thoughtful part of your intellectual process, at bay. Once that information gets in, it automatically has priority over anything new. It becomes the standard by which all new information is assessed.

What this means is that all future information you gather will be affected, tainted even, by what you have allowed in previously. All decisions you make going forward will be similarly affected, tainted even, by what has become an integral part of that clear, consistent, and cohesive picture of the world you have drawn for yourself. So you can see, as much as we'd like to believe we have properly analyzed every bit of information that we use as a basis for judgement, it's just not true, or even possible.

What can we do then to improve our decisions? Well, as the saying goes, "Garbage in, garbage out," meaning, if the information you've gathered is subpar, it's very likely that the decisions based upon that information will also be subpar, no matter how smart you may be. Therefore, in order to improve your decisions, invest time in assessing and improving your process for gathering information. Here is an incomplete list of tips for doing so.

First and foremost, it all begins with one seemingly obvious realization. *You cannot and will not ever know everything.* You can't read, see, hear, feel, and taste everything there is to experience. So stop pretending you can. No matter how many news feeds you subscribe to, newsletters you read, analysts you speak to and policymakers you have on speed dial, there will be a nearly infinite number of things you will not know. That means the time and energy you are wasting (or worse) skimming information cursorily in order to convince yourself you are in fact well informed, can be reallocated to endeavors that will deliver significantly better returns on effort.

Source Assessment

The halo effect is a cognitive bias we employ constantly, though we are rarely aware of it. Essentially, it describes how we let our overall impression of a person, firm, news source, etc. affect our feelings and thoughts about other aspects of that entity. If we like one aspect of something, we will have a positive predisposition toward everything about it, and even things associated with it. This works in both directions, both positive and negative. Be aware: anyone who seeks your attention is cognisant of your penchant for this particular heuristic and bias, so be on guard.

There is little we can do about how often we are affected by this bias, however, in knowing this we can take special care to be certain we are properly appraising people and entities. If you refer to an analyst as "Goldman's US guy" for instance, you can be fairly certain you've outsourced your appraisal of that analyst's skillset and the dependability of his accuracy to those who hired him. We joke all the time about how laughable it is to trust something we read just because it's on the Internet, but we do exactly that all the time with so many other sources.

The goal here is to put in the time and effort to properly appraise our sources like any good detective would. Then, in those moments when we do unwittingly fall prey to the halo effect (and it will be often) we will have lowered the odds of it doing serious damage.

Here are some ways attention seekers will capitalize on the halo effect, effectively gaining credibility by proxy perhaps without you even realizing it.

- Articles with the name of a highly regarded individual in its title. Example: "What Warren Buffett Is Doing Today."
- Ads with celebrity endorsers.
- Products distancing themselves from things perceived as bad. Example: "No high fructose corn syrup!"
- Articles written by a highly regarded individual, particularly on a topic unrelated to the basis for that high regard.
- Analysts quoting key policymakers or even implying an inside connection to them.

Engaged Reading

If you do a proper cost/benefit analysis on skimming articles, reading headlines, even having conversations while watching your screens, you'll stop doing all those things in an instant. The reasons are confirmation bias and the impact of familiarity. When we skim, our brains don't contemplate meaning or develop new context. We simply pull out words and word groupings that look familiar that enable cognitive ease and that fit neatly with our worldview. Have you ever noticed when something relatively obscure to you enters your consciousness that it suddenly appears everywhere?

When my sister became engaged to a man from Costa Rica, it suddenly appeared to my family and me as though this tiny little country was being mentioned everywhere. Of course Costa Rica hadn't suddenly taken on global significance, it had simply become familiar to us, and System 1 was now automatically drawn to any mention of it. The more we heard the country's name, the greater its weight in our worldview. The same happens in our research. If your information sources are all highly connected, they will become highly correlated for this very reason. (It helps explain why the greatest factor in determining correlation among hedge funds is geography.) If all your sources are mentioning the same thing, *that thing's weight* will increase dramatically in your worldview. It is a phenomenon known as the "mere exposure effect."

If instead of skimming, you select only a very few uncorrelated, highly reliable sources of information to truly engage with, to contemplate and further investigate on your own, your worldview will be far more balanced and reflective of reality. In those moments when connections develop between seemingly disparate topics covered by those sources, you'll know you've hit on something worthy of serious investigation.

Contemplation

What I mean by contemplation is the act of stepping away from everything. Having accepted that you can't read everything or speak to everyone, you should be free to truly absorb the information you have identified as worthy of gathering. Away from the scrolling headlines and incessant display of tick data, you are better able to see the world as it actually exists. Most importantly, you develop the patience and space to better understand context and connections. You will formulate better questions which will lead to more informed investigations.

Taking Care of Yourself

Studies have shown that our brains function similarly when we are sleep deprived versus when we are intoxicated. Israeli judges have been observed doling out radically different sentences just before lunch versus immediately afterward. We know sleep and nutrition affect us, but very often we sacrifice these things in favor of reading one more research piece or taking one more "peek" at the markets. The rational you knows that the marginal gain of checking your email for the fifth time before ordering appetizers is nearly zero, but the habitual System 1 isn't rational, it is impetuous. Hand your phone to your child at the dinner table. Leave your desk to read the research you value. Go on a hike. Eat a proper breakfast. Read a good novel. Learn a new skill. Unplug.

How Information Can Lead Us Astray

Cognitive psychologists like to use visual illusions to make the point that while we may be very intelligent, rational beings, our brains rely on heuristics, or mental shortcuts to gather clues about our surroundings and leap to conclusions based upon them. Although we tend to benefit greatly from this setup, very often those conclusions are severely flawed. It is easy to see the shortcomings visually, but recognizing when we make cognitive mistakes requires greater effort, in addition to mention a serious dose of humility.

The Problem with Flow Info

Recently I spoke at Drobny Global's annual macro conference in Santa Monica. Afterwards, I sat and chatted with an allocator from one of the large government pension funds who asked, "Don't you think flows matter?" Being a reader of *Seeds* for some time now, we were both aware that she already knew my answer, however it didn't mean that her question was a rhetorical one. It simply meant I hadn't yet convinced her. There are numerous reasons why I cut myself off from flow information long ago, all of them being statistical in nature. I'll explain my skepticism on the value of fund flow information with a story from an unrelated topic: education.

The Gates Foundation is widely accepted as the leader in education reform. The organization is of course backed by multibillionaire Bill Gates, viewed by most as one of the great minds of our time and an exceptional business leader. As it is with many similar organizations, the belief is that by applying the rigorous analytical tools that led to Microsoft's incredible success in software, the same can be achieved with the many social causes to which his foundation turns its attention. None of this is contentious, and in fact, the foundation carries so much weight, that the mere mention of its backing for a nonprofit or research finding will virtually guarantee a veritable avalanche of additional support from others as well.

In the United States, one of the great frustrations is that K–12 (kindergarten through 12th grade) education, once the gold standard for the rest of the world, has fallen well behind, despite nearly $650 billion being spent on it every year. Not only are public funds thrown at it, but it is a favorite pet project of many who come from the business world, armed with massive war chests, rivaled only by the confidence they have the ability to effect positive change. Theories abound as to how we got here and what should be done to fix the problem. School lunches, higher pay for teachers, and computers in every classroom are but a few of the solutions that have been proposed, received tremendous funding, and have been implemented.

In the late 1990s, the argument that smaller schools produced better results was gaining steam and powerful adherents. Research, such as that based on test results from the Pennsylvania System of School Assessments, had made a compelling argument in favor of smaller schools. Being based on cold, raw data, it was the kind of result that appeals to great business minds like Bill Gates, and the evidence was compelling.

They'd gathered scores from 3rd-, 5th-, 8th-, and 11th-grade math and reading tests, plus writing scores for 6th, 9th, and 11th grade. In analyzing the data provided by 1662 separate schools, they found that of the 50 top-scoring schools (the top 3%), 6 of them were among the 50 smallest (the smallest 3%). If the size of the school were unrelated to performance, the smallest schools should have represented just 3% of the top 50, but according to the data they actually represented 12% (6 out of 50). That's an overrepresentation by a factor of four!

The Gates Foundation was sold. They began pouring money into programs designed to support small schools, nationwide. By 2001, they provided roughly $1.7 billion in grants to education projects and were quickly joined by the upper echelon of not-for-profits, including the Annenberg Foundation, Carnegie Corporation, Harvard's Change Leadership Group, the Pew Charitable Trusts, and the U.S. Department of Education's Smaller Learning Communities Program. As Wainer and Zwerling so accurately stated in their follow up research, "The availability of such large amounts of money to implement a smaller-schools policy yielded a concomitant increase in the pressure to do so, with programs to splinter large schools into smaller ones being proposed and implemented broadly in New York, Los Angeles, Chicago and Seattle."

In market parlance, the smart money flows became evident, and had become a powerful force in the direction of education reform in their own right. Lives were uprooted and impacted for years to come. Westlake Terrace High School, a suburban school in Seattle with 1800 students was broken into five smaller schools, enabled by a Gates grant of nearly $1 million. It was just one of many such changes being carried out across the country. School boards were taking action, not based on the underlying data that had created the flows, but on the flow itself. Articles were written about the flows, who was behind them, and the action being taken as a result. Politicians jumped on board ideologically and financially.

Then, in 2005, the Gates Foundation made a stunning announcement. They were moving away from converting large schools into smaller ones. They decided that improving classroom instruction was more important to improving schools rather than breaking down the size. What led them to stop after leading the charge seemingly midcourse? Turns out their initial analysis was severely flawed, and both it and the follow-up data made a very strong case that not only were smaller schools not better, they may actually be worse.

The researchers who made the argument that smaller schools were better than larger ones had shown an exaggerated faith in small samples, a very common problem in research of all kinds, even today. Recent advances in cognitive psychology have taught us that we pay more attention to the content of messages than to information about their reliability.

As Daniel Kahneman points out in *Thinking, Fast and Slow*, "Many facts are due to chance, including accidents of sampling. Causal explanations of chance events are inevitably wrong."

That's what happened in the case of the findings regarding smaller schools. You might look at the fact that the data included 1662 schools and think that's a sufficient sample size from which to draw conclusions, but that isn't the problem. The error occurred in not recognizing that each of the small schools represented a far smaller sample size than those of the big schools. What you should expect when dealing with small sample sizes versus large ones is a higher degree of variability. As an example, the chances of tossing a fair coin 5 times and having it land on heads every time is far greater than if you tossed it 500 times. The researchers, Gates, Harvard, Pew, and the others that had reviewed the data focused on only one side of the results. Had they gone one extra step and looked at the opposite end of the spectrum exclusively they would have arrived at the exact opposite conclusion.

Going back to the Pennsylvania System of School Assessments data, among the 50 worst-performing schools, you will find that 9 of them were among the 50 smallest schools. In others words, there was an over-representation by a factor of 6! Far bigger even than what they found on the positive side. Truth is, drawing conclusions based solely on that information would have been just as flawed as the other way around. All it proved is that smaller samples generate data with greater variance. When a regression was done of all the data it showed no relationship between results and school size. However, when applied to those of high school students only, the regression line showed a significant positive slope. In other words, the larger the high school the better the scores.

The Gates Foundation recognized the error and stopped out of the position. Harvard, Pew, Carnegie, and the others followed suit shortly thereafter. Unfortunately, the students, teachers, and communities were left holding the position with no one around to help them put the schools back together. No new funding to fix the problems. Principals at the larger schools that had been broken up were held accountable for the diminishing returns on their students. School boards had to answer for the inefficiencies that resulted from the greater overhead of administration per student required for the smaller schools. In other words, those who had invested based on the smart money flows were left holding the bag. If instead, they had done their own research, dug into the data themselves, and recognized where their time and effort would have been better spent, they would have been years ahead of everyone else, being held up as the standard by which all others would aspire to.

So when you ask me why it is that I don't want to know about trading flow information, my simple answer is that it is more noise than signal. Whatever limited selection of flow information that might make its way to me is but a small sample of the total, leading to the very same problem experienced by the Gates Foundation. I'd prefer to depend upon fundamental data, which if you think about it, is also flow data, representing behaviors that are affecting price action, but from a much larger sample set, and therefore worthy of much greater confidence.

Besides, if I were to generate poor returns and an investor or client came to me after the fact to ask why, I never want my answer to be, "Well, everyone else was doing it."

Postscript

In a speech at a global macro conference I made the argument that markets were exhibiting extreme risk aversion, to which I received some serious pushback. Audience members suggested (quite vehemently at times) that the rally in equity markets, and particularly the compressed spreads served as evidence of quite the opposite of what I had proposed. I will go into why these arguments are flawed later, but I thought it worth noting that immediately following my talk and the counterarguments, the conference hosts posed a number of questions to the audience related to positioning. Nearly every single one of them showed an almost perfect bell-shaped-curve result, prompting the host to remark that he'd rarely seen results so symmetrical, with the preponderance of audience members selecting *No Position*, and a rapidly diminishing distribution as you approached either *Very Overweight* and *Very Underweight*. In other words, the very people who were arguing that the markets were not exhibiting indications of extreme risk aversion had just provided clear evidence of exactly that in their own behaviors.

Chapter 6

Cerebral Junk Food

10 Reasons Listicles Are Bad for Your Health

More often than not we know what we should do. We are well aware that we should choose salad over French fries, water instead of soda, and take the stairs rather than the escalator. Everyone knows these things, and yet in that moment of choice, no matter how many times we've said, "never again" or swore an oath to ourselves and others, we simply can't resist. Many times our very own bodies are actually working against us, nudging us to make the wrong decisions. The mere sight of something sugary or salty automatically triggers the production of excess saliva, hence the term *mouth watering*. To make it worse, because we tend to have a natural preference for the wrong option, it doesn't take much to tip us over in that direction and very often it's our friends and family, the ones who should be helping us do the right thing, who play the role of that little devil whispering in our ear, "You only live once. Go for it. You know you want it." And so we do. We rationalize the irrational act and postpone the difficult choice for some time in the future when we will do better. "I promise."

Unfortunately, it isn't just our physical wellbeing that suffers as a result of our poor choices, our mental fitness is also plagued by many of the same bad influences. The surge in popularity of the "listicle" is an example. The listicle is to your brain what a bag of greasy, sodium-packed chips is to your waistline.

What are listicles? They are those pervasive stories you've seen spreading like a virus on your social media feeds, and are now infecting traditional media and even institutional research. They have titles like "5 Things You Should Know About … ,", "7 Secrets to … ," "8 Keys to … ." Get it? Combine *list* with *article* and you have the *listicle*.

Why have they spread like type 2 diabetes? Well, much like images of sugary foods, our brains have a biochemical auto-response to lists. They are similarly satisfying in the short-term (and often just as damaging in the long run). The reason they are so appealing to us is that they hold the promise of simple solutions to complex problems, delivered via bite-sized, easy-to-digest nuggets of wisdom. Bottom line, our automated thought system doesn't like to work hard, and when given the option between an open ended discussion in which a wide range of possibilities are explored, and a finite list of bulleted answers, we are severely biased toward the latter.

Why It Matters

Like it or not, we are influenced by an article's headline, and those who are trying to draw our attention know it. Fundamentally, headlines are meant to perform two functions: summarize and attract attention to the full text of the article. However, a number of studies have shown that headlines typically do not accurately represent the articles they introduce. In fact, they have concluded instead that headlines make a loose, inadequate or misleading substitute for full-text news reports in a number of ways. Therefore, the purpose of headlines has degraded into solely attracting attention to the full text.

Writers and publishers know what will attract readers, but since publishing went digital, it's no longer enough to get you to buy the newspaper or magazine. Now they are judged, and often paid, according to how far down they get you to scroll, with God-like status reserved for those who get you to click to the next page. You see, they have to go beyond simply grabbing a reader's attention so that they buy the paper or open the article, now writers and publishers must hold that attention right to the end. As a result, the rules for writing headlines are now being applied to the entire article, leaving little more than a "loose, inadequate or misleading substitute for the full-text reports" as the content itself. Bottom line, we are consuming more empty calories, and content, leaving us simultaneously bloated and undernourished, both physically and mentally.

> The country is entertained, but not engaged. It is drowning in information and thirsty for knowledge.
> **Charles Pierce, *Idiot America: How Stupidity Became a Virtue in the Land of the Free***

You've Been Framed

One of the fundamental tenets of rational decision making is something known as "description invariance." What it means is that it shouldn't matter *how* available options are presented to us. We should consider them all consistently, and without bias. Unfortunately, we humans are extraordinarily susceptible to the manner in which information is delivered, a finding that is supported by a wealth of empirical data. This bias has been named the framing effect.

Figures 6.1 and 6.2 show a couple of examples showing how information can be presented in different ways, evoking different responses.

As much as we'd like to believe that we investors are too smart to fall for such things, there is compelling evidence that its effects are pervasive in our industry as well. Take, for example, the concept of P/E, the price-to-earnings ratio. As everyone knows, P/E is offered as a way to draw a direct connection between the price of an equity stake in a company and the earnings that business generates. Although it implies a connection and we may like to believe there is one, technically there isn't,

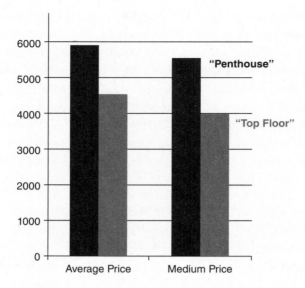

Figure 6.1 Rental prices for top-floor NYC
apartments based on the label ($0–$10,000).

Figure 6.2 How to make smoking seem healthy.

except in our minds. A stock can trade at 12, 17, 25, or even 100 times earnings, and nothing about the laws of physics argues that any one of them is more "correct" than another. In other words, there is no way to arbitrage a stock market merely because it is valued at 100 times earnings.

Sure, you could argue something like, "anytime it's traded 'up there' it's been a good short" or "it's 'undervalued' down here," but if you think about it, these are merely acknowledgments of a behavior pattern. In other words, P/E and any other measures like it, are little more than technical indicators, making terms like *undervalued* and *overvalued* functions of historical behavior patterns. The reality is, they serve as anchors for us to create order out of chaos and randomness.

Thanks to the way these simple formulas are presented, combined with our ability to graph, compare, and analyze correlations among them, it gives the impression that they actually mean something. The fact that they don't mean anything more than the words used to describe a top floor apartment, doesn't keep us from pretending that they do. We can say things such as it doesn't make sense that the stock market would rise at a significantly faster pace than the underlying economy or it isn't sustainable, but the reason it's so difficult to predict the top of a bubble is because there is no "correct" value, no way to arbitrage it. In fact, it *is* sustainable. Although some argue if there is no one else left to buy the price will go lower, but this simply isn't true. If there is no one wanting to buy and no one wanting to sell, you have market equilibrium. The price goes nowhere.

Yes, equities that are priced below the business' liquidation value can be arbitraged. The further we are from that level, the greater the extrinsic value relative to intrinsic value the stock price represents, and the more like trading baseball cards, artwork, and gold it becomes.

As the *penthouse* versus *top floor* example shows, we often value identical things differently based on how they are presented to us. It is irrational behavior. I believe the same could be said for those who are bullish for gold *because* they believe stocks and most other assets are in a bubble. You see, the only thing that separates gold from every other asset, including equities, is that it isn't anchored to anything. It has no actual use, no real demand, because we as a society don't *need* it for anything. There are no earnings or yield to anchor it. Therefore, it can't be proven to be relatively cheap or expensive, undervalued or overvalued. On the other hand, there isn't a whole lot of it and not much in the way of new supply, which is why people categorize it as a *pure* investment, when the reality is, that is what makes it the very embodiment of speculation itself. It has value only because we bestow value upon it. It is the ultimate fiat currency, ironically, the very thing from which gold bulls typically seek refuge.

The true definition of a bubble as it exists in our minds is when an asset's valuation doesn't reflect what it represents. By this definition, one could easily argue that the stock market, at the time of writing, is in a bubble, since stock prices keep rising while growth in earnings continue to recede. In order for us to maintain our belief in the construct of markets as having meaning rather than as a house of cards, we must argue that it isn't sustainable. When stock markets rally in spite of poor growth prospects, when bonds continue to rally despite negative yields, when commodity-dependent emerging markets find buyers for their debt at "low" yields even as commodities collapse, it creates cognitive dissonance. How can these things happen if financial asset prices are based on something concrete? The simple answer is, they can't, and yet they do. The reason is that financial assets are exactly like gold. Ultimately, their price is tied to supply and demand for the instrument itself, not the anchor.

A Picture Is Worth a Thousand Biased Words

Figure 6.3 shows the global production of what we traditionally think of as cameras, from 1947 to 2014. Photographer Sven Skafisk then thought to add sales of smartphones to the chart, which makes sense given how many people use their phones instead of cameras to take pictures now. Sven chose to maintain the y-axis scale, which puts the explosive sales growth in perspective (Figure 6.4).

It's a powerful image for sure, but does it *really* help put the growth in perspective, or does it distort it? To answer that question, take a look at the image on the next page, showing the same data (camera plus camera-phone sales) versus an exponential growth rate of 21% per year. In other

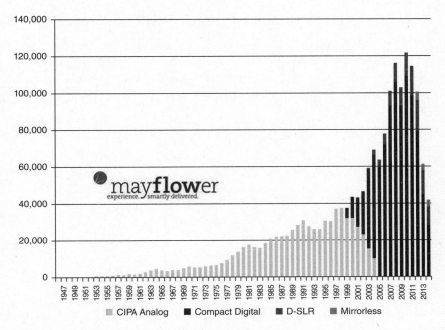

Figure 6.3 CIPA camera production, 1947–2014.
SOURCE: Mayflower Concepts.

words, begin with the actual camera sales from 1932 and grow sales at a constant 21% per year. Perhaps, we are affected by how information is delivered to us after all.

How We Manufacture Uncertainty and Volatility

In Figure 6.5, you will see the counties in the lowest decile of the kidney-cancer distribution. As soon as we see an image like this, our brains immediately set about the task of explaining why it is that the healthy counties appear to be mainly rural. Perhaps it is a result of breathing unpolluted air, consumption of farm fresh food, or maybe readily available clean water delivered straight from tranquil streams. As it turns out, the explanation has nothing to do with the environment or lifestyle, but I'll come back to this in a moment.

Figure 6.4　Sven
Skafisk's presentation of
CIPA camera
production,
1947–2014.
Source: Mayflower
Concepts and Sven Skafisk.

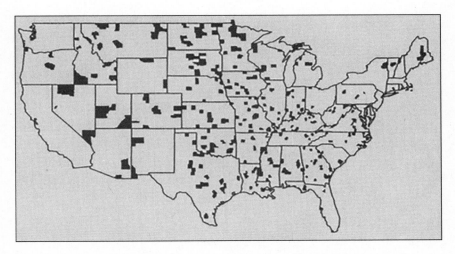

Figure 6.5   Counties with the lowest 10% age-standardized death rates for
cancer of the kidney/ureter for U.S. males, 1980–1989.
SOURCE: Howard Wainer and Harris L. Zwerling, "Evidence That Smaller Schools Do Not Improve
Student Achievement," *The Phi Delta Kappan* 88, no. 4 (December, 2006), pp. 300–303. Reproduced
with permission of SAGE.

A young auto racing team has had a phenomenal year, finishing in the
top five in 12 of the 15 races it completed. Unfortunately, the car failed
to finish due to a blown engine in the other seven outings. A decision
needs to be made whether to enter the final race of the season on this
particularly cold morning. Several major sponsors have taken notice of
the team's performance and the team is on the cusp of moving from
struggling upstart to a power player with significant financial resources.
If they finish in the top five again today they will certainly hit the tipping
point to success. However, another blown engine will likely send them
back to square one, or worse. Their engine mechanic, a true "grease
monkey" believes the problem has something to do with ambient air
temperature, but the chief mechanic, an engineer, disagrees. As proof,
he provides the air temperature for each race in which they experienced
a blown gasket, highlighting the fact that the problems occurred across
a full range of temperatures. More on their decision in a bit.

Baseball has just entered the postseason, that moment when the
30 teams that have been competing to win the World Series are

reduced to the top eight. It's also the time when experts begin making predictions. As it is with all sports, the experts place great emphasis on momentum, particularly recent momentum. As an example, here is how one article on SBNation.com begins: "Rule No. 1 of predicting the postseason: Pick a very strong team. The Blue Jays are rolling. They have the best team, clearly." It isn't just the so-called experts though. We all do it. For instance, if you were attempting to predict the outcome of the very next at-bat for a major league baseball player, which of the following do you believe would offer the most predictive value?

- His batting average over the past five plate appearances
- His batting average over the past five games
- His batting average over the past month
- His batting average over the season so far
- His batting average over the previous two seasons

If you're like most people, you would order the predictive power exactly as it is shown in the preceding list. However, when Moskowitz and Wertheim[1] studied all MLB hitters over an entire decade, it was the batting average of the previous two seasons that offered the most predictive value. In fact, if you wanted to order the preceding list from most valuable to least in predicting the outcome of a batter's next time at the plate you would completely reverse the order of the list. Interestingly, they found the same results when applied to the NBA, NFL, NHL, and European football.

Let's return to the question facing the owners of that auto-racing team. Unfortunately, because the chief mechanic had framed the data in a narrow way, the key decision-makers hadn't thought to ask the simple, but important follow-up question, "What were the temperatures when the engine did not fail?" Had they done so, they would have quickly discovered that temperature was indeed a key factor in the failures. This story of the racing team as presented here is a fictitious one, created by Jack Brittain and Sim Sitkin as a case study for decision-making. However, the data provided and the decision of "go" or "no go" was a very real one faced by the engineers at NASA ahead of the launch of the space

---

[1] Tobias J. Moskowitz and L. Jon Wertheim, *Scorecasting: The Hidden Influences Behind How Sports Are Played and Games Are Won* (New York: Three Rivers Press, 2011), p. 228.

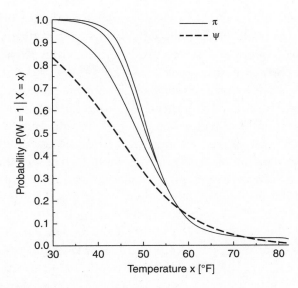

Figure 6.6   Probability of o-ring failure
SOURCE: C. Maranzano and R. Krzysztofowicz, "Bayesian
Reanalysis of the Challenger O-Ring Data," *Risk Analysis* (29
July 2008). Reproduced with permission of John Wiley & Sons,
Inc.

shuttle, *Challenger.* Unfortunately for all involved, because the problem
was initially framed very narrowly, some very valuable data, the kind that
surely would have resulted in a "no go" decision on that cold morning
(see Figure 6.6), was missed.

This is such a powerful story because it shows that even the smartest
among us are vulnerable to poorly framed problems resulting in all the
difficulties that come with overvaluing small sample sets. The annals of
history are littered with similar mistakes by equally intelligent, educated,
and successful individuals, which is why it shouldn't be hard to believe
that this same mistake is made on a regular basis by professional investors,
including the most successful ones.

Let's return to the question about why it is that rural living results
in lower incidents of kidney cancer, but first, some additional information before we get too deep into the creation of an intelligent sounding
narrative. Figure 6.5 shows the counties in the *top* decile of the kidney
cancer distribution. Once again, rural areas dominate. If you had been

presented with this image first, you would likely have jumped to the conclusion that the high rates might be due to higher poverty rates, limited access to proper medical care, a greater propensity for smoking and drinking alcohol, or perhaps diets that tend to be higher in fats.

In reality there is no valid narrative that can accurately explain the phenomenon. It is merely a statistic phenomenon of studying a small sample set. But rather than attribute it up to the random, highly variable nature of small sample sets, we intuitively set about the task of generating a story that can explain it. Unfortunately for us, regardless of what we desire, small towns represent small sample sets, and small sample sets typically exhibit greater variability and tend to be overrepresented in the tails, both of them. It really is that simple.

Back in 1985, a little known paper[2] was written by Robert Abelson of Yale University, in which he proved mathematically that the percentage of variance in any single batting performance for major league baseball players explained by skill is less than one-third of 1%. The author's hypothesis, which led to the proof was that "many games are decided by freaky and unpredictable events such as windblown fly balls, runners slipping in patches of mud, baseballs bouncing oddly off outfield walls, field goal attempts hitting the goalpost, and so on … The ordinary mechanics of skilled actions such as hitting a baseball are so sensitive that the difference between a home run swing and a swing producing a pop up is so tiny as to be unpredictable, thus requiring it to be considered in largely chance terms" (p. 129). Although he proved that skill played a minuscule role in an individual swing and at-bat, he did acknowledge that over sufficiently lengthy periods, skill was indeed a significant factor.

Considering the high degree of variability and uncertainty inherent in very short term results, not to mention the volumes of research proving that small sample sets are more volatile, less predictable, and less informative, it should make us question the decision-making ability of portfolio managers, CIOs, and asset allocators who, in the face of turmoil and uncertainty, actually shorten their investment horizon. Although it appeals to our intuition and therefore feels right, focusing on progressively shorter-term price action in order to gain greater control of P&L volatility is quite simply irrational.

---

[2] "A Variance Explanation Paradox: When a Little is a Lot," Psychological Bulletin 97, no. 1 (1985): 129–133.

By shortening our time horizon, allowing both short-term price action and every individual data point, including nonfarm payrolls, to drive our investment decisions, we are in fact increasing the influence of noise over signal, randomness over predictability, and injecting volatility into both our thought process and results. Ironically, as more and more investors and their money managers attempt to reduce volatility and increase their sense of control by becoming hyperfocused on what has just happened, their decisions become more sensitive to noise and their results more volatile. With this behavior having become so pervasive, it's no wonder markets appear more volatile and less predictable these days. When we shift our focus away from the big picture, where trends are far more apparent and explicable, it's only natural that the world would appear to be less certain, more volatile.

It is important to recognize that we can't actually explain every tick in the S&P 500 or weekly move in wheat. In the scheme of things, these are little more than random events. When we continuously attempt to create seemingly coherent narratives to explain what are essentially random events, we will naturally experience more moments when our expectations are proven wrong than when we weren't so myopic. Rather than accept responsibility for the mistake, we tend to place blame externally, which, in this case, leads to the explanation that the world no longer makes sense, that it is more volatile and uncertain. But, if we step back a bit, push those short term charts away, consider what the really big forces are that are truly driving global economics and financial markets, we can see that the world hasn't actually become more uncertain. The uncertainty is merely a function of how the problem is being framed, which is leading to poor decisions, lower returns, and greater volatility en masse. When that occurs, risk parameters tend to be tightened up even more, thereby exacerbating the problem, which is where we often find ourselves today.

What Dieting Taught Me About Consuming Information

In 2007, I was on the verge of breaking the 200-pound barrier, in the wrong direction. A lifetime of dietary habits that would have made

Morgan Spurlock's "Super Size Me" look like a healthy alternative had finally caught up with me. I had just moved from London to Santa Barbara, which seemed a logical time to make some adjustments that would nip this problem in the bud. The problem was I had no idea where to start. So I did what anyone who wants a six-pack stomach would do. I asked someone with rock hard abs for advice. In my case, it was my wife's new yoga instructor. "Sugar," she said. "You have to avoid sugar if you want to get rid of the layer of fat that is hiding your abs."

Exactly what I was hoping to hear. A succinct, simple formula that I could focus on to accomplish my goal. For the next 48 hours, I read every label and investigated the composition of every food that didn't have a package. I was a man on a mission to eradicate sugar from my diet. In no time, I would be walking shirtless everywhere I went.

Entenmann's doughnuts? No more. Honey Bunches of Oats cereal? Nice try. Sounds healthy, but it's got sugar. Box of raisins? Wait, raisins have sugar? I was like a deer caught in the headlights. I couldn't find any food that didn't have sugar in it, so I went two full days without eating a thing.

What sounded like a simple formula for achieving my goal was actually an impossible task. I was so focused on this one thing, I missed all the other important elements, including how sugar factored in to a complete diet.

This wasn't the first time I had rushed into an idea with vim and vigor. Years earlier, I announced to my wife that I wanted to learn how to speak German. A few days later she tells me that the kid who washes her hair at the salon is from Germany and that he would be happy to teach me. "Really nice guy," she said. It was great. He came to the house on my schedule and the lessons were inexpensive. I worked with him for a few weeks before it dawned on me that I had in no way vetted his linguistic skills other than knowing that he was from Germany. "What if he is teaching me the equivalent of street slang or even just poor grammar?" I had no way of knowing, so I stopped the lessons immediately and opted for a more structured and reputable methodology.

Getting back to my six-pack conundrum, it was clear I had committed the same error here as I had with my language lessons. By simply exhibiting the characteristics I desired, in this case six-pack abs, I jumped to the conclusion that this woman actually understood how she came to possess them, and that she had the ability to transfer that knowledge on to me. I was wrong on both counts, for a second time.

I decided to take matters into my own hands. It was clear that I needed an education, but the first step had to be vetting potential sources of information. I went to the bookstore in search of a book about food, and how it affects our bodies. I needed to understand how it all works together. With so many talking heads on television, infomercials, hundreds of books on dieting, thousands of fad diets, weight loss solutions and gimmicky products designed to help me achieve my goal, I needed a checklist to weed out the charlatans and block out the noise. With as little as I knew about this topic, I did know one thing for certain. Almost all individuals who attempt to lose weight and improve their health seem to fail. For many it is over before it even begins. For others, it slips away over time. For most, it is a roller coaster ride of success and failure, repeated ad nauseam, fueled by a lack of discipline and knowledge.

I was determined to avoid failure, so I set out for the biggest bookstore I could find, in search of a book(s) on the subject of food that abided by two rules, at a minimum. It could not have the word *Diet* in the title and it could not have a picture of someone wearing their old "fat pants" to show how much weight they had lost. You see, just as simply being from Germany doesn't qualify you to teach the language, having lost weight at some point in your life, no matter how much weight, doesn't necessarily qualify you to teach someone else how to do it.

I opted for the very bland looking, well-written, fact supported collection of diet-related information titled, *Eat, Drink, and Be Healthy: The Harvard Medical School Guide to Healthy Eating* by Walter Willett, MD. I read, highlighted, reread the book, and then condensed what I learned down to a few very simple, easy-to-implement guidelines that I would follow. By doing so, I got back to my fighting weight of 175 and have stayed there ever since.

So how does this relate to the consumption of information? People have developed shortcuts as a way to become more efficient. We pigeonhole, categorize, and bucket information without even knowing it. Most importantly, we outsource the vetting of information, often times to people we've never met and without knowing their qualifications as vetters.

Credibility is inferred through connection, even flimsy ones. It happens all the time, and often with disastrous consequences.

Bernie Madoff understood this and took full advantage. His connection to a charity bestowed credibility onto him in the eyes of a few wealthy elites, which then endowed him with further status. One connection after the next relied on the first, effectively outsourcing their critical thinking to an entity many times removed.

In an age when the original source of misinformation can be very quickly lost in a web of reposts, forwards, and cut-and-pastes, we must be even more diligent in our vetting. When smart people forward articles even before they've read them, the problem becomes infinitely worse for society as a whole, for it is the intelligent, particularly those with a reputation for it, to whom we most often outsource our vetting process.

The *availability cascade* is defined as a self-reinforcing process in which a collective belief gains more and more plausibility through its increasing repetition in public discourse (i.e., repeat something long enough and it will become true). It's a dangerous flaw in our cognitive process, because it can easily be capitalized upon by the deceitful and the hucksters. We are their prey and our only defense is to be more critical in our thinking.

I'm not suggesting that you should be overly cynical about every bit of information that comes your way but simply that you take a minute to vet the sources you depend on for the majority of your information. By doing so, you can actually let your guard down a bit, leaving you to absorb the truly valuable thoughts and information.

By the way, what the yoga instructor should have said when I asked her how to get a six-pack, was, "Calories consumed minus calories burned equals weight change. Burn more calories than you consume and, *voilà!* – you will likely lose weight. To reduce the calories consumed, eat things that keeps you full longer. To increase the calories burned, move more today than you did yesterday. It's that simple." Would I have paid for that sage advice? Probably not. So, if you think about it, I had incentivized her to provide me with information that was less valuable for *me* – similar to how we investors incentivize providers of research and analysis to deliver content even when there is nothing worth saying.

Chapter 7

The Input Paradox

Bowflex Behavior Modifier 2000

Last year US consumers purchased nearly four billion dollars' worth of new fitness equipment for use at home. The level of technological sophistication included in many of these products is astounding. Thanks to virtual classes with the world's best instructors now available in our own homes (see pelotoncycle.com), the 34,000 brick-and-mortar gyms are one step closer to obsolescence. Availability of the latest, most advanced equipment for home fitness is nothing new though.

Year in and year out, billions are spent by consumers who want to get in shape but lack the will to make it happen. For decades, the fitness gurus have been pumping out an endless supply of equipment that promises to tuck tummies and trim waistlines without requiring a great deal of effort. The commercials show scantily clad, incredibly fit average Joes not even breaking a sweat after working out for just seconds on a machine that requires "just minutes a day" to get the body we've always wanted. It's that easy. But of course it's not, which is why many of them fold up for easy storage. After all, tucking it under the bed keeps the dream of using it alive without having to be reminded every single morning and evening, that we've failed again.

From the ThighMaster to the elliptical, the Nautilus to the Bowflex Stairmaster, the technology represents great potential, but there's no getting around one very simple fact. Unless you actually put in the hard work and use it properly, that high-tech contraption will do little more than lighten your wallet. Actually making it worse than useless.

Thanks to cheap computing power and the availability of open source coding tools the investment world finds itself awash in the FinTech version of Thigh-masters and treadmills, each selling the promise of better returns free of cognitive bias and behavioral mistakes. At least once a week I am approached by a software developer offering to demonstrate the latest and greatest solution to behavioral bias. They promise access to all kinds of data which we can then slice and dice every way possible in order to make more rational, objective, and consistent decisions for our investment portfolios. They offer a potential panacea for those struggling to generate alpha. Just write a check and suddenly your firm will be smarter about the risk it takes and better able to generate those returns you desire.

Here's the thing about every single one of these products that I've seen demonstrated. Not one of them does anything you couldn't do with an Excel spreadsheet all by yourself for free. You don't even need to know how to program or code. None of them offers any value unless you employ the cognitive strain required to ask the right questions about the outcome, states, and acts, and challenge your own beliefs. They don't possess any more magic than the Bowflex Stairmaster Elliptical Weight Trainer 5000. Yes, if you work your tail off on that machine, you will lose weight and get fit, but no more so than running the stairs in your office building or the hill behind your house.

As much as we'd like it to be the case, you can't buy your way out of the hard work and discipline in pursuit of rock hard abs. Simply buying Jenny Craig's meal plan won't keep you from sneaking that slice of cheesecake. Neither will purchasing a glorified spreadsheet help you avoid the cognitive strain required to make better decisions.

Data is a tool, nothing more. If *gathered* and used properly it can help deliver insight. As any investor knows though, simply having access to even the cleanest data isn't enough. You must know what to do with it. It requires talent and skill to convert fundamental and technical data into alpha. The same goes for data regarding process.

Interestingly, the purchase and use of these products, intended to reduce cognitive bias, may actually make you more vulnerable.

Dieter's Paradox

Despite the exponential proliferation of "healthy" products being offered to the American public we are getting fatter at a worrying pace. According to the latest Gallup poll, 28% of the population is obese. That's an amazing 10% increase since 2008 alone. The Centers for Disease Control estimates that 70% of Americans are either overweight or obese. (By contrast, a mere 1.8% are classified as underweight.) Although we tend to associate obesity with diabetes, its effects go much deeper than that. One-third of all cancers are related to it as well. In fact, if you look at the major causes of both death and disability, weight is a key factor in every one of them. One study estimates that absenteeism due to weight related health issues costs the US $153 billion in lost productivity annually. However, that figure doesn't come close to reflecting the true impact were you to add in medical expenditures, both privately and publicly funded.

The big question is, how is it possible that every food product on the shelves these days is seemingly free of gluten, high fructose corn syrup, saturated fats, preservatives and artificial flavors, while being packed with protein, yet we continue to get bigger and bigger? Interestingly, and ironically, there is actually a positive correlation between eating healthier meals and becoming less healthy. The reason lies not in how our bodies process food, but in how our brains process information. We explore this phenomenon here, because it helps explain how it is that we can be so hyperfocused on diversification as a means for reducing P&L volatility, while P&L volatility is on the rise, thanks to diversification.

Negative Calorie Foods

Researchers at Northwestern University discovered an interesting phenomenon when they asked subjects to estimate the calorie content of
a series of unhealthy meals and then again for those same meals, but
with a healthy addition. For example, one of the unhealthy meals was a
hamburger. The average estimate among self-proclaimed *weight-conscious*
subjects was 734 calories. When the same hamburger was accompanied
by three celery sticks, the average estimate provided by the same group
dropped to 619. Think about that for a moment. When food was added
to the meal, respondents perceived the bigger meal to contain 15.6%
fewer calories. The same occurred when a small apple was added to a
bacon and cheese waffle sandwich, a small salad without dressing was
added to chili with beef, and a celery/carrot side dish was added to a
meatball pepperoni cheesesteak.

I know what you're thinking. These people are fools. How could
more food contain fewer calories? Don't they realize that a small apple
doesn't contain negative 66 calories? Well, actually, they do. When
assessed independently, people properly attribute calories to both the
hamburger and the celery sticks. However, we tend to assess things as
they are presented to us. That is the nature of framing, and the reason
it is so important to understand how it affects our decision making.
When shown a hamburger, we bucket it as a vice, whereas the celery
sticks are perceived as a virtue. Take a large vice, add a small helping
of virtue to it, and voila, you have a smaller vice. When we eat an
unhealthy meal and add a healthy option to it we perceive it to be less
unhealthy.

Our brains are fantastic at swapping out one hard-to-answer question
for a simpler, yet very different one, often without us even knowing
it. In this case, our brains erroneously perceive the words *healthy* and
low calorie as interchangeable. People behave as though healthy foods,
such as fruits and vegetables, have benefits that extend to all aspects of a
meal, including its effect on weight gain. It is a bias that, like all others,
leads to suboptimal decision-making, and marketers are aware and take
full advantage of it.

Diversifier's Paradox

Diversification is the name of the game these days. The portfolio manager diversifies her portfolio to reduce P&L volatility. The CIO looks to create a diversified portfolio of portfolio managers for the same reason. Endowments, fund of funds, family offices, and other institutional investors seek to build a portfolio of diversified funds, and end investors do the same – not to mention nonfinancial companies are diversifying their revenue streams and funding sources to reduce their reliance on a single source.

The concept of diversification is predicated on incorporating holdings that are uncorrelated, or possibly negatively correlated. Simply adding a long in Brent crude to a long in WTI won't likely reduce my P&L volatility. If I build a portfolio of longs in Brent versus an equal number of shorts in WTI, it's possible I could make or lose money, but in order to generate the same returns that are possible on a portfolio comprised of longs in one or the other alone, I'd have to size up the positions considerably.

Let's look at the concept of a "market neutral" strategy using long/short equity positions. I believe XYZ Company is undervalued, because I believe their earnings will be better than the market's expectations. When the earnings announcement comes I believe it will be repriced so that the company's stock once again trades at a multiple similar to the industry average. In anticipation, I want to get long XYZ's stock, but by doing so, I will expose myself to a possible adjustment in the industry multiple, general equity market risk, and a whole host of other factors separate and distinct from the company's earnings expectations. So I identify a stock or group of stocks that represent the same industry, similar revenue streams, dividends, etc. and short them in an appropriate proportion so as to isolate the one aspect of XYZ Company to which I want exposure. This leaves me exposed purely to the earnings announcement repricing for which I have high conviction. If the stock market moves down, I am protected with my short. If industry multiples come off, I am protected. Essentially, for everything exogenous to the earnings announcement, I am protected.

Now, since I have hedged (a form of diversification), I have reduced my risk, perhaps significantly. Therefore, I can size up the position significantly as well. Think about what that does for the risk/reward profile on the underlying view. Very little exposure to extraneous factors, and if the earnings positively surprise I generate a much greater return for the portfolio. It's a perfectly rational, compelling story, and a concept that is very appealing to our intuition.

But let's take a step back. I have increased the position significantly, not just on XYZ Company, but I have also gone short an equivalently large amount of the stock in a company or group of companies for which I have no strong opinion. Somehow, I believe this to be less risky than a significantly smaller position in XYZ alone, but is it?

On paper, perhaps it is. I'll run an analysis, or more likely, my firm will generate a factor by which I can determine the appropriate size for the hedge, whereby my risk will remain unchanged. Maybe the factor is beta or something more sophisticated, but in the end it's based on a historical correlation. It might be the past three months, six months, or two years, and for conducting a stress test, perhaps it will examine the exposure during particularly violent moments for markets. Without asking too many questions about the limitations of the analysis I'll establish the position, both the long in XYZ and the *appropriate* short against it. Now, it's just a matter of waiting for the earnings announcement.

What I've just described sounds so simple, thoughtful, and stress free. It's the story told by countless fund managers to even more investors, year in and year out. When it is told by a fund on a roll, it takes on an air of certainty.[1]

The reality is that correlations themselves have been increasingly volatile, so the "correct" notional for the hedge hasn't been so easy to determine. That in itself has led to far more volatile returns for market-neutral managers. Perhaps more devastating for many of them has been the timing of the moves between one side of a trade and the hedge on the other. When the side you have no opinion on moves 5%, 10%, even 30% in a day, in the wrong direction, yet your long doesn't

---

[1] Just read *Bloomberg Briefs'* annual analysis of hedge fund returns for 2015 and you'll see what I mean.

match it, are you willing to hang on for a few days in order for the hedge to retrace or your long to catch up? It's very unlikely and often impossible given internal risk limits. And that is exactly what has been wreaking havoc among many market neutral energy traders. Rather than having a relatively simple and small long equity position in the stock of a company we believe in, with clearly defined goals, both on the upside and downside, we add complexity and size, believing that we are somehow reducing the risk. It is a myth.

Of course when it works in your favor it's not seen as luck, but rather as astute trading. And that is how you have market-neutral funds topping the performance charts and seeing huge inflows, whereas others are closing shop at an astounding pace. A paradox indeed.

Illusory Invulnerability

We are inundated with data these days. At the touch of a button we can calculate our heart rate, monitor the number of steps we've taken, and estimate the calories we've burned. Many coaches suggest that you wear a heart monitor while exercising so you can determine if you're working hard enough. The FitBit is now fashionable, and even our phones can track much of the same data with free apps.

Now, thanks to the FinTech revolution, we can do the same for our portfolios. I sat with a client as he took me through the daily email he receives from his firm which is chock full of graphs and charts meant to help him better understand the composition of his portfolio and the attribution of his P&L. It was very impressive. With that kind of information so readily available, it could revolutionize the way he invests. Perhaps it could, but only if he has any idea what it all means. He doesn't, and neither do most people when they wear a FitBit.

We know we should take in fewer calories and burn more through exercise. We know we want to control our blood pressure and that our bodies require a proper balance of vitamins and minerals. We know that less volatility is preferable, as are higher returns. What many of us don't know is why we don't do what is best for us, or how we can change that.

FitBit premium offers an endless array of data about your sleep patterns, an unbiased activity assessment, and allows you to track your *progress* (yes, it assumes progress even though the odds favor regression). The beautiful charts and graphs are similar to those offered by many of the FinTech programs for portfolio health and progress. Odds are, neither a hedge fund's risk managers nor its CIO are likely to spend any time whatsoever understanding the math behind the calculations. They will simply assume it offers value. After all, something is better than nothing, right? Wrong.

When purchasing and using these systems, we have objectives such as better risk management and making better decisions. Simply by purchasing it and mandating that it be used boosts our related self-concept. In other words, the purchase and implementation reinforces the perception of ourselves as disciplined, thoughtful, and objective decision-makers. It matters little that we don't understand how it works or what value it actually delivers. It doesn't matter if there are shortcomings or that it may be misleading. What matters is that we made the effort. That effort reinforces a positive self-concept because we are taking action, much like purchasing the most expensive BowFlex.

Unfortunately, without an understanding of the mechanics of decision making, how cognitive bias occurs and why it matters, technology has the potential to exacerbate many of our most problematic issues. Consider the use of vitamin supplements. There is a general acceptance that vitamin supplements are good for health and well-being. However, there doesn't exist any evidence that a higher consumption of vitamin C is associated with a lower incidence of lung cancer, nor do people perceive there to be. However, in a number of studies, smokers who are given vitamin C supplements smoked more than the control subjects. Some researchers call it *illusory invulnerability*, whereas others use the related term, *licensing effect*. Which term you choose isn't nearly as important as understanding the concept.

When we work out, regardless of how hard or intensely, we feel good about ourselves. We feel as though we've sacrificed and therefore deserve a reward. The workout, like a smoker taking vitamin C supplements, represents a good deed, which in effect gives us *license* to do a bad deed.

Recall the negative-calorie food phenomenon. When we employ something we perceive as being good for us very often we mentally overemphasize its positive effect. That inflated valuation of a positive opens the door to the likely indulgence in a negative perceived as commensurate, that we would have otherwise rejected, thereby potentially producing a net negative return on the investment of time and/or energy without realizing it.

Codifying Mistakes Through FinTech

One of the keys to improving our decision-making is to shift from a belief-based system to an evidence-based one. Technology provides a terrific tool toward that end. However, unless it is employed properly and consistently, it can actually do as much damage as good. There are the usual issues related to the old "Garbage in, garbage out," and the ones mentioned earlier, but it goes well beyond those. Tech based tools are no different than any other tool meant to aid in decision-making. They must be developed within the context of the decision-making process rather than the other way around. In other words, we must first define the problem we are trying to solve, along with the criteria by which we will define success or failure. Then we must define the factors that affect our ability to solve the problem but that we do not control. Only then can we consider which acts will provide the greatest odds of solving it. To reiterate, the employment of technology should be for a specific purpose that is first properly defined.

More often than not though, the employment of technology occurs because there is an intuitive belief that it *should* be employed. Over and over, clients and potential clients tell me that they are exploring different FinTech solutions. They spend valuable time listening to pitches and trying to pick from the different options. Yet when I ask the simple question, "What problem are you trying to solve with this?" the overwhelming majority seem to be at a loss.

Then there is what you do with the output. A client recently had an interaction with his manager about the effort he is putting forth to shift his investment process from the industry-standard reactive process to a proactive one. The portfolio manager lamented about how much work it is to properly plan a trade, including the identification of relevant signals and delineation of the specific actions he will take over the trade's life. The manager's response? "According to the data you generate the majority of your alpha in the first two weeks of your trades' lives. So don't overthink them or you might miss the opportunities." The narrative is so flawed it could be considered laughable, but because it is *supported* by data, it carries weight. Poor decision-making by a poor decision-maker has now been codified into a poor decision-making process that will influence an entire firm, and given the proliferation of misguided FinTec implementation, perhaps an entire industry.

Bottom line is this. Just as buying the most expensive BowFlex Collapsible Elliptical StairMaster 5000 won't make you a professional athlete or give you a six pack abdomen, purchasing a FinTech version of the same won't make you an expert investor, or even a better decision-maker. In fact, there's a good chance it may make you worse.

Chapter 8

Auditing Mental Accounting

Example 1: Wasteful Education

In 2007 I began a five-year research project wherein I attempted to understand what is truly ailing the K–12 education system in America. Along the way I discovered a disturbing practice that is relevant to the topic of this book.

While touring an elementary school in South Florida, I passed a classroom that caught my attention. The door was open, but lights were off. I flipped them on to discover a room filled from wall-to-wall and floor-to-ceiling with nothing but desks and chairs. When I asked the principal about the display, she explained the rationale behind it. Turns out, every year the school gets a budget. Well, actually not *a* budget, but rather many budgets. Among them is one for teacher salaries, one for textbooks, one for maintenance, and yes, one for furniture. If the principal comes in under budget on say, school furniture one year, she can't apply the savings to something she might need more of at that moment, like maybe a new coat of paint for the gymnasium. If she doesn't spend the furniture budget that year, the money remains in the county coffers. Here is where it gets really interesting though. If she comes in under budget for furniture this year, there is a high probability they will reduce her furniture budget for next year. So, rather than risk having her budget reduced for anything in any given year, she will continue to buy furniture with her furniture budget even if it means shoving it into an empty classroom or using the facilities budget to build a shed out back to store it all until it can be fully depreciated and thrown away.

I know, I know. You're befuddled by the waste and stupidity of the education system. If you're anything like I was when I stared into the abyss of that classroom, you're probably shaking your head, mouth agape, wondering how it's possible that things like this still go on. However, if you think about it, given the system as it exists, her logic is actually unassailable. Given her constraints and how she is assessed, would you behave differently?

Over those five years I found episode after episode of similar situations and amazingly, every single time, the people in charge were as frustrated with the state of the education system as you and I. Even more incredible, when I would meet their bosses and their bosses' bosses they all had a similar story to share. Each had a pet peeve about the system that caused them to make decisions that could be perceived as irrational to those on the outside, but made sense to them given the constraints.

No doubt by now you're ready to tear the hair out of your head, prepared to march straight down to your school board to either raise hell or take a position on the board so that you can singlehandedly straighten out these knuckleheads. But before you do you might want to continue reading because, very shortly, I will argue that the same cognitive flaw responsible for this colossal error in judgement among the leadership in education is also responsible for a systematic error in judgement exhibited by nearly all institutional money managers (traders and allocators alike), and yes, it probably applies to you too.

Example 2: Drunken Economics

Back in 1998, behavioral economist Richard Thaler teamed up with Eldar Shafir to learn about the thought process among wine enthusiasts. They asked subscribers of Orley Ashenfelter's newsletter, *Liquid Assets*, the following question:

Suppose you bought a case of a good 1982 Bordeaux in the futures market for $20 a bottle. The wine now sells at auction for $75 per bottle. You have decided to drink a bottle. Which of the following best captures your feeling of the cost to you of drinking this bottle?

1. $0
2. $20
3. $20 plus interest
4. $75
5. –$55 (I drank a $75 bottle for which I only paid $20)

Interestingly, respondents were fairly evenly dispersed with the percentages for each answer being 30%, 18%, 7%, 20%, and 25%, respectively. Put another way, in the mind of more than half the respondents, drinking the wine either cost them nothing or it actually saved them money. The researchers found the results so fascinating, they followed up a year later with a related experiment. Their findings were later published in a paper with the very literal title, "Invest Now, Drink Later, Spend Never." It's worth noting that the great majority of respondents were people who most would consider to be financially sophisticated individuals, including many professional investment managers and economists.

Example 3: Bet the House

On the back of Kahneman and Tversky's Prospect Theory paper, Thaler conducted a study in 1990 to see how decisions are affected by prior outcomes – namely, gains and losses. In the study MBA students gambled with real money and were given the following three problems. (The percentage of students choosing each option is provided in brackets.)

Problem 1: You have just won $30. Now choose between:
a. A 50% chance to gain $9 and a 50% chance to lose $9. [70%]
b. No further gain or loss. [30%]
Problem 2: You have just lost $30. Now choose between:
a. A 50% chance to gain $9 and a 50% chance to lose $9. [40%]
b. No further gain or loss. [60%]
Problem 3: You have just lost $30. Now choose between:
a. A 33% chance to gain $30 and a 67% chance to gain nothing. [60%]
b. A sure $10. [40%]

As it happens MBA students are really no different than the typical gambler at a Las Vegas casino. Gamblers who are up money often create a separate mental account for "house money," which is somehow distinct from the rest of their wealth. It's a phenomenon aptly named the *house money effect*, because the casino is often referred to as *the house* and so when gamblers are up money at the casino they tend to think of those winnings as the house's money. Many gamblers will even go so far as to physically separate their money from the house's money, putting one in the left pocket and the other in the right.

What is significant about Thaler's study, along with many others that came before and after, is not so much that a separate mental account is created, but that the money in these two accounts are actually treated differently. As the results show gamblers playing with house money exhibit a greater propensity for risk. Those who were experiencing losses tended toward risk aversion, *unless* the gamble offered a chance to break even. In other words, the very assessment of a bet's risk/reward is affected by whether individuals are betting with "their" money or the "house's."

Example 4: Half Off

James is a global macro portfolio manager with 20 years of experience. He purchased a one-touch option on the S&P Index with a barrier at 3000 for 10% of a $1 million payout. For those unfamiliar with one-touch options, worry not. For the purposes of this example all you need to understand is that James has bet the S&P Index will "touch," i.e. trade at, the 3000 level at some point between the day he purchased the option and the day it expires. If it trades at 2000 during that time frame, he gets 100% of the payout or $1 million. If it does not touch, he gets nothing in return for the $100,000 premium he paid up front. Based on the payoff profile, it would be fair to assume the chances of it touching 3000 are low.

Two weeks later, the S&P Index jumps up and the option is now worth 20% or $200,000. James decides to unwind half the position in order to "recoup" his initial investment of $100,000, thereby leaving only the house's money at risk.

Well done, James. That's a very wise decision that serves as evidence of your ability to remain disciplined. A decision that would be applauded by even the most experienced traders. After all, it's an age-old strategy that has been passed down from generation to generation.

Unfortunately, it's also irrational.

In fact there is absolutely no difference between what James did and what gamblers in Las Vegas do on a daily basis. James created a mental account that differentiated between *his* money and the *house's* money. There are numerous issues to consider here.

Firstly, money is fungible, which means there is no difference between money in your left pocket and money in your right, money earmarked for furniture and money earmarked for textbooks, $75 in your bank account and a bottle of wine that you can sell today for $75. As for James, all $200,000 is money to do with as he pleases.

I know what you're thinking. The risk/reward has changed and so too should his assessment of the trade's value. I wholeheartedly agree, so long as it is assessed based on the merit of the trade itself. The issue is that the doubling of James' original investment is purely a function of where he bought it (10%) and what it's valued at today (20%), neither of which are inherently relevant to either market fundamentals or technical indicators. The only relevance "20%" has is that it creates an opportunity for him to put his initial investment of $100,000 cash back into his account while creating a separate mental account for the $100,000 he still has at risk.

To reiterate, the problem isn't simply that mental accounting has occurred, but that the two accounts are actually treated differently. Having "pocketed" the original investment and now playing with the house's money means the gambler, err, I mean trader will be more risk tolerant with the remaining position. This is inconsistent with the tenets of expected utility theory. In other words it is irrational.

Beyond that, what Thaler and others have proven is that this generally accepted strategy of taking off enough of a position in order to cover your initial investment wasn't the result of decades of experience or wisdom being passed down from generation to generation, but rather flawed intuition shared by MBA students, gamblers, and experienced investors alike. As a result of simply being repeated time and again by market participants, the wisdom behind it is rarely questioned, even though it should be.

Ultimately, the goal for all decision-makers should be objectivity. If your assessment of one bet with one set of characteristics and one set of outcome probabilities is affected by whether the money you are betting with has come out of your left pocket or your right then you are not being objective. You are making a mistake.

The common thread that ties all the preceding examples together is that the law of fungibility has been broken leading to irrational decisions and suboptimal results. In the education example formal barriers in the form of segregated budgets created the inefficiencies that frustrate us all. For the wine enthusiasts, because the current value of $75 hadn't been realized (i.e. converted to cash), it was difficult for them to see the fungibility of that money, and therefore the true cost of the wine they were drinking. Fundamentally, there is really no difference between the MBA students in example 3 and James in example 4. In both cases (and that of the typical gambler), the law of fungibility was broken when the distinction was made between their own and the house's money. Even though it may feel right and make intuitive sense, fundamentally it is as irrational as ordering more furniture to be stacked in an empty classroom.

How to Stop Turning Winners into Losers

To give an example of how this impacts dynamic trading, two weeks before a Bank of Japan meeting, a client – let's call him Max – purchased a dollar call spread in the US Dollar (USD) versus Japanese Yen (JPY).

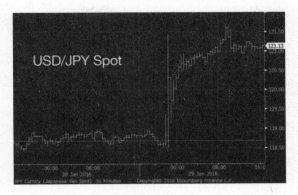

Figure 8.1 USD/JPY spot
SOURCE: Bloomberg Finance L.P.

He risked 25 basis points (0.25%) of his assets under management (AUM) based on his view that the Bank of Japan (BoJ) would cut interest rates. The BoJ action slightly exceeded the expectations he stated ahead of time in his trade write-up. The market immediately reacted by buying USD and selling JPY, pushing it from 118.50 to a high of 121.65 (+2.65%) within a matter of hours (Figure 8.1).

Max's call spread was showing a profit of 1.8% of AUM with less than 24 hours to go before expiration. The options' expiration is significant, because it sets a line in the sand for the idea, and its expression. What Max was effectively saying by structuring his trade with that expiration date is that whatever the BoJ does, the impact is likely to be quick and powerful, with 123.00 (the call strike he was short) representing the upper boundary of his expectations. He was proven right.

At that moment, the call spread had a delta of 80. In other words if the call spread had a notional of $100 million per strike, then the P&L on the position was behaving similar to that of an outright cash position of $80 million. With the expiration looming near Max decided to unwind the call spread and convert it into that cash equivalent. He set the stop/loss "just below where spot was when the announcement came out." Within a matter of days, the stop was hit and the trade was over. Max had turned a 1.8% winner into a 0.3% gain.

The questions we aim to answer: Did Max make a mistake, if so what mistake did he make, what can cognitive science tells us about his thought process, and can we use decision architecture to improve on the process going forward?

The Mistake?

Max followed the process beautifully including thoughtful research and analysis regarding policy expectations and the resulting price action it would likely trigger, as well as the development of an appropriate strategy for expressing that specific view. He did a proper trade write-up complete with rationale, expectations, premortem, and reassessment triggers, and when one was triggered, he executed according to the script. In other words there wasn't a single mistake in the trade that he named "JPY14." He even recognized that the cash position was a new trade, separate and distinct from JPY14.

However, when a new trade is established it isn't sufficient to merely acknowledge it as such. A new trade write-up needs to be written, complete with its own unique rationale, premortem, supporting evidence and reassessment triggers. In this case it wasn't done. Why? Max says he was busy with other things and since it was effectively a continuation of an idea he'd already written up it wasn't a priority. *That* was a mistake. Although he recognized this should be considered a new trade, separate and distinct from JPY14, he clearly hadn't mentally processed it as such.

Had he followed the prescribed protocol, one specifically designed to help nudge him toward better decisions, he would have created a new trade write-up, thereby forcing him to mentally process it. He would have expressly noted the capital at risk (max downside) for the trade as 150 basis points. A sixfold jump from that which he thought appropriate for JPY14. Although you might argue, as he did (briefly), that given the fact that the BoJ decision was now known, JPY15 involved less uncertainty, and therefore should be sized accordingly. I disagree for two reasons.

First, the jump in spot reflected the new policy and therefore shifted spot to its new reference point. Where spot would move in relation to that new reference point involved a different set of factors, each of which engendered their own uncertainty. Secondly, even if you take issue with my first point, the question is was he now six times more certain about the future of USD/JPY as his relative position size implied? It's possible, but highly unlikely. Instead, the more likely explanation for the increased exposure was related to the profitability of JPY14 (1.5% versus 1.8%) and the original risk relative to the protected profit (25bps versus 30bps). In his mind Max was playing with house money, and research tells us we are far less risk averse with house money than we are with "real" money. Which leads us to the science behind this mistake.

The Science: Hedonic Framing

Back in 1998, Read, Lowenstein, and Rabin wrote about a concept they called choice bracketing to explain why it is that decisions are often made and assessed as a group, rather than one at a time. What is most interesting is that the brackets should theoretically and mathematically have absolutely no effect. In other words, if you consider the value function for outcomes x and y, it should look like this: $v(x+y) = v(x) + v(y)$. Yet their research showed that it wasn't typically the case. Due to our very human aversion to loss, it often means that $v(x+y) \neq v(x) + v(y)$, and vice versa.

Consider, for example, how you would feel about winning a single lottery of $75 versus winning one lottery for $50 and a second one immediately after for $25. According to research done by Richard Thaler, 64% say the two-time winner is happier (read: experiences greater utility). Think about this for a moment. The outcome is exactly the same. In both cases you wind up with $75, yet because of the way the winnings are bracketed you have the following: $v(\$75) < v(\$50 + \$25)$. In the pursuit of happiness, our actions can defy the laws of logic. Does it really matter? The answer is a resounding "Yes!"

Thaler coined the term *hedonic framing* for the phenomenon and devised a set of principles to help us predict people's behavior given what we know. Keep in mind Thaler isn't condoning the behavior, he is merely attempting to model it. In doing so, we stand a better chance of identifying when we are likely to act irrationally, and that in turn can help us take action to defend against our own natural instincts. According to Thaler, the principles we follow for maximizing utility when we evaluate joint outcomes which assume the prospect theory value functions are as follows:

1. Segregate gains: (because the gain function is concave).
2. Integrate losses: (because the loss function is convex).
3. Integrate smaller losses with larger gains: (to offset loss aversion).
4. Segregate small gains (silver linings) from larger losses: (because the gain function is steepest at the origin the utility of a small gain can exceed the utility of slightly reducing a large loss).

The Science: Mental Accounting

Some time ago one of my graduate students submitted a decision log in which she described how a friend had purchased two tickets to a Beyonce concert for $900 each. When the person she was due to attend with backed out she faced a decision. Should she go alone and sell the other ticket, offer the other ticket to the young daughter of a friend who had done her a favor recently, or sell both tickets online for the prevailing price of $5,000 per ticket?

Her friend saw the first option like this. She paid $1,800 for the pair of tickets - $5,000 she would receive from the sale = She would effectively have been paid $3,200 to attend the show, and that made her very happy (read: high utility). According to copious studies on the subject that's how most people would analyze the decision, but it's dead wrong. The reason is that money is fungible. If she can exchange her ticket for $5,000 then that ticket is equivalent to $5,000. It may not look like $5,000 cash looks but it is exactly the same. Let's look at her change in wealth after each of the following scenarios.

She buys two tickets and sells one: +$3,200
She buys two tickets and gives one to friend's daughter: −$1,800
She buys two tickets and sells both: +$8,200

This way of framing the decision shows how the ticket holder viewed it. Essentially, her reference point was her initial wealth and so attending the concert alone was viewed as a gain. However, if the problem were reframed using the maximum return as the reference point, it would look like this:

She buys two tickets and sells one: −$5,000
She buys two tickets and gives one to a friend's daughter: −$10,000
She buys two tickets and sells both: +$0

Due to our natural aversion to losses it's very likely my student's friend would have come to a very different decision had she framed the problem in this way. She also would have seen just how much she was "paying" her friend for the favor. Of course, we haven't considered the utility (read: happiness) gained by attending the concert (a) alone, (b) with a friend, or (c) with the friend's daughter, but the point of this exercise is to show that it matters how the options are framed. In other words, where the parentheses are placed may not affect the math, but it certainly affects the behavior, and that in turn affects the outcome.

As it relates to Max, it matters whether he tagged the JPY cash position as a unique trade, separate and distinct from JPY14. Although it's true that $(1.8\% - 1.5\%) = (1.8\%) - (1.5\%)$, the decision-making along the way is different.

Decision Architecture: Avoiding the Mistake

There are three things that stand between the way we make decisions and the way we should make them:

1. Ability
2. Cognitive bias
3. Motivation

Anyone reading this has the ability to make proper decisions. We tend to falter when it comes to bias and motivation. Unfortunately, it requires hard work to overcome bias and avoid its corrosive effects, even if we do recognize it. Unless we make the direct connection between the bias and our performance it's unlikely we will muster up the motivation necessary to avoid its deleterious effects.

Over the time we have been working together Max has made great strides in understanding how his decisions are affected by cognitive bias. Just as importantly, he has made a tremendous effort to incorporate the tools devised to help him avoid it into his daily process. In fact I consider him to be a model client, exhibiting the kind of curiosity, introspection, and motivation required to improve.

In the case of the episode discussed earlier, several processes have been put in place to help him *bracket* his decisions in order to better analyze his decisions and reach optimal conclusions more often. The detailed trade write-up including all the requisite components is one. Giving trades distinct names in order to isolate the specific, unique objectives of the structure is another. Calculating and writing down the capital at risk (CaR) in combination with writing a premortem is designed to make the experience of the potential loss more salient prior to establishing the risk. This results in more appropriate position sizing and allows the decision maker to be better prepared for that eventuality should it occur down the road. By doing so it reduces the emotional impact in the future, thereby reducing the likelihood that the affect heuristic will lead to a flawed decision at some point over the life of the trade.

In the end though, this one slipped through the cracks. As his decision architect I must develop additional safeguards that improve the odds that he will implement the process as prescribed next time. What makes it so challenging for many portfolio managers is that they are essentially left to their own devices as far as process goes. They don't have to turn in time sheets or fill out a requisition form explaining why they need capital for a new project as it is for most line managers in other industries. That gives portfolio managers the freedom to be sloppy and undisciplined. The next step is to create a fictitious version of that external accountability for Max, but it must at least carry the perception of validity teeth.

Part II

Decisions in the Financial Context

Chapter 9

Mistakes at the Heart of Investment Management

A Common Risk Management Mistake

Jim is a portfolio manager (PM) with a positive track record over the past four years that he's worked for your fund. He began 2016 managing $400 million with a 1% value at risk (VaR) limit and by the end of August was up 10% for the year (+$40 million profit). Given his track record and recent performance you doubled his allocation to $800 million beginning September 1. He can now build a portfolio with as much as $8 million in VaR. Unfortunately, he's run into a rough patch and as of November 1 is down 5% from his August peak (−$40 million from the peak; $0 million on the year). As a result, according to your risk management rules, he must cut his risk in half, which he does. As of December 31, he's back to his high watermark (+$40 million profit).

Table 9.1 shows what Jim's track record looks like for 2016.

There's just one small problem. That isn't Jim's track record. It's the track record of your firm's decisions as they relate to Jim's portfolio. Let's delineate all of the decisions that led to those results.

Table 9.1 Jim's performance by month and year.

	Jan	Feb	Mar	Apr	May	Jun	Jul	Aug	Sep	Oct	Nov	Dec	2016
AUM	$400	$400	$400	$400	$400	$400	$400	$400	$800	$800	$800	$800	
Notional	$5	$5	$5	$5	$5	$5	$5	$5	–$20	–$20	$20	$20	$40
%	1.25%	1.25%	1.25%	1.25%	1.25%	1.25%	1.25%	1.25%	–2.5%	–2.5%	2.5%	2.5%	10%

The CIO made four decisions:

1. Allocate $400 million to Jim on January 1.
2. Allocate $400 million more to Jim on September 1.
3. Treat the allocations homogeneously (back to this in a moment).
4. Mandate that VaR be cut by 50% if a PM experiences a 5% peak-to-trough drawdown.

Risk Management made one decision:

1. Recommend that VaR limit be cut in half at 5% drawdown.

Jim made all remaining decisions.

Each of those decisions impacted the firm's track record as it relates to Jim's portfolio, however because of the way we track and monitor decisions in this industry, only Jim owns them. Since the end result is a good one, he's unlikely to kick up much of a fuss, nor is anyone else, but if we are to reduce mistakes going forward a number of changes should be made.

Let's make just one minor adjustment to this scenario. Instead of cutting Jim's VaR limit in half in November, risk management recommends that the CIO take back half of Jim's allocation and reallocate it to other portfolio managers. What would Jim's track record look like then? (See Table 9.2.)

Table 9.2 Jim's performance with updated allocation.

	Jan	Feb	Mar	Apr	May	Jun	Jul	Aug	Sep	Oct	Nov	Dec	2016
AUM	$400	$400	$400	$400	$400	$400	$400	$400	$800	$800	$400	$400	
Notional	$5	$5	$5	$5	$5	$5	$5	$5	–$20	–$20	$20	$20	$40
%	1.25%	1.25%	1.25%	1.25%	1.25%	1.25%	1.25%	1.25%	–2.5%	–2.5%	5%	5%	15%

Jim makes his decisions as a proportion of the risk he is allocated. How much VaR he can take on as a percentage of assets under management (AUM), how much AUM he is allocated, and how his compensation is determined are all beyond his control. All he controls are the decisions he makes *given* the rules of the game as determined by the CIO and risk management. Jim's actual return on AUM for 2016 is 15%. The difference between the 15% Jim delivered and the 10% shown in the previous table should be owned by management. This isn't a theoretical loss, it is negative alpha and it should be attributed to the CIO.

After all, it is the CIO's job to maximize the returns on the portfolio of PMs they have chosen to invest in. Their ability to generate alpha can be broken down into its components. Comparison to a benchmark tells part of the story, but there are multiple factors that go into those results. Which PMs should they employ? How much should they allocate to each of them? Given the correlation among them, should they overallocate, and if so, by how much? When should they reduce, cut, or increase their position size (allocation to a PM)? In effect, the CIO is a portfolio manager of portfolio managers. The value he delivers as a decision-maker overall, and as it relates to each of these questions, should be tracked as it is for any other allocator.

Why would a CIO instruct a PM to cut their risk? There are two reasons commonly given: (1) To help the PM get their head straight again. This is invoked because the CIO believes the PM has become emotionally effected by the loss itself, leading him or her to become suboptimal decision-making. To break the emotional connection and get the PM to invest strictly based on market factors, they reduce the position sizing to something far less consequential. That's at least the idea. (2) To reduce the impact of the PM on the fund's performance. In other words, the CIO has lowered his expectation that the PM will generate positive results going forward. Naturally, if your expectations for that PM have gone down, you want to reduce their ability to affect your fund returns. Effectively, you cut back on your investment in that PM. *That* is a trading decision, and like all trading decisions, it should have P&L attributed to it. In order for it to be tracked it must be clearly recorded as a decision. That is why it is important for management to cut the PM's AUM rather than cut their VaR.

Over time, we can then see if this decision to reduce allocations at a random moment such as the 5% drawdown is optimal. (Of course it rarely is) However, it is easier to implement speed bumps than the more optimal alternatives of (1) ensuring that all PMs have proper investment/decision- making processes in place to reduce the potential for emotion to creep in and (2) developing a better process for assessing whether a portfolio manager adds value over time.

An Uncommon Solution

After eight months Jim was up $40 million. If his payout is 13%, he was looking at taking home more than $5 million. Then suddenly, without any say in the matter, management allocates another $400 million to his portfolio. It creates a very real quandary for him. The rational thing to do, of course, is increase his position size proportionally going forward. Well, that's not entirely accurate. If his objective is to maximize returns on his portfolio over time, then yes, he should make a proportional adjustment to his position sizing. However, if his objective is to maximize his take home pay over time, the rational decision may be to make no adjustment.

On January 1 the firm's and Jim's incentives and objectives were aligned which led to optimal behavior. As soon as profits or losses are generated though, they begin to diverge. When objectives diverge rational actions may diverge as well. Unless management understands the dynamic, how to monitor it, and the appropriate actions to mitigate the impact, it can lead to mistakes that reduce returns. On the other hand, if management can and does take the appropriate actions the mistakes are reduced and returns improved.

To find a simple solution, we need look no further than what happens when an investor allocates more to the fund itself. Typically, it is treated as a series. In other words, the initial $400 million investment is treated as a separate series from the additional $400 million. As of October 31, it looks like Table 9.3.

If the year were to end here, the fund would be paid a performance fee of $4 million (assuming 2/20). However, Jim would be paid zero. The reason is that Jim's entire capital allocation is treated homogeneously. There is no distinction between new and old capital. Therefore, when Jim's allocation is doubled, it becomes twice as easy for him to give back

Table 9.3   The initial $400 million investment, as a separate series from the additional $400 million.

	Jan	Feb	Mar	Apr	May	Jun	Jul	Aug	Sep	Oct				2016
						Series A								
AUM	$400	$400	$400	$400	$400	$400	$400	$400	$400	$400				
Notional	$5	$5	$5	$5	$5	$5	$5	$5	−$10	−$10				$20
%	1.25%	1.25%	1.25%	1.25%	1.25%	1.25%	1.25%	1.25%	−2.5%	−2.5%				5%

	Jan	Feb	Mar	Apr	May	Jun	Jul	Aug	Sep	Oct	Nov	Dec	2016
						Series B							
AUM									$400	$400			
Notional									−$10	−$10			−$20
%									−2.5%	−2.5%			−5%

everything he's made up to that point. That has real implications for Jim's decision-making, likely making him more risk averse with the additional capital. A simple solution is to treat the capital allocated by the fund to their portfolio managers in the same way as capital allocated by investors to the fund.

This is intended merely as a primer to help management understand that your actions have implications and that even subtle, seemingly insignificant adjustments can have real P&L consequences. For the alpha-generating CIO, properly implemented risk management can deliver a significant competitive advantage.

Why Risk Takers Stopped Taking Risk

In the NFL, after a touchdown is scored the coach has the option to either kick for an extra point or attempt a two-point conversion. Historically, extra points have a 97% success rate, whereas two-point conversions are successful 55% of the time (this analysis is prior to the extra point attempt being moved further away from the endzone). Since the expected return for the two-pointer is greater ($0.55 \times 2 = 1.1$) than that of the extra point attempt ($0.97 \times 1 = 0.97$), you'd think most coaches would opt for the two-point attempt. Better yet, when you consider that two-point conversions executed with a run play have a 75% success rate and therefore an expected utility of 1.5, you'd think any coach that went for an extra point would be ridiculed for making such an irrational decision. Alas, you'd be wrong. In reality, coaches opt to kick the extra point in all but the most dire circumstances, and I can't recall a single time any of them have been criticized for making such a suboptimal selection.

Actually, it's a bit more complicated than I've suggested. Although the two-point conversion is the optimal choice if your goal is to maximize the number of points scored, that isn't necessarily what coaches desire.

You see, in football, the coach's objective is not to score the most points over time, but to win games (which means scoring the most points within a segregated time period). In fact, it is easily possible for a team to score the most points and even the most net points over the course of a season, and yet not make it into the playoffs. (See Table 9.4.) So while opting to attempt the two-point conversion is clearly the more rational option for someone looking to maximize total point accumulation, it's not necessarily the right decision given the parameters as defined by the rules of the game.

Think about that for just a moment. For those of us in the business of making rational decisions in the face of uncertainty, one of the fundamental tenets is that we seek to maximize expected returns. In other words, we play the odds. As an investment manager, if I were facing a decision with the historical probabilities already presented, the only logical decision would be to attempt a two-point conversion. After all, as investors, we don't have segregated time buckets for which we need be concerned. I mean, a 2% return on January 31 means the same to me as a 2% return on February 1. Therefore, I don't have to make suboptimal decisions. Instead, I can make choices with the sole goal of maximizing my returns over time, right?

Wrong. Well, it used to be that way, but the rules of the game have clearly changed to more closely match that of the NFL. We'll get into one of the reasons why it has happened in a moment, but for now let's explore the ramifications.

Bracketing occurs in our industry in a number of ways, all of which create segregated buckets of time, causing a shift in objectives away from maximizing expected returns, just as it does in the NFL. As a result, it's understandable that the thought process of investment managers today shares more in common with NFL coaches than it does with those who sat in these seats just 10 years ago.

Table 9.4   NFL 2014 season: points scored and games won.

Team	Points Scored	Games Won
Green Bay	486	12
Denver	482	12
Philadelphia	474	10
New England	468	12
Dallas	467	12
Indianapolis	458	11
Pittsburgh	436	11
Baltimore	409	10
New Orleans	401	7
Seattle	394	12
Miami	388	8
Atlanta	381	6
New York Giants	380	6
Houston	372	9
Cincinnati	365	10
Kansas City	353	9
San Diego	348	9
Buffalo	343	9
Carolina	339	7
Minnesota	325	7
St. Louis	324	6
Detroit	321	11
Chicago	319	5
Arizona	310	11
San Francisco	306	8
Washington	301	4
Cleveland	299	7
New York Jets	283	4
Tampa Bay	277	2
Tennessee	254	2
Oakland	253	3
Jacksonville	249	3

It's self-reinforcing too. Just as NFL coaches are applauded for choosing the suboptimal route of kicking the extra point, investment managers are rewarded for shortening their time horizons, window dressing their portfolios around month-end, quarter-end and year-end, and for focusing more on p&l volatility than returns.

If you think about it, the reason time horizons are truncated in sports is to make every moment more exciting, more uncertain: the shorter the season, the fewer the games, the fewer the opportunities to make up for a bad run, the more exciting the spectacle. What the promoters of sports seek is fans sitting on the edge of their seats exhilarated by the fact that even the worst team can beat the best team on *any given Sunday*. What they count on is the fact that the shorter the time horizon, the greater the likelihood for an outlier result, essentially that noise will overwhelm signal. Granted, over the course of a season or tournament, the best teams often rise to the top, but in sports like NCAA football, a single loss can take a team out of contention for the entire season. It's what makes college football so much more exciting than the pros, and it's also why, even though the rules of the game are nearly identical, the way the game is played is so radically different. This difference in approach also explains why the greatest college quarterback of all time, Tim Tebow, garnered so little interest from NFL scouts and why so few fantastic college coaches have been able to successfully make the transition to the pros. It becomes a fundamentally different game, with different play calling, demanding different skill sets, and generating different results, and yet the only significant difference between college and pro football is the frequency with which conclusions regarding success or failure are drawn.

There is a fundamental difference between sports and investing though, and this difference is the source of numerous problems that have developed over time, including lower returns for the industry and a rise in the impact of noise relative to signal on price action across all markets. You see, the end investors do not seek excitement for their money. They do not want noise to have a greater influence than signal on their returns. They do, however, seek to maximize expected returns, even if their behavior often appears at odds with that desire.

This isn't a phenomenon unique to football or the current state of markets. Decades of research regarding human behavior have attempted to differentiate the phenomenon I've been discussing to this point known as "narrow framing" to cognitive psychologists and "myopic loss aversion" to behavioral economists as opposed to the more recognizable term "risk aversion." One notable study conducted by Mehra and Prescott in 1985 attempted to understand the equity premium puzzle, with *premium* referring to the outperformance of US equities over a safe investment like US Treasuries, and *puzzle* referring to how high it had been for so long (roughly 6% per year for 70 years). The real question they were asking is, if stocks have so outperformed Treasuries over such a long period of time, why are they perceived as more risky? Ultimately, the conclusion they reached is that the "risk attitude of loss-averse investors depends on the frequency with which they reset their reference point." Richard Thaler estimated that in order to "solve" the equity premium puzzle, the most prominent evaluation period for investors would need to be 13 months. In other words, if you had a portfolio consisting solely of, say, the S&P Index and US T-Bills, and only looked at your returns every 13 months, you'd perceive them to be equally risky. If you did so, your allocations would be very different – and so too would the returns on your portfolio – from what they would be if you observed them more frequently.

Myopic loss aversion is the term used to describe this behavior because the "frequent evaluations prevent the investor from adopting a strategy that would be preferred over an appropriately long time horizon." In other words, the longer your time horizon for investing, the less frequently you should be observing the returns in your portfolio. Simply by checking on your investments more frequently you perceive risk to be greater which leads to more risk-averse behavior. We tend to think we can control our tendency towards risk aversion but enough research has been done to prove you'd be an extreme case if that were true. A simple study by Benartzi and Thaler proved this point quite well. They asked two groups of university professors how they would invest their retirement money if they had to choose between two investment funds, one of which was based on stock returns and the other on bonds. To the first group they provided charts showing the distribution of one-year rates of return, and the other was shown the distribution of 30-year rates of return. Those in the first group elected to put the majority in bonds, whereas the other group invested 90% of their funds in stocks.

With the proliferation of hedge funds came the proliferation of firms and products designed to help you assess them which has led to standardization. Benchmarking became common practice. Seemingly innocuous and arguably random selections were made, such as using monthly data to analyze returns *and volatility* creating a standard for which all future analysis would be conducted and funds compared. This standardization of time bucketing then led to the unintended convergence in both the assessment and, just as importantly, the perception of risk among two otherwise disparate groups: short-term and long-term investors. Now, even investors who describe themselves as having longer-term horizons are likely to suffer from myopic loss aversion, even if they don't realize it.

For the hedge fund manager who seeks to maximize expected returns, one solution is to release your returns on a frequency you believe would allow investors to more accurately assess your true inherent risk. If you offer quarterly liquidity, release your returns at the same time.

For investors, do your own analysis of returns and the volatility of returns using a period better aligned with your investment horizon. In other words, if you're truly a long-term investor, review the performance of your investments less frequently. Gather the data less frequently or have your analysts parse the monthly data into buckets more aligned with your objectives *before* you see it. Ask yourself whether it makes sense to review and analyze return data with the same frequency as hot money investors. As long as you keep watching short term performance your resulting behavior will more closely match that of a hot-money investor rather than the long-term investor you perceive yourself to be.

Chapter 10

Manager Selection

Designing a Manager Selection Algorithm

Is Warren Buffett a good investment manager? It seems like such a seemingly simple question, but is it really? How do you define *good*? What factors should you consider? Is his entire track record relevant? The past 10 years? Five years? Last year? Should we consider only his average annualized returns? Calendar years or rolling 12 months? What about his drawdowns? Volatility?

Would your process differ if you were attempting to assess a hot-shot trader from one of the big investment banks who doesn't have a track record as a CIO or even as a portfolio manager? How about a manager who's been generating exceptional returns on a small portfolio out of his garage, but has never worked at a large institution? Does it make sense to fast-track one, but not another?

These are the questions that allocators should grapple with long before they invest a penny, but few do. Instead, fund managers are asked to fill out due-diligence questionnaires with 400 or more questions. Consultants produce extensive reports and conduct intensive on-site assessments. For what? Just as most portfolio managers never truly contemplate the impact that sizing has on their investment returns, most allocators have done very little to understand the role that experience, assets under management, research techniques, personal investment, or any of the other factors that they diligently gather information about have on a manager's returns.

For all the meetings, questionnaires, consultants, and *expertise* employed, you would be hard pressed to find an allocator who consistently generates alpha, and a great many often find it difficult to even keep up with beta. Rather than admit that the problem lies in their analysis, the prevailing theme is that fund managers can't generate alpha consistently, therefore, the objective should be to generate beta at the lowest cost possible.

When people give up because a task requires cognitive strain in order to be done properly, it often means there is an opportunity to capitalize for those willing to put in the effort. We believe this to be the case here. So when a few large allocators came to us looking for help with manager selection we used it as an opportunity to build a new manager selection process from scratch. As always, we applied the fundamental principles of normative decision theory to the problem while using decision architecture to help allocators avoid the predictable cognitive land mines. The result is a truly unique approach that allows for an *objective* assessment that can be *consistently* applied to managers across asset classes and investment styles while also allowing for freedom of expression. I highlighted *objective* and *consistent* because those are the two key aspects that allocators and consultants almost universally lack, but without it the analysis has little value whatsoever, no matter how many questions are asked and on-site interviews conducted. I'll come back to the reason freedom of expression (i.e. beliefs) is not only valid in this process, it is actually necessary.

We began by asking our clients a simple question. "What questions do you need answers to in order to properly assess a manager?" With guidance from us along the way, after weeks of internal discussions, they honed in on their specific questions. For example, they wanted to know how much of their net worth the managers had invested in their own fund, the ratio of fee income to expenses and how many years of experience the CIO has. We then examined the purpose of each of those questions to understand *why* they needed the answers to each of them. What value did they deliver? What would they do with that information and how would they go about factoring it into an actual decision?

We then asked them to weight the value of each individual question (variable) where the total sums to 100%. We also bucketed the questions according to three key factors: business risk, investment risk, and investment opportunity, as well as subsectors within them, and asked them to apportion weights accordingly. Again, they must add up to 100%. Interestingly, the results were different between the two queries. In other words, the very same variables were weighted differently, depending on how the we framed the query. That's a red flag, but a highly predictable one given what we know from the cognitive sciences.

A five-point scoring system was devised for each question, which was then weighted and summed in order to deliver a grade for the factor categories and variables.

It seems so simple, but as they say, the devil is in the details. For example, consider the following question under *Investment Risk -> Management Quality -> Experience of Senior Investment Team*. It could be asked as simply as:

How experienced is the senior investment team?
A. Extremely experienced.
B. Very experienced.
C. Experienced.
D. Somewhat experienced.
E. Inexperienced.

However, this range of options leaves a great deal up to the analyst's interpretation, and that means there could be great inconsistency even between funds being considered by a single analyst. One way to resolve that is to have these options:

A. More than 20 years combined in investment industry.
B. 15–20 years combined in investment industry.
C. 10–14 years combined in investment industry.
D. 5–9 years combined in investment industry.
E. 0–4 years combined in investment industry.

It's an improvement, but of course not all experience is the same. Perhaps we should break this one question down into two.

Combined years as buy-side risk-taker/decision-maker?
A. More than 20 years.
B. 15–20 years.
C. 10–14 years.
D. 5–9 years.
E. 0–4 years.
Combined years as sell-side risk-taker/decision-maker?
A. More than 20 years.
B. 15–20 years.
C. 10–14 years.
D. 5–9 years.
E. 0–4 years.

However, anyone who has ever managed a group of portfolio managers and overseen risk for a fund knows there is a difference between that job and managing a trading desk at an investment bank, and certainly a difference between it and managing a portfolio. So perhaps it would be appropriate to include the following questions and answers, first for the buy-side and then for the sell-side.

Combined years with directly attributable track record?
A. More than 20 years.
B. 15–20 years.
C. 10–14 years.
D. 5–9 years.
E. 0–4 years.
Combined years managing risk-takers?
A. More than 20 years.
B. 15–20 years.
C. 10–14 years.
D. 5–9 years.
E. 0–4 years.

You can see how it is that these questionnaires grow to be over 400 questions. You can also see how easy it is to get so bogged down in the minutiae that you lose sight of how each of these details contributes to the overall purpose and the final decision. Eventually, the entire process becomes little more than a collection of *stuff* haphazardly collected and then applied according to intuition and gut feel. The output is riddled with cognitive bias, and offers little value beyond simply ticking boxes and covering behinds.

Flipping the Frame

There's one indisputable fact that must be acknowledged up front. We don't *know* how the number of years of experience as a fund manager contributes to returns. We don't *know* how the proportion of a CIO's wealth invested in their fund correlates with the returns of that fund. We don't *know* the relationship between the returns of a fund and just about all the answers to those 400-plus questions we love to ask with a purpose. The reason is that we are so confident in the value of our intuition and our assessment of what is "logical," that we don't see the need to gather evidence to support it. So here we are, decades into this process and we have little to no evidence to support the great majority of the allocation decisions being made. Trillions of dollars being allocated on little more than gut feel, and the results stand as proof.

In properly defining the decision problem we are attempting to solve we must acknowledge this as a "state." In other words, it is a factor that affects our ability to achieve the goal of allocating to better performing managers, but one we do not control ... yet. Yes, although we don't yet know what factors are important, and to what degree, one of our key objectives is to ascertain that information. This is why we must allow the allocators to incorporate their beliefs, for those beliefs serve as their hypotheses. In order to prove or disprove their hypotheses they must apply them, observe them, and collect their findings. For only then can we move from the age-old belief-based system of manager selection to an evidence-based one.

As it is for all scientific inquiry, it is vital that we create a controlled experiment, using a repeatable and consistent process each and every time in order to collect the data. As the findings are gathered we can then learn, make adjustments, and improve the process. In developing this controlled experiment we need to allow for the freedom of hypothesis development within the rigor of an objective, systematic process.

There's one additional factor that is fundamental to the objective of the experiment, and it relates to the nature of the query itself. What we seek is improvement to generate better results. As it is for all improvement, gains are achieved by reducing mistakes. In other words, gains are reductive, not additive. This applies to the manager selection process as well. Rather than attempting to identify the next stand-out manager who will produce upside outlier returns (a low probability event), we seek to predict the probability that a manager will make mistakes (a high probability event), and discount the expected returns accordingly. When you reframe the decision problem in this way, and then revisit those 400-plus due-diligence questions, it will become obvious that is exactly what they are meant to deliver. They help us understand who will underperform due to mistakes, and why.

Consider the question, "What is the ratio of fee income to expenses?" Why would we ask that? The reason is that if the fee income doesn't cover expenses there is a greater chance that the partners and employees will be concerned about the long-term prospects of the firm. That concern is a distraction from the task we want everyone's attention to be focused on – namely, the task of generating investment returns. So, if we begin with a baseline expectation for returns, and that expectation assumes 100% of the investment team's attention will be focused on generating investment returns, potential distractions should be a reason to discount those expectations. As it relates to this particular question, the allocator must define how low they believe the ratio could go without becoming a distraction.

If a variable does not create a distraction, the baseline expected return should be unaffected. Let me restate that for emphasis. No distraction means no impact on expected returns. In other words, just because my expenses are covered several times over doesn't mean you should expect me to generate returns greater than my benchmark. However, if we're barely breaking even it could be cause for discounting those expectations.

Every question we ask is designed to help us discover whether a manager is more vulnerable to making a mistake. That's it. Just identify the probability of making a particular type of mistake and then apply an appropriate discount to the baseline expectation in exactly the same proportion for every manager who exhibits the same shortcoming. It works for everything, from years of experience to the quality of financing partners.

Now that we understand the function of the questions and answers, we must determine an appropriate baseline return expectation. As it is for almost every entrepreneur, when you ask a fund manager what the appropriate benchmark is for their style, most will say their approach is so unique that it's hard to find a comparable benchmark. Nonsense. Even if there isn't a single index that is directly comparable, there is certainly some combination of indices that will allow for the creation of a synthetic benchmark.

Then the question is, what is the appropriate historical time period from which to set your expectations for the future? 30 years? 10 years? 5 years? 1 year? Do you weight each year equally? What about for a manager that has a track record? Should you completely replace the synthetic benchmark with the manager's returns? If you do, you are effectively saying that their returns are an absolute function of skill with no contribution from luck. Is that really what you believe? If not, then you should weight the synthetic benchmark and manager track record accordingly, but whatever your weightings, time horizon, and weighting of luck to skill, everything must be applied consistently to all managers.

We call this approach the Bija Manager Discounting Method. We've described it using broad strokes in order to focus on the fundamental difference between this approach and the industry standard. As you can imagine, there are a number of additional, very important components I have not mentioned, including levers for risk aversion, macro expectations, and other adjustments. The discounting method is but one component of an objective, evidence-based, and consistent investment process for allocators that enables improvement over time.

Stroke of Genius

Golfers like to say that the game is one of inches, millimeters even. The slightest of adjustments can yield dramatically different results. Take our eye off the ball or dip our head, and we're likely to send it on the wrong trajectory, adding strokes to the final outcome. Performance is so finely tuned that etiquette dictates you should never talk during someone's backswing, it's bad manners to allow your shadow to cross between another player's ball and the cup while they putt, and sand traps must be raked smooth after use.

In truth, so many factors affect performance. There are the broad, static physical characteristics, external to the golfer, whose details are typically provided on scorecards and signage throughout the course. They include distance from tee to hole, shape and width of the fairway, placement, shape, and size of hazards, and even pin placement. Although they are the most commonly considered physical factors, there are plenty more that can have a significant effect on the success of an individual shot. Temperature, humidity, weather, and speed of play are just a few of the other factors external to us that can have an impact on our scores. When it comes to improvement though, little thought goes into the environment.

Instead, we tend to focus on what we believe we can control – namely, our bodies and the equipment that serves as an extension of us. Bigger, lighter, more spring, larger sweet spot, more comfortable grip, better feel, and that's just the club. Shirts that let your skin breathe. Balls with dimples that are scientifically designed to capitalize on microscopic changes in course conditions, and pressurized to be finely tuned to our swing. Shoes, gloves, hats, sunglasses, bags – there is no end to the ways we can purchase a better golf score. Considering the more than $4 billion per year that Americans alone are spending on golf equipment it's clear that improvement is desired.

Yet, with all the advancements in technology over the past 15 years and the insatiable desire among players to employ it, the average golfer's handicap hasn't shown improvement. They still require roughly 100 shots to complete 18 holes. Surely, in the hands of highly trained professionals, scores must have collapsed, right? Actually, they haven't really seen improvement either. In fact, you could argue that technology has actually stifled the impressive decades-long trend of improvement among professional golfers (see Figure 10.1).

I've heard all the reasons that the true impact of improved technology has yet to be reflected in golf scores, but the most common among them

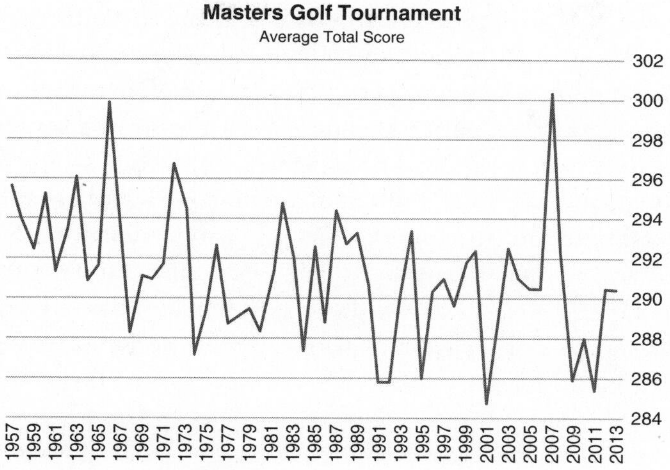

Masters Golf Tournament
Average Total Score

Figure 10.1 Masters golf tournament.
SOURCE: Bija Advisors.

is that they've made the courses longer, specifically to offset the effect of the new clubs. The evidence, however, does not support this argument. I gathered data from the Masters Tournament in order to weed out the noise and what better place to do that than Augusta. Rather than use winning scores (a far less time-consuming task), I compiled the average total score for all golfers who made the cut, so as to focus on the generic trend. If the injection of titanium heads were a major factor, we should be able to point to the year that it happened without any hesitation. If the delayed extension of the course's length had a great impact, we should likewise be able to point to the year the scores clearly reversed trend. Can you guess when technology transformed the golf club and the year when Augusta lengthened by 5% just by looking at the chart? (Hint: If you think you can you're mistaken.)

Turns out, in order to explain the outlier spikes and collapses in scores, you'd be better served looking to the weatherman, than the golfer's bag. Apparently, rain delays are a score killer and clear skies are like manna from heaven.

It's funny really. Anyone who has ever set foot on a golf course knows full well that it is a game of inches not yards. Yet, for some reason, we still believe a club that adds yards to our game, and time spent at the range or with a pro focused on the distance aspect is where we will find some dramatic improvement. There are so many ways we can improve our game. For me, nothing comes close to the simple act of proper club selection. I don't mean knowing the club Rory would use in a particular instance, or even the one I or someone who scores similarly to me would use, but the one that fits my natural swing, flaws and all. When I have absolute confidence that I have the correct tool in my hand for the task ahead I swing more naturally, fluidly, and accurately. I am relaxed, and can focus on the other aspects of the game where my attention is better served.

For years I had two golf games. In one, I was all over the place. My club selection was haphazard, and every swing came with uncertainty. It was the kind of uncertainty that lead me to hold back or push harder at the very last nano-second of my swing. My scores were an accurate reflection of that confusion. In my other golf game, I was confident and inspired. My scores were consistent, and on average, 15 to 25 shots lower. The difference? I played with an experienced golfer who understood my swing. He never commented on my tendencies or suggested improvements. Neither did he offer me the latest weapon in his bag. He simply knew who I was as a golfer, and made my club selections for me. I had absolute confidence in his selections and so those misgivings that would normally tweak my swing, sending me off into hazards, disappeared. For those who have seen the movie, *The Legend of Bagger Vance,* you will understand when I say, it allowed me to "get out of my own way." When I golfed with this friend, I could "see the field," and my scores reflected it.

Unfortunately, Andrew King, my friend and guru of club selection, died in the World Trade Towers. I haven't experienced the game in the same way since.

The Definition of Actionable Intelligence

In many ways the game of golf serves as a metaphor for business and investing. Very often we spend the great majority of our time and effort focused on the aspects of our job that provide the smallest potential for improvement while ignoring those that are far more likely to generate significant gains. Hours a day are spent talking to others, reading reports, and agonizing over the latest data, all in the hope of gleaning some insight that will improve our returns.

Trade ideas and market analysis are to investors what golf clubs are to golfers. You can feel them in your hand. You can hear that "ping" as the ball connects and the idea resonates. They are the go-to for investment performance improvement. I get it. I also get that the connection is more about convenience and availability than reality. The big gains come by analyzing our own tendencies, strengths, and weaknesses, individually and collectively as humans. The greatest improvement gains come when we can get out of our own way, and see the world more clearly.

As mentioned earlier, at one point I was asked to take over the investment process for a hedge fund. Considering the individual and fund performance until that moment, you might think my first points of order would involve tightening up risk parameters, improving our forecasting by hiring new analysts or subscribing to more research, or organizing more meetings in which we could share the market intelligence each PM was gathering individually. It's a natural assumption. I mean, if we could just improve our assessment of the markets we would improve our returns. We needed to get focused. Get down to brass tacks. Spend more time pouring over data, on research calls, in meetings, and of course, tighten up risk parameters.

I elected to do none of that. Rather than suggesting a club suited for Rory McIlroy, I spent time understanding each individual's natural tendencies, as well as those of the group, and then gave them the tools to improve their own individual games. I presented evidence for my findings and with each day, as returns improved, they began trusting my club selection, freeing them to swing more naturally, and their scores reflected it.

Through *AlphaBrain*, I'm not handing you the hottest new driver in my bag or even necessarily selecting the right club for you to use today. Instead, my goal is to help you make better club selections for yourself. That is how I define *Actionable Intelligence*.

What Allocators Can Learn From Paper Traders

Why is it that results generated through paper trading, meaning the trades aren't actually executed, are discounted relative to those that are actually generated? If you think about it, in both cases research is done, views are formed, expectations are set, instruments are selected, entry levels are determined, and decisions are made regarding trade exit. Doesn't that cover what almost every institutional investor spends just about every moment focused on?

Of course, for anyone who has actually managed capital, the difference is obvious. What the paper trader's experience lacks is the emotional impact of gains, losses, regret, and accountability. When real money is at stake repercussions from a misstep can involve serious consequences, and that effects the decision-making process. *That* is what distinguishes the results generated through paper trading versus actual investment management.

The fact that paper trading returns are discounted, rather than the other way around, implies that it is more difficult to generate returns when dealing with those emotional factors. I'd be hard pressed to find anyone who disagrees with anything I've said so far, which begs a few questions that surprisingly are rarely asked. If it is easier to generate returns when emotion is removed, why is so little time and effort spent focused on doing exactly that, and why do so many widely accepted, fundamental tenets of this industry serve to inject emotion into the decision making process rather than remove it?

What we are talking about here are decisions made with "affect-rich" outcomes versus those made with "affect-poor" outcomes. When risky decisions involve outcomes that can conjure considerable emotional reactions they are considered affect-rich. When they don't, they are categorized as affect-poor. It turns out, when we face decisions that have a greater potential to effect us emotionally, particularly those invoking negative feelings, we more often rely on our intuition and other mental shortcuts when considering our options while disregarding probabilities. In other words, our decisions become more emotionally driven and less probabilistic in nature which is exactly the opposite of what you want when attempting to improve the odds of a successful decision.

Although dozens of studies dating back to the 1990s have focused on and proven this case, one conducted recently took it one step further. For the first time researchers showed the existence of systematic preference reversals between affect-rich and affect-poor choices *within* individuals. In other words they showed that individuals who faced a problem with an affect-rich outcome would come to the polar opposite conclusion to the very same problem when it was later attached to an affect-poor outcome, and vice versa. This study – conducted in Germany and Switzerland – proved exactly what we've all suspected. There is a difference between managing a paper portfolio and managing a real one. These researchers proved that even the very same person, with the very same skill set, analytical tools, views, and expectations, when facing the very same decision, will make the opposite choices when emotions take over.

Think about that for a moment. When real money is on the line we are more likely to make *worse* decisions, and we know it! Now, think about some of the things we do on a regular basis that actually inject emotion into the decision-making process of those who are managing our money. Take, for instance, the common practice of requiring a CIO and other hedge fund partners to invest a substantial portion of their personal wealth in their fund. What is the rationale for such a requirement? To ensure that their goals and those of the investor are aligned. Well, if the investor's goal is for the leaders of that hedge fund to make decisions that are more probabilistic in nature, and less emotionally driven, thereby improving the odds of better returns relative to risk taken, the best way to align that goal with that of the manager is to *not* force them to invest a such a large portion of their wealth that is likely to turn an affect-poor decision into an affect-rich one. Ironically, that is *exactly* what the investors should hope to avoid but is precisely what they are accomplishing.

When I make this argument, particularly to asset allocators, I get more than a little pushback. Some will argue that it doesn't effect the managers, that they don't become more risk averse, which, if you think about it, is an odd argument to make. After all, isn't that precisely the intention, to keep the manager from behaving like a cowboy with your money? So, if you don't believe it actually makes the manager more risk averse, what exactly does it mean to be "aligned"? Research shows that when you convert decisions from affect-poor into affect-rich ones, you don't only simply make choices more risk averse. As I will discuss next, there are times when affect-rich decisions will have the opposite affect. The only true constant is that the decisions lack the kind of objectivity and probabilistic foundation you want from someone managing your money.

Chapter 11

Prophecy of Value

From Scalping to Trading

It began with this text from my wife about our son Jackson: "Jackson wants to buy an extra Austin City Limits ticket to sell later on, presumably for a profit. What do you think?" For years, I've been trying to find a way to teach my kids about trading in a way that would capture their interest. Finally, I had my opportunity. I said, "Yes, but it's not a gift, it's an investment that he will make from his savings." (I will preface this chapter by stating up front that reselling tickets for a profit is legal in the state of Texas.)

Jackson's argument for purchasing the extra ticket for $255 is that every year he sees tickets sell in the online aftermarket "at the last minute for as much as $500." If he could do that, he would effectively be able to go for free. That's when I let him know that he was trading. He was making a bet based on his experience. He had identified a trend in price action and was positioning himself to capitalize on it. He immediately made a classic mistake by framing the decision irrationally. He is correct, he could effectively go for free, but because money is fungible, the cost of the ticket he is actually using is completely irrelevant. All that matters is how much he is risking relative to how much profit he expects to gain. It's a mistake that traders often make.

He acknowledged that there was a risk that he wouldn't be able to sell the ticket for at least what he'd paid, which is the lowest he'd be willing to sell it. By refusing to sell it for less than he paid, he is effectively saying he'd rather lose everything, than lose even a little bit. As is often the case with traders, he saw that risk as something close to zero. Even if that's the case, the price he paid for the ticket is irrelevant going forward. It means nothing to other concertgoers, and should mean nothing to him also. From that point forward he is simply trying to maximize his return.

His argument for getting into the trade is sound. Every year the tickets sell out within two days, and he just bought one more ticket than he had in any other year. "So you could assume that there's at least one person who's normally getting a ticket that was unable to." If you think about it, he's talking about market positioning now. There are two issues with this logic. First, he has ignored the fact that there is also at least one person who normally buys just one ticket who now has two. So, while demand may have grown by one, so too has supply. This has implications for the second issue.

As it is for traders, he doesn't have perfect information about market positioning. How many others have purchased extra tickets for the sole purpose of selling at a higher price? How many are professionals? What is their risk tolerance? How quickly does the excess demand normally get satisfied? In other words, what is the optimal time to sell? That doesn't necessarily mean the highest price, but that point where the reward relative to risk has peaked. "You're playing to people's need to not be left out of stuff and the closer it gets the more of a panic people get into." He's right, but again, he's ignoring the supply side, which will feel the same pressure. The longer he waits, the more desperate potential buyers become, but if he waits even a minute too long, the ticket will be worthless, and so at some point, that puts pressure on sellers.

"However, when all of the other people doing this put tickets on sale for $500, if I'm desperate, I can put mine up for $400, still make money and have a definite sale since its $100 less than competitors." On paper, as a hypothetical, this strategy appears sound, but only because it glosses over some very difficult to define, yet essential aspects of the decision process. How do you define desperate? Will you know when you have become desperate, and if so, will you be able to contain the emotion so that you can still make a rational decision? I suggested to him what I suggest to all of my clients. Make a plan ahead of time. Up front, before emotion takes over, set reassessment triggers in both price and time. In other words, rather than trying to sell at the absolute high, set a price target and stick to it. If the target isn't hit by a particular date, resolve to sell it then, at the clearing price.

There is one final, but very important point that came to light when he said "I saw one go for $650 last year, which is absurd." He says it is absurd, but because he didn't sell his ticket for $650, he effectively paid $650 for the ticket he used. Therefore, he has defined his own action as absurd. How did I arrive at this conclusion?

He has a ticket. That ticket could be sold for $650. Therefore, there is no difference between $650 cash and the ticket. If instead of holding that ticket, which represents $650, he was actually in possession of $650 cash (and no ticket), he could not attend the concert. However, to get back to holding a ticket, he would have to exchange that $650 in cash for it. Therefore, he paid $650 for his ticket. My son remains unconvinced, but he's not alone.

This is similar to the mistake made by the wine connoisseurs mentioned earlier. You know, the ones who didn't realize they had actually paid $75 for a bottle of wine for which they'd only paid $20.

How Regret Makes Us Do Things We'll Regret

There is a well-known psychological study in which participants are posed the following question:

> There have been several epidemics of a particular strain of flu that everyone contracts, and it is fatal for 10 out of every 10,000 children under the age of three. A vaccine for the flu is available, which causes death in 5 out of every 10,000 children. Would you vaccinate your child?[1]

---

[1] David A. Asch, Jonathan Baron, and John C. Hershey, "Omission Bias and Pertussis Vaccination," *Medical Decision Making* 14, no. 2 (1994): 118–123 (journals.sagepub.com/doi/pdf/10.1177/0272989X9401400204).

Although the answer is obvious to an objective observer, the majority of parents who participated in the study opted not to vaccinate their children, because the vaccination *caused* five deaths. It didn't matter to these parents that their children faced twice the risk of death without the vaccination. The reason they gave for the decision is that they would "feel responsible if anything happened because of the vaccine," yet they dismissed the notion that they'd feel responsible if they failed to vaccinate. In other words, they would feel responsible for an outcome that followed their own actions, but not if it resulted from a lack of action.

Evidence of this type of bias is embedded in the very fiber of our society. For instance, the Hippocratic Oath that doctors take compels them to "Do no harm" rather than "Do some good." If someone physically holds another person's head under water until they drown they will have broken the law and will face a very stiff penalty. However, if someone is drowning and an onlooker who is capable of saving him elects not to, it is not a crime.

Richard Thaler ran a related experiment wherein participants were posed the following question:

> Assume you have been exposed to a disease that, if contracted, leads to a quick and painless death within a week. The probability you have the disease is 0.001. What is the maximum you would be willing to pay for a cure?[2]

They then faced this slight variation:

> Suppose volunteers would be needed for research on the [aforementioned] ... disease. All that would be required is that you expose yourself to a 0.001 chance of contracting the disease. What is the minimum you would require to volunteer for this program? (You would not be allowed to purchase the cure.)[3]

Although both scenarios involve exactly the same odds for contracting exactly the same disease and the same likelihood of death, participants

---

[2] Richard Thaler, "Toward a Positive Theory of Consumer Choice," *Journal of Economic Behavior and Organization* 1, no. 1 (1980): 39–60.
[3] Ibid.

required a fee to volunteer that was roughly 50 times greater than they were willing to pay for the vaccine.

In all of the preceding examples, the fundamental difference in the choices they face comes down to a decision of omission versus commission. Although the outcomes may be identical, and in some cases far worse, the feelings of responsibility, and potentially regret, are what drive the systematic errors in judgment, and we are all vulnerable to it.

What Would You Do?

Scenario 1

You are one of many portfolio managers for a large hedge fund. As you do every day you've just reviewed the contents of your portfolio to be sure it contains only positions that you believe present attractive risk versus reward profiles from current levels, and considering your views and expectations, all are sized in appropriate proportions. Without warning, you receive an email from your CIO informing you that your capital allocation has been doubled, effective immediately. One of the positions in your portfolio has appreciated substantially since first putting it on several weeks ago. Having already realized the move you had initially anticipated, a few days ago you unwound all but 1/6th of the position, leaving the small remainder on in case the move continues.

Question 1a: In light of your new capital allocation, should you adjust the size of this position?

Answer 1a: For many experienced risk-takers this scenario presents a very real quandary. However, if your goal is to always make optimal, purely objective decisions, the only rational answer is yes, you should double the size of all positions in order to maintain the same proportional exposure to the portfolio. Of course, this is predicated on the assumption that you had made a balanced and objective decision regarding this position before you received the email from your CIO.

For example, if you had decided this position should represent 50 basis points of risk to your portfolio before the increase, it should represent 50 basis points of risk after it. If instead you choose to do nothing, you will actively reduce your exposure to 25 basis points, thereby effectively ceding control of a trading decision to an unwitting third party. If you are willing to do so now, why not make all trading decisions in a similarly random manner, such as by the flip of a coin? The only reason not to make the adjustment is if the current offer is at or above your take profit level (and vice versa for a short position). There is the possibility that you remain unconvinced, and in that case you have proof that your portfolio review prior to the email was lacking in conviction. If this applies to you, take note of just how biased you are toward doing nothing.

Question 1b: Would your answer change if you were the only portfolio manager in the fund and, rather than receiving an increase from your CIO, the unexpected increase was from a sudden inflow from an investor?

Answer 1b: No. Whether you are a portfolio manager independently managing capital allocated to you by your firm or directly invested with you by an investor, the decision-making process should be identical. If your previous answer was riddled with uncertainty, but made clear when rephrased in Question 1b, you have a potential tool for improving your decision-making going forward.

Scenario 2

You are one of many portfolio managers for a large hedge fund. You have an excellent track record both as a producer and disciplined risk manager. Although the fund has a policy of cutting capital allocations on a 5% drawdown, it is also well known that this speed bump is more relaxed for portfolio managers of your caliber. In fact, you've witnessed other portfolio managers who have been down more than 8% before having their capital allocation reduced. As a result, you decide to manage your portfolio as though the speed bump is an unknown, so, as you have always done, as you recently began to experience a drawdown you gradually reduced the risk in your portfolio. Now down 4%, this has been a particularly bad run for you, and management believes the stress is beginning to affect you. As a result, they've suddenly decided to reduce your allocation by 50%, effective immediately.

Question 2a: In light of the fact that you have been reducing your risk along the way, do you need to make any adjustments to your positions when your capital is unexpectedly reduced?

Answer 2a: This tends to be more of a dilemma for former proprietary traders than those who began their careers on the buy-side, because they have been trained to manage notional risk rather than capital. Once again though, the answer is clear. The portfolio should be adjusted in exactly the same way and for exactly the same reasons as discussed in scenario 1, with the same caveat regarding entry price but this time relative to the stop-loss. To make the argument that risk has already been reduced ahead of the capital reduction is to ignore that you are managing capital. Without a definitive speed-bump procedure, the portfolio manager should manage the allocated capital without bias. Although reducing your risk when your conviction is waning is a prudent decision, doubling it because an unwitting third party attempted to reduce its exposure to your portfolio is not, and that is exactly what you will be doing if you don't cut your positions proportionally. If you argue that you cut your risk in anticipation of your capital being reduced at some point, then you are presenting evidence that you have been underinvested relative to your conviction, which begs the question, at what point did you actively cut your capital, and why didn't you notify the CIO at that time?

It's important to make a distinction between reducing risk due to waning conviction and reducing it because you are managing less capital. If you don't make and recognize that distinction in a deliberate manner, you make it easier for this bias to regularly affect your investment process.

Question 2b: Would your answer change if you were the only portfolio manager in the fund and if, rather than the reduction in capital coming from your CIO, it was the result of unexpected outflows?

Answer 2b: See Answer 1b.

Scenario 3

You are the CEO and CIO of a young hedge fund with several portfolio managers each managing independent portfolios. The end of your second calendar year in business is fast approaching and your firm has had a good run. So good, in fact, that if you were to close down all positions today, the performance fees alone would allow you to fully fund your entire business for another year, after all bonuses are paid out. Recognizing this as a crucial time in the development of a young hedge fund, you are inclined to reduce risk dramatically into year-end.

Question 3a: Should you (a) tell all portfolio managers to reduce their risks immediately or (b) reduce capital allocations to all portfolio managers?

Answer 3a: As CEO, your objective is to ensure the viability of the business. As CIO, you are tasked with maximizing returns relative to the risk taken in the investment portfolio, just as it is for each portfolio manager and the capital allocated to each. The CIO effectively manages a portfolio of trades like any other risk-taker, assessing the merits of each component both independently and as part of the overall portfolio. In order to maximize the benefits associated with each portfolio manager, they should be allowed maximum autonomy within well-defined constraints that they are able to account for in their planning and positioning. If we believe it is better to make decisions under certainty than uncertainty, then as CIO we should do our best not to be the source of uncertainty for our own portfolio managers. Therefore, the best answer must be "b." The only reason to opt for "a" would be to avoid responsibility and potential regret should the decision to reduce risk be seen as a bad one at some point in the future.

The very possibility that any of these scenarios could invite debate serves as evidence of our very human preference for doing nothing.

P&L Driven P&L

I recently gave a talk to hedge fund clients of one of the largest investment banks. Among other things, I once again argued against the use of speed bumps. To review the way a speed bump works, if a portfolio manager or fund is down a certain percentage from its high-water mark, the portfolio manager must cut risk by a specific proportion. The thinking is that occasionally risk-takers aren't seeing things clearly, but they are somehow blind to that fact. Rather than letting the wheels come off completely, the speed bump serves as a formal process for avoiding the downward spiral. Think of it like a time-out for a troubled child. It forces them to take a step back and think about their actions. I don't believe the time-out helps the troubled child avoid further problems, it simply gets them out of the parent or teacher's hair for a while. Same goes for the speed bump. Like nearly all other risk management tools this industry has come to depend upon, the speed bump is a reactive one. Worst of all, it accomplishes one of two things. Either it reduces the returns of a good portfolio manager or it extends the life of one that should be fired.

Interestingly, this was one of the rare times I didn't run into fervent opposition to my argument from the audience. Instead, I was asked a simple, but very telling question. "How can you be opposed to speed bumps while simultaneously arguing that stop-losses are an essential component of an intelligent investment process?" I began to salivate, because the question itself highlighted an equally problematic issue. Stop-losses are often seen as a way to limit losses, to avoid the downward spiral, and in a way they are. There is, however, a seemingly subtle, yet very important distinction between my approach to stops and that of most others that begins with position sizing.

Very often a portfolio manager will determine the size of a position by how much he hopes to make, or even just by picking a nice round number. The stop-loss level is then chosen by how much he is willing to lose given the resulting notional amount. In other words, the level is determined by P&L. That is the mistake, and it's the same one made by those who use speed bumps, which is why the question was posed. The person posing the question saw my support for stop-losses and opposition to speed bumps as inconsistent because he saw them both as being driven by P&L. He's right, but only if you implement stop-losses as I've described, which I do not.

Determining the position size is the very last step in my investment process. Before the notional amount is set, I first identify the correct level that the position should be unwound if my expectations are not met which is my stop-loss level. It is the nearest market price that should not trade so long as my underlying thesis holds true. The last thing I want is to be taken out of a position while I still believe in the underlying view.

I know that if I stop out of a position meant to express a view that I still hold, eventually I will be compelled to express that same view again. If that is the case, what was the point in stopping out of the position? The reason is that it creates the illusion of discipline, an illusion designed to fool others – and ourselves.

Here's an example of how it plays out in practice. You identify an assortment of evidence arguing for company XYZ's stock to go up. The stock is trading right in the middle of a well-defined yet fairly wide trading range. You go long. You set a "tight stop," well within the trading range, in order to "cap the downside." If the stop is triggered, you will lose 20 bps of your AUM. In other words, you have decided that given your level of conviction for the underlying view, you are willing to risk a maximum of 20 bps on the idea. A few days later, the stop is hit and you realize the 20 bps loss. Two weeks later, the stock rallies back to the original entry level. All the reasons you initially believed in the trade remain in place, so you enter the trade again, with the same "tight stop." Now you have risked 40 basis points (bps) on the idea that you initially deemed worthy of just 20 bps, but it doesn't end there. This is often repeated over and over and over again.

Eventually, your view is proven correct. The stock rallies and you make 60 bps having risked just 20 bps. We see this happen all the time. Remember the short EUR, the long JPY and short S&P trades that cost funds for years before finally "paying off?" If portfolio managers are being honest with themselves and with investors, all those trades should be combined in order to properly assess the return on investment (and risk) over time.

Tight stops are a good idea, but only when it is due to the entry level being very close to a price that is significant to many market participants. A simple way to say this is, "so long as my view holds true, the stop-loss level should not trade. If it does, something has significantly changed and I no longer want to have that position." This is a dramatically different approach to the stop-loss from the one described earlier. The decision involved is driven by the view, the portfolio manager's expectations, and the market, not based purely on P&L. That is how you want decisions to be made.

Going back to the question posed by the audience member. He was correct if you approach stop-losses like most in the markets do. It is inconsistent to argue against speed bumps and in favor of stop-losses, because, in both cases, decisions are being made driven solely by P&L, without consideration for markets, views, or expectations. When utilized in this manner stop losses are last line of defense against an investment process that is impulsive and poorly planned. However, if the stop-loss is an integral part of a proactive investment process, derived as a result of a thorough analysis, fact-based research, and a firm view, it no longer has anything in common with the speed bump. That leaves the speed bump as the only decision being made indiscriminately.

Chapter 12

Mind over Matter

Painfully Aware

Consider a turkey that is fed every day. Every single feeding will firm up the bird's belief that it is the general rule of life to be fed every day by friendly members of the human race "looking out for its best interests," as a politician would say. On the afternoon of the Wednesday before Thanksgiving, something unexpected will happen to the turkey. It will incur a revision of belief.
—*Nassim Taleb*, The Black Swan

I've had several old mercury fillings replaced and two root canals done over the past decade, all of which have been performed without anesthetic of any kind. No, I'm not a masochist, but rather a hyperrealist; one who enjoys an honest risk/reward analysis and welcomes a serious mental challenge. There are four things I always hated about visiting the dentist: (1) sound of the drill, (2) shrapnel that threatens to slide down my throat while my mouth is wedged open, (3) multiple, painful Novocain shots in the gums, and (4) numbness that leaves me drooling and unable to eat or talk normally for hours after the office visit is over. The first two can't be solved and the last two are actually self-inflicted. I've found that even with Novocain getting cavities drilled out and fillings put in is a

161

painful endeavor. Ultimately, the question is whether the combination of Novocain shots + lingering numbness + reduced procedure pain produces a more pleasant cumulative experience than no shots + no numbness + heightened procedure pain. Since no one I know including the dentists and endodontists themselves had ever attempted to do without it, I had no idea just how painful it would be. I was therefore missing a key piece of the equation. After the dentist (and every assistant in the practice) attempted to talk me out of it, I elected to forge ahead and answer that question for myself. I won't lie, it is painful. And root canal, a surgical procedure performed directly on the tooth's nerve, is even more so.

I've elected to do without the anesthetic numerous times now (and they still try to talk me out of it every time), so clearly I believe the cumulative experience sans Novocain is preferable. However, it's not that straightforward. You see, the pain comes in shocking jolts that seem to pierce your very being, and it does so without any forewarning. It means you sit on edge as the dentist drills and drills, until suddenly, it feels as though someone has driven a needle into your tooth with a sledgehammer. There's one additional element to consider though. You cannot move when the pain comes, otherwise that high speed drill could do some serious tangential damage. No matter how startling or painful that shock is, there must be no externally visible expression of my internal experience. Therein lies the greatest mental challenge I've ever faced. It's important to note that I don't clench my fists, hold my breath or tighten up in any way. I also don't zone out or ignore the pain, otherwise I might be startled by the inevitable shock, causing my body to lurch. In fact, I zero in on the pain, seeing it for what it really is; a signal being delivered from the nerve ending to my brain. I contemplate its purpose, which is to warn my mind that there is a problem in the tooth that requires attention. Because it is already receiving that attention, the pain is simply an artifact.

Some people refer to what I put myself through as "torture," but I disagree. Although the intensity of the experience may be similar, what makes pain torturous is not knowing when or even if it will end. In my case, the instant the instrument is removed from the nerve, the pain disappears. The dentists and endodontists always remark afterward how nice it would be if every patient could go without anesthetic because

I am able to provide real time feedback on the effectiveness of the procedure. I can feel when a crown isn't fitted properly or if the nerve hasn't been properly deadened. In other words, there is a tangible benefit to remaining lucid and objective throughout even the most painful moments.

The reason I share all of this with you is that it serves as a powerful metaphor for my investment style versus the norm. Losses are painful for everyone. According to the research, losses hurt twice as much as a commensurate gain feels good. However, losses are also an inevitable part of the job and how you deal with them says a lot about your ability to generate long-term returns. Most portfolio managers hold longs or shorts in outright positions, using "tight stops" to protect the downside. The problem is, even after the tight stop is hit, they often have no qualms about reentering the same trade upon a similar setup or "better" entry levels, with yet another tight stop. Every time the stop loss is triggered, a loss is realized. Whatever risk allocation they initially make to that view/idea is somewhat disingenuous, because it must be multiplied by the number of times they will ultimately attempt to express it. I'd rather acknowledge the possibility of being wrong on the view up front; structuring a position that remains alive until something has fundamentally changed and the view itself is proven wrong. If I am proven wrong, I'd prefer the pain to be of a finite duration. To me, the idea of repeated tight stops being triggered would be torturous.

A colleague once remarked that we all need time-outs when losses are experienced because they are painful and can keep you from seeing things clearly. Clearly we do not all respond to pain in the same way. Some require a Novocain shot for a deep teeth cleaning whereas some can lucidly work through even the most excruciating pain without any lingering affects. Learning how to manage and diminish the pain of losses should be a primary goal of every risk taker.

Fooled by Stability

Between 1971 and 2002, Philippe Petit performed 35 major high-wire performances. The most well known of these occurred in 1974, when he traversed the 138 feet between the roofs of New York's Twin Towers.

For 45 minutes, he walked, laid down, danced, and knelt down along an inch thick cable strung nearly a quarter mile above the crowds below. Port Authority Police Officer Charles Daniels later described the scene to reporters: "He was bouncing up and down … His feet were actually leaving the wire," and yet he had no safety net or harness binding him to it.

However, Petit, like most high-wire performers, did take certain safety precautions. Most notably, he and his crew installed stabilizer cables, known as guy lines, to keep the main wire from swaying too much. In addition, in order to increase his control over his torque, Petit carried a weighted balancing pole, which allowed him to counterbalance the occasional powerful wind gust. Ultimately, the goal of all of his precautions was to reduce sway, the side-to-side motions as he walked back and forth across the wire.

In the end, Petit successfully made eight passes across the wire that day. If we took the distance he covered walking up and back across that wire (return) and divided it by the side-to-side distance covered (risk), we would come to the conclusion that he accomplished a great deal relative to the risk taken. Of course, the side-to-side motion actually experienced reflected neither the sway potential nor the dramatic difference in outcome should that sway have been increased even a fraction of an inch more.

Naturally, if Petit had done the walk without a balancing pole you would perceive the feat to be inherently more risky, and you'd be correct. However, if there was no wind and the stabilizer cables had done their job, the side-to-side distance he would have actually experienced that day would likely be exactly the same as it was with it. Therefore, using this equation, his return relative to risk taken would incorrectly appear to have been unchanged.

What if Petit had swapped the balancing pole for a safety harness that tethered him to the wire or a safety net installed just below the wire, thereby increasing the dangerous sway while dramatically reducing the potential for calamity? Based on the previous equation, his return on risk taken would have gone down, since the return was unchanged, whereas the perceived risk would have gone up because his side-to-side distance would have increased. This equation has no way to account for the true change in risk.

Why am I talking about high-wire walking? I often hear allocators, and even PMs and CIOs refer to the Sharpe ratio as a measure of returns relative to risk taken, but it is as misguided as using the preceding formula to measure a high-wire walker's return on risk taken – and for the exact same reasons. Realized P&L volatility, especially short-term volatility, does not provide an accurate measure of risk taken. It is fraught with hindsight bias, a lack of appreciation for the dynamics of risk and even the different types of risk that exist. Just as anyone who would use the preceding equation in assessing the risk/reward of a high wire act would be viewed by most readers as naive (and potentially dangerous), so too would I characterize anyone who would use the Sharpe ratio as a way to measure returns relative to risk taken. In fact, you could equate its use in the analysis of a PM or fund to that of the turkey in its assessment of its human feeder. If you are one of the Sharpe (or Sortino) advocates, the only question is, when will you experience a "revision of belief"?

The 20/80 Rule

I was a mediocre student growing up. Every report card had the same comments, "Stephen is highly intelligent and very capable, if only he would settle down." My parents were creative in their attempt to incentivize me to obtain top grades. They drove me around the wealthy neighborhoods pointing out the most ostentatious mansions, took me to the expensive car dealerships, and brought home brochures of beautiful boats, all with the hope that an innate desire to acquire nice things would trigger a shift in my priorities. In high school they even offered to buy me a new car if I was able to finish a semester with nothing but A's on my report card. I give them credit and I'm thankful that they cared enough to worry about me. Unfortunately, what they didn't understand is that I wanted to settle down and get straight A's as much as they did. A lack of motivation was never the problem.

Being a late bloomer, both physically and emotionally, I was perennially immature. Right up until I left for college, that immaturity was the explanation given for my hyperactivity and inability to focus on any task for more than a few minutes. However, when I continued to struggle with the same issues in college, it was clear there was more to it, but what could I do?

Every year, I followed all the usual advice and mimicked the behavior of the best students, but the results remained the same. My mind would drift and my energy knew no bounds. The first two years of college were a struggle even though I desperately wanted to do well, get good grades, and show everyone what I could accomplish. Finally, after struggling academically for 14 years I had an epiphany. Rather than worrying about the outcome (grades), I would focus my effort and attention on the only thing I could actually control, the process itself. What it required was a departure from the annual fool's game I played, where I would pretend that suddenly this would be the year when I would settle down and be able to focus on anything for more than 5 to 10 minutes at a time. Instead, I accepted that my boundless energy and inability to focus is a factor that affects my ability to achieve the outcome I desire, but it is one that I cannot control. It was a state. Therefore, in order for me to improve the odds of achieving the outcome I desired I would need to consider alternative actions, a different approach, one that would take my inability to settled down and focus into account.

I devised a radical new learning process for myself whereby I broke everything down into the most minuscule of tasks, what I later came to define as *bija*. Each of those tasks required me to focus for just five to ten minutes. When I finished a task, I would get up, walk around, maybe shoot the basketball, draw a picture, or get a drink of water. Then, a few minutes later, I'd return to my studies. Not necessarily the same assignment or even the same subject, but to another education-related task that required just 5 to 10 minutes of my attention.

I created repetition exercises to essentially trick my brain into cataloging information properly. My system required constant vigilance, but was specifically adapted to accommodate my natural inclinations, allowing me to jump around from topic to topic in short intervals. It fundamentally flipped the traditional approach on its head. Whereas most students put in some work throughout the semester with the occasional burst of intense activity as exams approached, my method required short bursts of intense activity at the moment when material was introduced and dwindled down to literally nothing as exams approached.

So, while the libraries were packed until 5 a.m. with caffeine-infused students during exams I had absolutely nothing to do, no notes to review, no books to read, and no practice exercises to do. Nothing. It's difficult to explain just how uncomfortable I felt at those moments. I mean, I had no track record of success to give me any reason to believe that the system I devised for studying was better than the one followed by previous generations of incredibly smart students, not to mention every student on every campus at that exact moment. I was torn.

On the one hand, I believed wholeheartedly in my method, because every facet of it was deliberately designed to be rational and effective, but that didn't quell my doubt. Although I was incredibly relaxed and confident in my knowledge of the material, ironically, possession of that state of mind worried me when everyone around me was so uncharacteristically stressed. In the end, my concerns were unfounded. I achieved straight A's, not just that semester, but every semester that followed. For the last two years of my undergraduate studies as well as my time in graduate school at NYU I was consistently on the Dean's List and President's Honor Roll.

I learned many great lessons from the experience. Perhaps most important of all was the realization that we can't control the outcome, only the process that leads to it. When you improve the process, when you make hundreds of tiny decisions even marginally better, you can dramatically improve your odds of achieving the results you desire. Ultimately, *that* is what you control. As it relates to education, what is within the student's control is the development and execution of a process that improves their odds of learning the material. When that happens, the grades inevitably follow.

The same goes for generating alpha. Daily, weekly, monthly, quarterly, and even annual returns are not something you can choose. Instead, they are merely a reflection of the quality of the process that guides the millions of decisions made along the way. The better the process, the greater the likelihood each of those decisions will improve the odds of generating better returns. Simply coming to this realization can go a long way toward reducing your vulnerability to systematic errors in judgment, including hindsight bias. When all of the focus is on outcome, it can cause us to make mistakes in interpreting statistics, like overweighting small sample sets.

Consider another real-world example. One of my coaching clients shared with me that she tends to cut her positioning, following months when she had performed poorly, and increase it, after positive months. It's a very common process among investment managers. After analyzing her trading data it turned out she was more systematic in this process than she even realized. We then ran a scenario analysis over her seven-year track record as a hedge fund portfolio manager where we made just one adjustment to her process: we unwound all of those reactive adjustments. In other words, after every down month we erased the downward size adjustment for the following month and vice versa for the up months, leaving everything else constant. Her results, with this and only this adjustment are shown in Table 12.1.

Think about that impact on her returns over those seven years. She reduced her average annual return by a full 250 bps and her total return by 3,000 bps by focusing on the outcome rather than the process. By the way her version generated a better Sharpe ratio, but which return stream would you prefer?

Again, all we can control are our decisions, but not just those that are directly related to markets such as macro/micro analysis, valuation, technical analysis, and historical returns. There's so much more to generating alpha.

Table 12.1   Investment performance with and without systematic adjustments

	Actual Return	Return with Adjustment Removed
Year 1	9.5%	16.0%
Year 2	7.1%	5.5%
Year 3	10.1%	9.9%
Year 4	10.3%	16.1%
Year 5	3.5%	2.7%
Year 6	9.8%	12.1%
Year 7	9.2%	14.8%
Average Annual Return	**8.5%**	**11.0%**

Think about your typical day. How much of it is spent trying to figure out if the Fed will or won't, China will or won't, and so on? Now, how much of your day is spent doing a similar analysis and investigation of your decision-making process? How much time is spent quantifying your expectations, comparing your postmortem against your premortem analysis? How much effort do you put into developing and maintaining proactive processes ahead of the trade, versus fretting over the best course of *re*action later on?

With decades of cognitive, behavioral, and decisional research proving that we are all vulnerable to systematic errors in judgment, doesn't it make sense to make the effort and take the necessary steps to improve our decision-making process? In order to shift the odds of success in our favor we must be deliberate in our approach every step of the way. We must be vigilant in our defense against bias and suboptimal selections.

Think about your track record over the past year or even over the past 10 years. Would you say your returns are an accurate reflection of your market views? If you're like most investment managers you've probably underperformed them. I estimate that roughly 20% of your returns can be attributed to your investment and market analysis, with the remaining 80% being a function of your decision-making process. Meanwhile, most professional investors spend upward of 80% of their time and research budget focused on the aspect that contributes just 20% to their bottom line.

Think about it on a grand scale across all market participants. How else do you explain the incredibly high correlation in views shared by market participants accompanied by a wide dispersion in returns? According to Mark Buchanan's *The Social Atom*:

> The economics consultancy London Economics assessed the predictions of more than thirty of the top British economic forecasting groups, including the Treasury, the National Institute, and the London Business School. They concluded: It is a conventional joke that there are as many different opinions about the future of the economy as there are economists. The truth is quite the opposite. Economic forecasters ... all say more or less the same thing at the same time; the degree of

agreement is astounding. The differences between forecasts are trivial relative to the differences between all forecasts and what happens.

As a result, when I coach experienced investment managers, we spend very little, if any, time discussing the factors that account for the 20% impact. Instead we focus on the decision-making process itself.

Figure 12.1 depicts another actual example from a coaching client. In this case, it's a hedge fund CIO. We began by discussing the evolution of the firm's first year in business, which led to identifying key moments of significance, strictly from a managerial perspective. In other words, they bore no relation to market action or portfolio-manager performance. We also limited the analysis to consider only those issues that were identified in real time, thereby avoiding the benefits of hindsight. In the end, *he* identified four alternative decisions that would have been more objective at the time. The shaded dashed line reflected his actual allocation process. Holding everything else constant, including market views, execution, structuring, and sizing, the alternatives would have added between 400 and 1400 additional basis points to the fund's returns.

The point I am making here is that your returns are dependent on so much more than knowing whether the Fed will or won't. When you

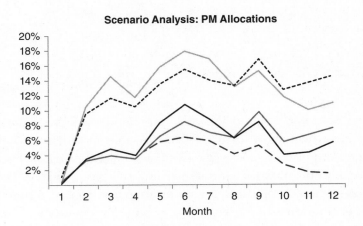

Figure 12.1   Scenario analysis: portfolio manager allocations

come to that realization, you will begin to ask new questions, explore new ideas, realize greater potential, and, I expect, enjoy the process a whole lot more.

Why Size Matters

Through the years, one aspect of trading has created more uncertainty, generated more volatility, injected more emotion, and had a greater negative impact on the returns of otherwise excellent managers than any other. Whether I work with a 25-year veteran of the industry or a brand-new portfolio manager, this is by far the one facet that perplexes almost every single one of them. It's the one that no one talks about and everyone is afraid to ask about for fear of looking like an amateur. However, whether I mention it in a talk, broach the subject in an investment committee meeting or raise the topic in a coaching session, it immediately triggers the undivided attention of everyone who manages a portfolio. If you are one of them, you already know what it is. I will argue that it lies at the heart of the reason that most trend followers have done so poorly over the past several years, a period that arguably should have been one of the best for investors of that breed. The issue is how to size positions.

Many traders readily admit that they make something close to 80% of their profit from just 20% of their trades. Rather than arguing here why that should not be the case, I will focus on what it does to the sizing process and the damage it causes. When you believe that only a couple of trades hold the key to your success in a given year you tend to approach position sizing with the idea that it has to be on a size that will "move the needle," if this one turns out to be one of those few. You think about where the stock can go and how much you need to have on for it to have a meaningful impact on the portfolio if it does. Of course, you recognize the possibility that it may not work out as planned, and so you set a stop loss for the underlying position based on how much you are prepared to lose.

If there is one thing cognitive science has taught us about ourselves it's that we are natural-born optimists, and this method for sizing is proof.

When entering the trade, it embodies all that is possible in a trade. We see far more clearly how it can go right than wrong. Why else would we enter it? If it goes in the right direction almost straight out of the gates and continues without much pain along the way that optimism grows, making it difficult to imagine how it could possibly go wrong. You feel confident in your abilities and see the price action as confirmation of your initial beliefs. With this newfound confidence you increase the size, moving up your stop-loss along the way. After all, that would be the prudent thing to do. (Or is it?)

Unfortunately, as was acknowledged at the outset, most of the trades don't wind up being big contributors to the portfolio's profitability, which is why we tend to use "tight stops" as a key risk management technique. After all, if a trade isn't going to be moving the needle in a positive way, we need to ensure that it doesn't dig us in such a hole that we can't ever get out. As soon as a trade exhibits any sort of uncertainty our overly optimistic expectations at initiation are called into question. With every tick in either direction the trajectory of that trade is extrapolated out into the future as either a positive game changer or ruinous disaster. Swings of such proportion can be mentally and emotionally exhausting, making us more and more nervous, less optimistic, and ultimately risk-averse.

Essentially, the fundamental problem with this sizing methodology is that at initiation, that moment when we determine the proper size, we are focused on the upside potential, and from the first moment that we realize it won't be the unobstructed slam dunk we'd foreseen, we become focused on minimizing the downside. That can be an issue in and of itself, but the impact of it has been exacerbated over the past seven years. You see, risk controls for portfolio managers and even many asset allocators have been tightened. Portfolio stops have gotten smaller and questions from the board come sooner than they used to. At the same time, our performance expectations have been slow to adjust in accordance. In other words, we expect to generate the same returns with tighter stops and risk constraints. So we get into trades (and add to those that work initially) by sizing according to our performance expectations, and get taken out (prematurely) according to the reduced risk limitations. Simply stated, we are oversizing positions by approaching it from this side.

Instead, position sizing should be approached from the opposite end of the spectrum. Sizing should be the very last step in the investment process. It comes after the view is developed, the asset and instrument is selected, and the structure is determined. When expectations are set for where the underlying should go if I'm right and where it just simply should not trade unless I'm dead wrong, *then* size should be considered. The stop-loss level should be determined by market factors, *not* as it relates to your P&L. Period. The next step is to allocate an amount of capital you are prepared to lose should things not work out as expected. In other words, what is the most you are willing to lose if you are absolutely dead wrong?

With both the appropriate, market driven stop-loss level and the maximum notional loss you are willing to accept having been identified, determining the *maximum* position size requires a very simple calculation. Divide the notional amount you are prepared to lose in the trade by the percentage distance from entry level to stop-loss, including expected slippage, and you have the maximum notional size for the trade. If, when you multiply that number by the percentage you expect to make if all goes as expected on the upside, it is not enough to "move the needle," you have a decision to make. You can either acknowledge that the risk/reward profile of the trade wasn't quite as good as you thought and pass on it, or accept that although this particular trade may not be the one that makes your year, it will be managed in a way that dramatically improves the odds of it being a positive contributor in the end. When you do that, you are likely to move away from having to depend on hitting the lottery a couple of times a year and toward more sustainable, consistent, and, most importantly, profitable performance results.

Lessons from Nick Saban and the Octagon

After going 14-0 in the 2016 regular season, Nick Saban's Alabama Crimson Tide football team beat fourth-ranked Washington to earn a spot in yet another National Championship game. As of that moment, in the four years preceding Saban's arrival, 'Bama won just a hair over 50% of their games and hadn't competed for a championship in 15 years. Since he took the head coaching job in 2007, however, they've become a perennial powerhouse of the highest order, winning 87% of their games, achieving the number-one ranking at some point in every season since 2008, and winning the national championship in 2009, 2011, 2012, 2015, 2016, and 2017. It's an impressive feat considering the obstacles.

There is an incredible amount of turnover on college football rosters year in and year out, and recruiting has never been more competitive, yet one of the Tide's strengths is their depth at every position. Amazingly, many of the best high school recruits will often sit out a season or two, just to have the opportunity to learn from and play for Nick Saban. Although that is an advantage, when you win as often as Alabama does, the competition is constantly nipping at your heels, trying to poach your talent – and rarely at an opportune moment. Case in point, with just days left until his team competed in the Super Bowl of college foot- ball, Saban had to welcome his fifth offensive coordinator in 10 years, after Lane Kiffin took the head coaching job at FAU. On top of all this, Alabama competes in the strongest division of the toughest conference in the country, meaning the strength of their schedule is notoriously challenging. How then is Saban able to keep Alabama so competitive year after year? Process.

As it is for Saban's mentor, Bill Bellichick and his New England Patriots, what makes 'Bama's program so unique isn't the roster or sup- port staff, but rather what he constantly refers to as "the process." It is the consistent approach to decision-making in training, practice, game planning, and execution, which focuses on minimizing mistakes that attracts the country's best talent and repeatedly delivers championships to Tuscaloosa.

What I know from my own conversations over the years in focusing on process in the investment industry is that many people confuse having a regimented process in place with being dogmatic and unwavering. That superficial assessment of process is naive, both in our industry and in football. In fact, one of the hallmarks of a good process is dynamism. It is purposefully developed to accommodate and adapt to change in the environment, not to ignore or defy it. Saban's approach serves as evidence of this fact. Although most who have achieved his level of success in any industry tend to plod along stubbornly following the same formula, Saban's system is built to adapt to the environment, rather than expecting the environment to adapt to it, no matter how much he might disagree with the direction in which it is headed.

He told ESPN.com, "It's unbelievable how much the game has changed, and it's really hard to coach defense now. But hey, it's on me – regardless of the way I think football should be played – if I don't change with it."[1]

In another major sporting event on the same weekend UFC's bantamweight champion Amanda Nunes defended her title against the former champion, Ronda Rousey, who was making a comeback after a one-year break. Nunes knocked Rousey out just 48 seconds into the first round. Ahead of the bout the UFC and the media focused almost exclusively on the return of golden girl Rousey who earned $3,000,000 to World Champion Nunes's comparatively paltry $200,000. Rather than worrying about being disrespected, Amanda concentrated on her process. In the post-fight interview the champ spoke the truth to those who follow her sport. The lesson translates easily to our industry and should be heeded by those of us who participate.

Nunes told ESPN.com that she trained strenuously so she would be able to respond to Rousey's every move, whether it was physical or mental. Rousey made no changes to her coaching staff or her style following her devastating loss to Holly Holmes and in preparation for Nunes. That didn't go unnoticed by her opponent. "Always when I see something wrong with my evolution, I try to make some changes," Nunes said. "I feel like [Rousey] doesn't know those things like a real fighter. I feel like if she doesn't know how to make some changes in her game, she's not a real fighter."[2]

Rousey was a dominant fighter leading up to her *shocking* loss to Holmes. She appeared to be unbeatable. Rather than recognizing that Holmes exposed Rousey's weaknesses, it seemed that everyone but Nunes dismissed the loss as little more than an unlucky kick to the head. A fluke. Instead, Nunes exposed the early career of Rousey as the fluke, but not before Rousey took the UFC and hundreds of thousands of pay-per-view fans to the cleaners.

---

[1] Quoted in Chris Low, "Nick Saban has adapted to and conquered a new style of college football," ESPN.com, January 3, 2017.
[2] Quoted in Brett Okamoto, "Amanda Nunes stops Ronda Rousey in 48 seconds at UFC 207," ESPN .com, December 31, 2016.

The lesson to be learned from Nick Saban, Amanda Nunes, and even Ronda Rousey is that a positive track record doesn't grant you immunity from a constantly evolving environment. If you want to continue to compete at the highest level you must adapt and evolve as well. You are finished the minute you rest on your laurels.

Doubling Down on Luck

While on holiday I spent some time at the craps table. I don't frequent casinos very often, but when I do, the only game that draws my attention is craps. If you think about it, it is the only truly social game on the floor. When a roller gets "hot" and everyone around the table is making money, the atmosphere is electric. People high-five, nicknames catch on, and bonds are developed among players. There is no other game like it in the building.

It is also a fascinating place to witness the pure, unadulterated flaws of the human brain in action. Otherwise smart, successful people unabashedly display a disconcerting level of naivety regarding statistics and the role of luck versus skill, rarely seen outside of financial markets. Yes, the craps table represents a microcosm of the broad financial markets, and the participants in both exhibit eerily similar behaviors.

First, there's the misguided idea that the next roll is somehow dependent on previous rolls. Clearly it's not. What makes this particularly fascinating is that it can be misguided on both sides of reality by the same person, simultaneously. For example, imagine a player has thrown several hard rolls (a hard eight is two fours, a hard six is two threes, etc.). Many bettors believe the odds favor it happening again as though the shooter possesses some magical ability to make two fair dice land with the same number on each facing upward. Hard bets are the house's favorites among the multiroll bets because they provide the house with the biggest edge. Winning a hard bet is an extreme long shot. When a hard bet pays off bettors should consider themselves incredibly lucky, take the money, and walk away. Unfortunately, they rarely do. More often than not they let it ride, thereby turning a winning bet into just another loser.

At the same time, when a shooter hasn't thrown a seven for quite a while, many bettors believe the odds favor her throwing one soon. This reflects a belief in reversion to the mean in the short run. So, simultaneously, the bettor is exhibiting a misguided belief in the hot hand as well as a misguided belief in short run reversion to the mean.

The reality of course is that the next roll presents the exact same odds as every other roll. No matter how it may "feel" when you are caught up in the excitement of the moment. That means the most likely roll of all will total seven (1 + 6, 2 +5, 3 + 4, 4 + 3, 5 + 2, 6 + 1, or 6 out of 36 possible combinations). Unfortunately for the bettor, the social convention at the craps table dictates that you shouldn't bet against the shooter (and the overwhelming majority of the other bettors at the table), which means most won't make the "Don't Come" bet, it's considered anti-social.

One bettor at the table would get very upset when the shooter didn't roll "with enthusiasm." What he meant was, the shooter didn't hit the opposite wall with his roll. This is a rule put in place by the casinos, because it ensures that a shooter can't line up the dice preroll, and lightly toss them so that they land in the same way. However, it wasn't the casino that was upset with the lack of enthusiasm, it was a bettor who was actually putting pressure on the shooter to reduce the odds of success for *himself!*

Another bettor criticized me for "betting like an amateur," because I only played "Don't Come" line and never let my winners ride.

Most bettors like to begin small and wait to see if a shooter gets hot before increasing their bets. By letting winning bets ride they are sizing up their positions as the shooter's momentum builds. Not to mention, they are playing with the *house's* money, so if it is lost it won't hurt nearly as much. Again, all of these behaviors are predicated on the misguided belief that the next roll is in some way affected by previous rolls.

Capitalizing on Change

The connection between the two topics just discussed and our job as investors should be obvious but they are particularly relevant in today's markets thanks to the rise of FinTech. Throughout my career the moments that presented the greatest opportunity have always been when modeling shortcomings were resolved through new algorithms delivered via user-friendly, graphical user interface (GUI)-packaged solutions. For example, when I first started in the industry, we were using Black-Scholes without skew to price options and manage risk. The methodology was clearly flawed, especially when applied to emerging markets, but it took years for it to come to light. Along the way, some traders learned to make manual adjustments and those adjustments created bifurcated markets. If you wanted to buy calls/sell puts, you went to one group of market makers, and if you wanted to sell calls/buy puts, you'd go to another. When some of the banks created skew models to revalue their positions the bifurcation grew to extremes. I distilled the different models down to their essence, then found the situation whereby the difference would be exhibited in its most extreme form, and picked at it until the differences disappeared. I remember the first trade as if it was yesterday.

US Dollar versus Brazilian Real was a $5 million market at the time. The at-the-money implied volatility was trading at 15 and so were the risk reversals. It was the most extreme skew in the market. Nothing else came close. I went to my boss and said, "I can sell a 15 delta call, buy a 35 delta call, and earn premium. How much can I do that on?" He responded by letting me know arbitrages don't exist in currency markets. They are too efficient. When I pressed him, he said, if you can do it, you do as much as possible. For the 35 deltas, I went to two of the biggest market makers that weren't yet pricing in skew, and for the 15 deltas, I went to two that were. I put the trade on in $100 million with each counterparty, and I earned $200,000. It was even better than an arbitrage because I was long a call spread and had earned premium. Unfortunately, in the end, I only earned the premium, but had USD/BRL exploded I would have made a fortune. Do that enough times and you have a very profitable career.

When new products are launched, they are often modeled by quants with little experience in trading. In currencies, these exotic options were modeled with the most liquid currency pairs in mind, where interest rate differentials, skew, and even underlying implied volatilities are fairly staid. The models are then loaded into the same user-friendly, GUI-packaged systems with which the traders, salespeople, and risk managers are familiar for all related assets. After all, a currency is a currency is a currency, right?

To this day, new products are rolled out by quants and delivered into the hands of trusting souls across the industry. The quants trust that those using their models understand their limitations, and the users trust that the developers wouldn't have released something unless it had already been properly vetted. Neither is typically true, but the divide is rarely discovered until someone suffers extreme pain as a result. At the moment, the divide appears to be quite wide in the factor modeling that has taken the industry by storm. Not a week goes by without several discussions with my clients about the impact of these models on their risk management and positioning. The conversations are often laden with exasperation and frustration. The constant adjustments demanded by risk management are causing real losses, and disrupting solid investment processes. Now, you can either continue complaining about them, proceed as usual, thereby being victimized by them and feign surprise at your poor performance at year end, or you can dig into the models, understand what they are designed to fix, discover what new flaws they have exposed, and make adjustments to capitalize on them.

As Coach Saban says, we don't have to like what is happening in markets, but if we don't make the proper adjustments to capitalize on them, it's on us. The proliferation of FinTech products, including AI, introduces many new sources of alpha generation, particularly now in the early stages when human intervention plays such a large role. You may never see such an abundance of opportunities to generate truly uncorrelated alpha again. The only question is, will you be a victim or beneficiary?

Chapter 13

Coaching

Why Coaching Is a Waste of Time and Money

A rather odd title given that I now spend a great deal of my time "coaching" clients, but it's true. Coaching at every level and in every field is, by and large, a farce. I don't care where they were certified or how many initials come after their name on a business card, the overwhelming majority of coaches and trainers fail their clients. Even worse, they know it.

Let's look at the role of the fitness trainer because almost all of us have had some experience with one making it easily relatable. According to the Bureau of Labor Statistics there are 279,100 fitness trainers in the United States, with the ranks swelling by approximately 8% per year, or 10 times faster than the overall population. They typically sport fantastic physiques, have the "hero pose" down pat and throw around terms like *transverse abdominis* with great confidence. In addition, they often possess at least a cursory understanding of how our bodies process proteins, fats, and carbohydrates, as well as which exercises will have an impact on each body part. They genuinely know what is required for you to get in shape and to shed those extra pounds. Meanwhile, the Centers for Disease

Control estimates that a full 70% of Americans meet the qualifications for being overweight or obese. Over the past seven years alone the obesity rate has risen 10%· to include an astounding 28% of the population. The nation's fitness trainers are failing us and they know it. I say that because commercial gyms require 10 times more members than they can handle just to break even. That means they must be okay with signing up new suckers as members, because they know we'll likely only show up a few times before disappearing forever.

Interestingly, even those coaches who know they are failing their clients don't necessarily know why. However one of them, a "fitness coach to the stars", asked me that very question recently. Following a successful career in finance she decided to pursue her true passion, fitness, as a profession. Over the past seven years, she has developed a terrific business, catering to a diverse clientele including time-starved CEOs, entire student bodies at elementary schools, *real* housewives, high-performance athletes, recovering addicts, and everyone in between. She has been able to thrive in a field with tremendous turnover and low success rates, and yet even she struggled to understand why it is that so many clients come to trainers for help and leave without realizing their goals.

The answer relates to every type of coaching and every industry, including ours. One of the fundamental assumptions made by most coaches is that the problem will be solved if they simply transfer their knowledge to the client. For example, fitness trainers typically see their jobs as developing exercise routines specifically suited to help their clients achieve their objectives: 15 leg lifts, 20 squats, 20 crunches, 30 minutes on the treadmill … four times a week. They help them perfect their form, count down the last few in a set and track their reps on a neatly organized clipboard. A recipe for success, flawlessly executed.

As anyone who has ever attempted to re-create something they saw on Pinterest knows, simply possessing and following a recipe to the letter does not guarantee success. The same goes for coaches. It begins innocently enough with the client needing to skip a session for their child's school play or to catch up on work. Then it happens again. Before you know it, they've joined the ranks of 80% of the trainer's clients. Just another name in the contact list. The trainer blames the client for the failure, and it's likely that the client does too. "If they would have just done what I told them they would have lost the weight." That's how they console themselves, and absolve themselves of the blame, but every time they do so, it practically guarantees it will happen again and again.

In a way it is true that the client is to be blame. The overwhelming majority of clients are liars. We lie to our trainers, but more insidiously, we lie to ourselves. We hire a coach because we want to achieve results we've failed to on our own. When we reach out for help we make ourselves vulnerable, admitting that we have had a hand in our shortcomings, and that can be uncomfortable, but also empowering. That moment is like drawing a line in the sand. From here on out I will change my ways and do what is necessary to realize my dreams. *That* is the lie. You've said it while praying to the porcelain god too many times to count. You swore it as you wolfed down your sixth slice of pizza on the Sunday night before your tenth diet began. And you're doing it again now as you bare your soul to your new trainer. To her detriment, and yours, she believes you and in that moment you both fail.

To know why that is the case it's helpful to review the key components of a decision. First, there is the outcome. It is what you are attempting to achieve. You don't directly control the outcome. Instead, you must understand the factors that affect your ability to achieve that outcome, but that you also don't control. These are known as *states*. This information is vital in selecting *acts* that will provide a high probability of achieving the outcome you desire. Here's the tricky part that very few people understand or are willing to acknowledge. Your habits are factors that impact your ability to achieve the outcome you desire *and*, for all intents and purposes, they are beyond your control. Therefore, you must account for them when choosing the most appropriate acts. In other words, your own behavior patterns are *states*.

The reason we fail is because in that moment when we are telling our trainers that we will do whatever it takes to succeed we are pretending that we are in control of our habits, and they believe us. So they put together a regimen that requires an adjustment to our habits which assumes we will cease prioritizing our actions in the same way we have been, and reorganize everything in that very moment. It's a lovely thought but carries a very low probability of success. Instead of pursuing this time-honored tradition of failure, good coaches will take the time to understand not just their client's goals, but everything relating to their habits, passions, schedule, priorities, and demands on their time and attention, because together, they make up the *states*. Only then can coaches choose the acts that provide their clients with the greatest odds of success.

Why Even the Best Seek Coaching

It's very likely the name David Cutcliffe doesn't ring a bell, and with good reason. He's been a football coach for almost 40 years, but never in the NFL. He ran the program at Ole Miss for a few years before being fired after his first losing season. Since 2007, he's been turning around the football program of perennial loser Duke University, leading them to their first bowl game in almost 20 years and their first-ever division title. Cutcliffe has developed an incredible track record for turning around programs and developing talent. He coached six quarterbacks who have gone on to play in the NFL, including two Super Bowl MVP's, and two who went on to careers in Major League Baseball. Unfortunately for Cutcliffe, neither turning around programs nor developing future stars tends to result in a frenzy of attention and accolades from the press (unless it directly results in a Super Bowl win or National Title). It has, however, earned him the respect of those who understand just how difficult it is to achieve the results he has delivered.

In June 2011, after struggling to regain the form that earned him a Super Bowl MVP years earlier, Eli Manning sought "Cut's" expertise to recalibrate his footwork and fine-tune the mechanics on his deep balls. The following season Eli enjoyed his most productive season ever and a second Super Bowl win.

The next year, Eli's brother and arguably the greatest football player who ever took the field, Peyton Manning, called on Cutcliffe as well. He'd just undergone his third and most serious neck surgery in just 19 months, and the Indianapolis Colts, the team he'd led to two Super Bowls and with whom he'd earned four MVPs, had just chosen Andrew Luck, the top quarterback in the draft. This was a challenging moment for Peyton, with many experts, including his own doctors, questioning whether it was possible for him to ever return to form, or to even play the game again.

A free agent at the time, he wanted to work with somebody he trusted to oversee his rehab and return to the NFL. More than a coach, though, he sought a teacher.

"I was in rehab state where I needed a quarterbacks coach," Manning told *The Times-Picayune*. "I needed a weight room. I needed physical therapy. But a big part of rehab was on the field. There's only so much a physical therapist can know as far as quarterback work on the field."[1]

Cutcliffe sent Manning through hour after hour of tedious drills, catching shotgun snaps, taking snaps from center, footwork, and hand drills. Day by day, throw by throw, Manning gradually started to regain his form. Then Cutcliffe introduced a radical idea. He had Manning run a play-by-play simulation of the Colts 30-17 AFC Championship win over the New York Jets from two years earlier, even flying in his former teammates and offensive coordinator to authenticate the simulation.

One teammate flown down was Colt's center, Jeff Saturday, who could see immediately how seriously Peyton was taking this, and he said everyone tried to match the energy expenditure and speed of the game.

Manning called plays in the huddle and made checks and hot reads at the line. When the script called for a run, they ran it. When it called for four wide recievers out of the shotgun in no-huddle, they did that also.

No detail was overlooked during the three-hour workout. Each play was run at full sped from the exact yard line and hash mark as the real game. The receivers ran the same route trees and Manning completed the passes to the same targets. When the script called for the Jets to be on offense, Manning and company retreated to the sideline and waited for the exact time of possession to expire on the play clock before retaking the field. They even scripted a 12-minute break for halftime. The only thing they didn't have were defenders.

It was an exact replica of the game.

In addition to providing a prime evaluation tool of Manning's mechanics and fundamentals, Cutcliffe said the game was a crucial

---

[1] Quoted in Jeff Duncan, "Duke Coach David Cutcliffe Played Key Role in Peyton Manning's NFL Comeback," NOLA.com and *The Times-Picayune*, October 26, 2012.

physical conditioning test. It had been more than 14 months since Manning had played an NFL game and this was the closest he could come to simulating a real experience.

"Afterward, he was sweaty and worn out, but he had a big ole smile on his face," Cutcliffe said of Manning.[2]

The Duke video crew recorded the game from both sideline and end zone angles. Cutcliffe and Manning then evaluated the game film from the workout and compared it side by side with the 2009 game, gauging his footwork, the velocity and trajectory of his throws, and the speed of his drop-back and release.

It was clear to everyone who participated that Peyton was back.

Four days later the Colts released Manning. In making the decision to sign Peyton to a five year, $96 million deal, Denver Broncos Head Coach John Fox and VP of Football Operations John Elway put a lot of stock in Cutcliffe's scouting report and the film of the simulated game.

Their confidence was well founded, and Cutcliffe's unconventional methods were once again validated. That year, Manning took the Broncos to the playoffs where they lost to the eventual Super Bowl champs. The following year, Manning earned his fifth MVP and the Broncos returned to the Super Bowl.

What stands out to me in stories like this has less to do with David Cutcliffe and more with Peyton Manning. Here is a man who has set just about every record for which he is eligible, who has accomplished more than almost every other athlete will ever dream of, yet he still believes he can improve, that he has more to learn, and knows that in order to do so he must rely on the expertise of others. What's really interesting is that he didn't go to Jon Gruden, the man who the media has anointed as the guru of quarterbacks, but instead he sought out a man whose name is almost unrecognizable to most in the business. Not only did he seek his guidance, he went all in, showing complete faith in the process, even when Cutcliffe suggested a most radical approach, and he was rewarded for it.

I don't know why it is but for some reason this same belief in coaching and teaching for top investment managers and allocators is reserved

---

[2] Ibid.

for the rare few. Sure, many employ "psychologists" or even spiritual guides, but how many do you know who enlist the expertise of coaches in the same way that Eli, Peyton, Serena, Roger, and other world class athletes do? How many are willing to forgo protecting their ego to invite the kind of deep analysis and detailed critique of *the very process that got them to the pinnacle of their success*?

Even when I am approached by portfolio managers for coaching, there is often a hesitance to truly reveal the company's inner workings. It's easy to feign humility, to say "I know I have room to improve and want to learn," but far more difficult to push our own ego out of the way. I've worked with whole teams, with each member visibly excited to get started, only to discover down the road that what they were each secretly expecting was for me to fix all the *other* guys.

This isn't especially surprising. One of the indisputable truths discovered through research in the field of cognitive science is that when we read about bias, more often than not we see evidence of it in everyone around us, but very rarely in ourselves. In my experience, simply accepting that you too are vulnerable to systematic errors in judgment opens the door to a spike higher in your learning curve, the likes of which you haven't experienced since your first day on the job.

The Power of Confronting Fear

Many of my coaching clients pay for our services out of their own pockets. Some say they do so because they see us as a competitive edge and don't want others to know about us. Others do so because they don't want others to know that they need our help. We are talking about people who, on average, directly manage $1.15 billion in AUM and have been in the business for 16.7 years. In other words, these are professionals who are well established in the business and have proven themselves to be exceptional at what they do over the course of many years. They openly take meetings with analysts, subscribe to data and research services, attend conferences, and seek guidance from salespeople for structuring ideas. Why then is there a stigma when it comes to seeking help with investment process and decision analysis?

Perhaps the belief is that our investment process and ability to make decisions is what defines our expertise. Therefore, as an expert, we shouldn't need help with those aspects of the job. If we do, maybe our bosses or investors will think we aren't the right people to be guiding the business or portfolio. What's ironic about this is that almost unanimously, at some point in our discussions, allocator clients float the idea of making it mandatory for managers with whom they invest to be coached by us. In other words, what some managers fear may be perceived as a weakness is overwhelmingly viewed as a strength by the very people whose opinion they value.

Despite this, there can still be a stigma attached to seeing a coach, especially in the financial industry. Hollywood portrayals of performance coaches and trading psychologists can seem pretty absurd. The character of Wendy Rhoades in Showtime's *Billions* is one example. Imagine my surprise in finding a *Fortune* article titled "Inside the Secretive World of Hedge Fund Psychiatrists and Performance Coaches." The writer had interviewed several of them who concluded that the *Billions* character "isn't too far off."[3] I couldn't believe what I was reading!

I can see how some might now lump me in with the trading psychology/performance coaching (TP/PC) crowd. I guess I bear some responsibility. After all, I did voluntarily choose to call what I do *coaching*.

I'd like to explain what I do when working with portfolio managers and CIOs as compared to what TP/PCs do. The distinction is important, because what lies at the heart of the difference between our approaches is what I see as the reason this industry perennially fails to generate returns reflective of the brain power dedicated to the task.

Performance Coaching versus Decision Architecture

Nearly everything we've come to take as gospel in the business of investment management is, by its very nature, reactive. Risk management,

---

[3] Clarie Groden, "Inside the Secretive World of Hedge Fund Psychiatrists and Performance Coaches," Fortune.com, February 4, 2016.

manager selection, asset allocation, and so much more, are all deeply rooted in reactive decision-making. Regardless of the disclaimer regulators make us add to our returns, most of what we do and think is a function of past performance. It's understandable that this would be the case; after all, it is how we are hard wired as a species. We are designed to maximize efficiency, which is another way of saying that we don't like to expend energy or effort unless it's absolutely necessary, both physically and mentally. As a result, we are designed to achieve and maintain a state of cognitive ease whenever possible. In this state, we don't feel threatened or at risk, so we don't have to mobilize the part of our brain that is in charge of thinking hard or deeply. Instead we can rely on our intuition and gut feel. It's how we live the majority of our lives, and make the majority of our mistakes.

In doing so we are attempting to avoid cognitive strain, and it turns out we are quite adept at it. We prefer to put out fires after they ignite rather than putting in the effort up front to reduce the odds that a fire will occur in the first place. We use mental shortcuts known as heuristics to help us avoid cognitive strain. Armed with scarcely more than a cursory glance we will make broad assumptions about correlations and causation, develop narratives and leap to conclusions with little concern for evidence supporting any of it.

When a performance coach gives you a "Rah-Rah" speech to get your head back in the game, it may feel good in the moment and appeal to your intuition. After all, if you could just shake those negative feelings then you will see things clearly again, right? Wrong. To prove it, you need only consider the premise from start to finish. Let's assume you were at one point on a fantastic roll, experiencing tremendous success. In that moment, you were likely feeling extremely confident in your abilities as an alpha generator. If all that is required to generate positive returns, to see things clearly, is confidence and having your head on straight, then how could you have gotten from there to a place that requires a coach to remind you of how great you are? In other words, once you're successful and confident it will breed more success and confidence, indeed resulting in a never-ending cycle of success and confidence. Therefore, if the TP/PC's approach is valid, you will never require their assistance. Their approach, like most in this industry, is reactive. It is about putting out fires. Clients seek immediate relief from what ails them and the TP/PC's approach is designed to deliver just that.

Technically speaking, I am not a trading psychologist or a performance coach. I am a decision architect. As such, my job is to close the gap between how my clients should make decisions and how they actually do. Behavioral psychology plays a significant role in helping us understand why we tend to deviate and when we are most likely to do so. It allows us to recognize what makes us vulnerable to mistakes. A TP/PC believes that by simply being aware of your mistakes and/or being aware of what you should do, you will do it. In other words, if they can get you to "snap out of it," you'll do what needs to be done. That approach ignores the decades of research produced by cognitive scientists which has gone a long way to explaining why smart people make poor decisions.

Trading psychology/performance coaching pretends that we don't have flaws, that there aren't moments when even the most disciplined among us will be undisciplined, and that even the smartest, most highly educated people can't behave irrationally given the right circumstances. Decision architecture does not. My job is to recognize an individual's vulnerabilities, to identify those moments when the mistakes are most likely to occur, and devise a process that reduces the probability that they will. It is about shifting from a reactive, belief-based decision-making process to one that is proactive and evidence based. Rather than propping up my client's egos, we develop an approach that reduces the likelihood that Rah-Rah speeches will ever be necessary.

Chapter 14

Trading Decisions

What Makes Trading So Difficult

In this section I will discuss why one of the most common approaches to trading is dead wrong. I'll also explain what makes it so appealing and why it will continue to be difficult to resist, even after I prove to you that it is irrational.

Let's begin with the basics of investing. You form a view and with it come expectations. See Figure 14.1 for an example. In this case the investor is bullish.

Of course, we aren't so naive as to believe that anything will move in such a straight line, so we have a range within which we expect it to trade (see Figure 14.2).

As time goes by the spot price ebbs and flows, sometimes moving higher confirming your view, while other times it moves lower calling your view into question (see Figure 14.3). When we look back on an asset's price action it actually appears to be this clear cut, and the job, with the benefit of hindsight, seems like it really is that simple. The reality, however, is quite different.

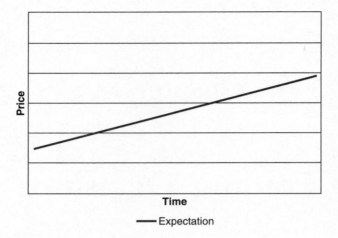

Figure 14.1   A bullish investor

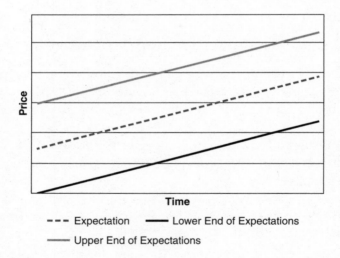

Figure 14.2   Expected trading range

Let's examine what happens when the price moves down toward the lower end of your expectations (see Figure 14.4). As long as all the reasons behind your establishment of the view remain in place, the only thing that has changed is the risk/reward. The closer spot gets to the lower end of your expectations, the more attractive the trade becomes

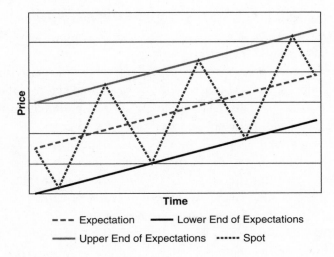

Figure 14.3   Price action

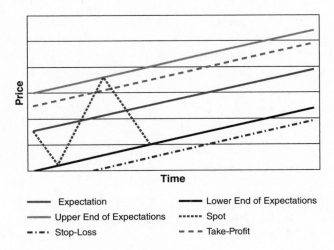

Figure 14.4   Price moves down

from a risk/reward perspective. As a result, it is the point at which the position should be at its maximize size. Think about that for just a moment. I am suggesting that you should max out your position size at the exact moment when your confidence is likely to be at its lowest. Why would it be low? Well, something must have happened to drive the price lower and that *something* is likely to be what everyone is talking about at that moment. It is also evidence against a bullish view. Why else would it have pushed the price lower?

So, in that moment you are likely to be bombarded with all the reasons you should *not* be bullish. The guy sitting next to you, the talking heads on TV, analysts and salespeople are all essentially telling you why your view and accompanying expectations are wrong.

Assuming your investment process is valid and you have identified up front what the important factors are that affect your view (the signals), then everything else is essentially *noise* as it relates to this position. Therefore, it shouldn't matter what the guy next to you or anyone else has to say. You should feel as confident in your view and expectations as you did on day 1. As a result, you should take full advantage of the move down and max out your position size.

Why is it that this moment creates so many problems for investors? Well, most don't invite cognitive strain up front during the planning phase of the trade. Most don't put in the effort to identify what represents a *signal* when they first establish the view and set their expectations. Therefore, when the noise is released, everyone is talking about it and it pushes the price lower, it becomes difficult to determine whether it is, in fact, signal or noise. You begin to question your view. Your confidence wanes. So, instead of sizing up as you should, you sit and wait for confirmation, or even worse, you cut it.

Now let's examine what happens as you approach the upper end of your expectations (see Figure 14.5). Your confidence is at its peak. Everything, especially price action, is supportive of your view. Everyone who told you your view was wrong is now explaining to *you* not only why it has gone up, but why it will make new highs and break out to the upside. Momentum traders have received confirmation and are beginning to really load up. You are giddy with excitement, knowing that you were right all along. The guy sitting next to you is now singing your praises, patting you on the back for being so amazing. He too has loaded up and is feeding you a constant diet of evidence confirming your view including information that you hadn't identified as *signal* when you first established the position. (Yes, even confirming evidence can be noise.) With everyone talking about it and so many profiting you begin

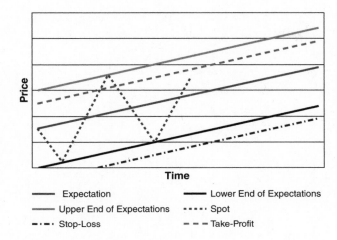

Figure 14.5   Peak confidence

to worry that others, particularly those who were arguing that it would breakout to the downside just days earlier, will profit more from your idea than you will. That is what makes it so difficult to begin unwinding the position, but that is exactly what you should be doing as the risk/reward has flipped to the opposite extreme. Being so close to the upper end of your expectations and so far from the lower end means your risk is now much greater than your potential reward. As a result your position size should be at or near zero. Take a second to contemplate what I am saying. At the moment your confidence is at its highest, your position size should be at its lowest. It sounds and feels counterintuitive, which is why it is so difficult to make the rational decision.

What do most traders do instead of unwinding the position? They move their stop-loss up, thereby effectively rebalancing the risk/reward. While it may appear rational, it is not. The reason is that the upper and lower expectation bands represent discrete moments. What that means is the probability of spot trading just above the upper band is disproportionately lower than the probability of it trading just below it (see Figure 14.6). So, if you want a high probability that your take-profit will be hit, you should set it below the upper band.

On the other hand, the probability of spot trading just below the lower end of your expectations is disproportionately lower than the

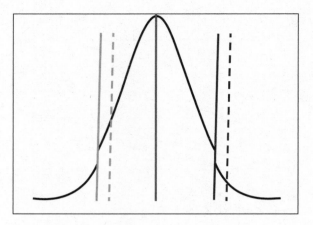

Figure 14.6   Spot trading probability

probability of it trading just above the lower end. Therefore, if you don't want to be stopped out while your view is still in effect, you should set your stop-loss just below the lower end of your expectations. If you were to raise your stop-loss with the objective of rebalancing the risk/reward, you are shifting the probability of triggering that stop-loss from very low to very high (see Figure 14.7). So, while you are reducing the

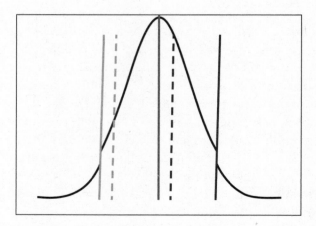

Figure 14.7   The effect of changing a stop-loss

magnitude of your potential downside, you are significantly increasing the likelihood of actually realizing that loss.

What I am saying is that the rational decision would have you reduce your position when momentum traders are loading up, and loading up when they are stopping out. If you are an investor who expresses a view based on fundamentals, momentum trading is incompatible with your approach. In fact, it is downright corrosive. Do it often enough and you'll find yourself saying, "I got my view right, I just didn't make any money on it."

The Freedom of a Straightjacket

I often hear investors talk about wanting to remain agile, not wanting to be *straightjacketed*. They believe it's important to be able to react to new information as it becomes available, to reassess the situation as it unfolds and adapt. Very often what they're really saying is they don't want to have to contemplate all of the likely future events, variables, and outcomes that can affect their investments today. They'd rather deal with them as they occur. However, decades of studies in the cognitive sciences suggest that this is a bad idea. By delaying the hard decisions you are avoiding cognitive strain in favor of maintaining cognitive ease. Factors such as losses, gains, and a whole host of emotional triggers are likely to skew your objectivity in that future moment, leaving you with the task of making difficult decisions at a time when extraneous factors, the kind that tend to create bias and result in mistakes, come to the fore.

In the typical "agile" process, decisions are made with the benefit of new information, but also under heightened emotions, increased time constraints, and bias-inducing influences, like P&L. This reduces the weighting that the new information itself can have on the decision (see Figure 14.8). If instead, we can identify the important information ahead of time, its possible effects, and the resulting adjustment you should make to your forward expectations, then there is no decision to be made in that future moment. It can be made ahead of time in a moment of greater objectivity and lucidity thereby increasing the odds of a better decision.

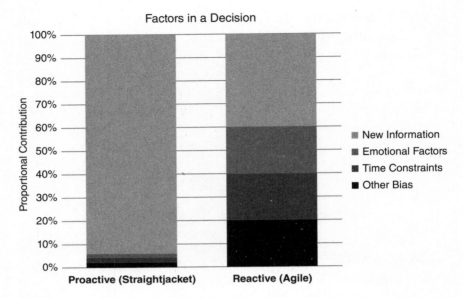

Figure 14.8   Factors in a decision

Let's use a decision tree to see how this works. Imagine you are contemplating going long in XYZ stock. The catalyst for your potential investment is an impending court ruling. Having done your research you believe the probability of a favorable ruling is 80%. If the ruling does turn out to be favorable, you believe the stock has an 80% chance of trading to $30 and a 20% chance of dropping to $10. If it turns out to be unfavorable, the odds flip (see Figure 14.9). Based on the probabilities you have assigned as a result of your research, and the expected profit/loss in each scenario, when you fold back your decision tree, you come to the conclusion that you should purchase XYZ stock.

It's likely that the analysis to this point isn't very different from what goes on in your own head. You've done it so many times over your career you probably don't see the need to take the time to lay out your thoughts on a decision tree or write down your expectations as they exist today. You believe that your expectations (i.e. probabilities assigned) today will remain constant, requiring adjustment only when new information is produced. You will reassess the situation after the ruling comes out.

Initial Decision

XYZ Stock at $20

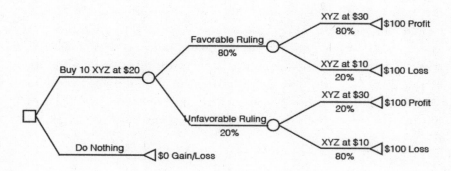

Initial Decision

XYZ Stock at $20

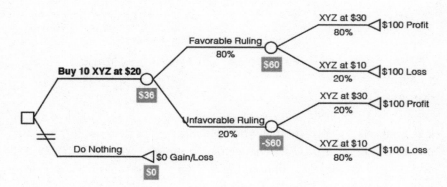

Figure 14.9 Initial decision tree (left) compared with probability-guided decision tree (right)

If you read that last sentence without skipping a beat you've already made a mistake. You see, in your initial analysis, the one that led you to purchase XYZ ahead of the ruling, you set your expectations for the valuation of XYZ *given* that the ruling was favorable. Therefore, any adjustment to your "post–ruling expectations" after the ruling is announced will be the result of bias, not the ruling itself.

Prior to the announcement, you believed there was a 68% chance that the stock would trade at $30 (80% chance in the case of a favorable ruling + 20% chance if it were unfavorable.) See Table 14.1. Once the ruling is announced, the only thing in your decision tree that should change is the odds of a favorable versus unfavorable ruling (see Figure 14.10). Strictly as a result of that adjustment your expectation of achieving a loss on the investment has dropped from 32% down to just 20%. No flexibility or adjustment in the moment is necessary. The decision you made initially is the only one you need to make. If you raise your price expectation based solely on the fact that the

Table 14.1   Prior to court ruling

Stock Price	Expected Return	Prob of Upper Tgt	Rtn at Upper Tgt	Prob of Lower Expec	Rtn at Lower Expec	Max Downside	Notional
30	−21.33%	68%	0.0%	32%	−66.7%	−1,000,000	1,500,000
29	−18.00%	68%	3.3%	32%	−63.3%	−1,000,000	1,578,947
28	−14.67%	68%	6.7%	32%	−60.0%	−1,000,000	1,666,667
27	−11.33%	68%	10.0%	32%	−56.7%	−1,000,000	1,764,706
26	−8.00%	68%	13.3%	32%	−53.3%	−1,000,000	1,875,000
25	−4.67%	68%	16.7%	32%	−50.0%	−1,000,000	2,000,000
24	−1.33%	68%	20.0%	32%	−46.7%	−1,000,000	2,142,857
23	2.00%	68%	23.3%	32%	−43.3%	−1,000,000	2,307,692
22	5.33%	68%	26.7%	32%	−40.0%	−1,000,000	2,500,000
21	8.67%	68%	30.0%	32%	−36.7%	−1,000,000	2,727,273
20	12.00%	68%	33.3%	32%	−33.3%	−1,000,000	3,000,000
19	15.33%	68%	36.7%	32%	−30.0%	−1,000,000	3,333,333
18	18.67%	68%	40.0%	32%	−26.7%	−1,000,000	3,750,000
17	22.00%	68%	43.3%	32%	−23.3%	−1,000,000	4,285,714
16	25.33%	68%	46.7%	32%	−20.0%	−1,000,000	5,000,000
15	28.67%	68%	50.0%	32%	−16.7%	−1,000,000	6,000,000
14	32.00%	68%	53.3%	32%	−13.3%	−1,000,000	7,500,000
13	35.33%	68%	56.7%	32%	−10.0%	−1,000,000	10,000,000
12	38.67%	68%	60.0%	32%	−6.7%	−1,000,000	15,000,000
11	42.00%	68%	63.3%	32%	−3.3%	−1,000,000	30,000,000
10	45.33%	68%	66.7%	32%	0.0%	−1,000,000	0

Initial Decision
XYZ Stock at $20

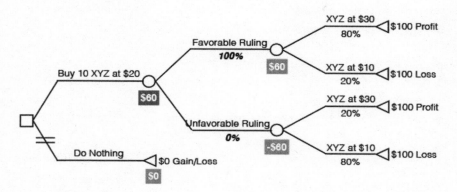

Figure 14.10   Post–announcement decision tree

ruling was favorable you're making a mistake, likely the result of a cognitive bias.

Of course, given that a great amount of uncertainty has been removed the expected return on the investment has changed (even though the price target hasn't). Therefore, it makes sense to reassess the investment from this point forward. Perhaps, it is wise to double down. I know what some of you are thinking. So you *do* have to make a decision in the moment! Actually, no. This decision can and should be made prior to the initial investment as well. Leaving only the execution for today.

In Figure 14.11 you will find the tree for the post–ruling decision to sell, hold, or double down. Based on your expectations and the current stock price of $23, the expected return is positive, and doubly so if you were to double down from here. (Note: The original price paid is no longer relevant.)

There is a difference, though, between simply making the decision to be long and the decision about *how* long you should be. Let's say you want your expected upside to be twice your expected downside. Initially that required an entry price below $20.30, which is why you had purchased it when it dropped to $20. Now, the decision is whether

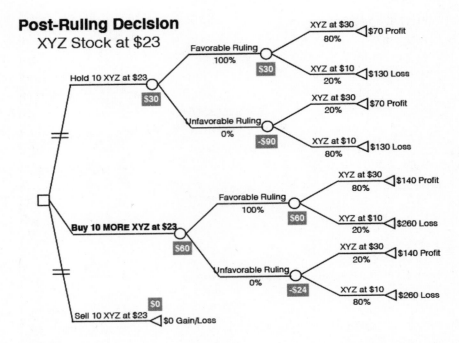

Figure 14.11   Post–ruling decision tree

to hold, double down or sell it all. Again, you decide that you will double down after the ruling *if* the expected upside is at least 2x the expected downside. If the ratio is below that you'll stick with what you have, and if it's at $30 you'll sell it all. Therefore, given your post-ruling probabilities, you should double down if the stock is below $23.33.

Note that those parameters can, and should, all be set prior to entering the initial trade. Since those parameters *are* the decisions as they relate to this investment, no actual decision needs to be made as new information becomes available, only execution of those made in a moment of maximum objectivity.

The Natural Beauty of (Decision) Trees

Table 14.2 shows a decision matrix created to assess the expected returns for a hedge fund manager that an allocator is considering

for an investment. In the second column are the returns projected
by an analyst for the seven mutually exclusive potential outcomes as
he has defined them. The next column contains the probability that
each of those scenarios will occur. We know these outcomes are both
exhaustive and mutually exclusive because the sum of the probabilities
of the seven scenarios totals 100%. As you know, the total expected
return is a function of the expected returns for each scenario and their
respective probabilities. If the first four columns were all we knew it
would be difficult to find a flaw in the analysis. However, the content
of column five calls everything that came before it into question. Let's
explore why that is and what can be done to avoid this mistake going
forward.

Table 14.2   Decision matrix

	Expected Return	Probability	Weighted Expected Return	Reason
Scenario 1	−5.0%	3%	−0.2%	2008 occurs again, xxxx performs better due to high quality focus of portfolio.
Scenario 2	−2.5%	7%	−0.2%	Market declines 7.5%, xxxx creates no alpha.
Scenario 3	6.0%	10%	0.6%	Market is relatively flat, xxxx creates 6% annualized alpha.
Scenario 4	8.4%	20%	1.7%	Markets hits historical return profile of 8%, xxxx creates 300bps of alpha.
Scenario 5	13.1%	40%	5.2%	xxxx matches historical return profile.
Scenario 6	24.1%	15%	3.6%	xxxx is able to benefit from volatile market and generate material alpha on both sides of the portfolio.
Scenario 7	33.7%	5%	1.7%	US economy outperforms, benefiting small and midcap companies, allowing xxxx to materially outperform broad market strength.
Total Expected Return			12.5%	

One factor mentioned in several of the scenario "reasons" comments on the performance of the "markets," thereby implying that there is a beta component to this fund manager's returns. In other words, there is a correlation between market returns and this fund's returns. Based on the description in Scenario 1, that correlation is thought to be positive. According to this analyst there are three other key variables that contribute to the fund's returns – alpha, market volatility and the US economy.

In order for the probabilities of all seven possible scenarios to add up to 100% they must be mutually exclusive. Scenario 1 is very specific, calling for −35% returns for the Russell 2000 (very negative) over the next 12 months. Scenario 2 calls for a 7.5% decline (slightly negative) in R2K without any alpha generation. Scenario 3 calls for zero return in R2K, but positive alpha. Scenario 4 calls for R2K to rally 8% (slightly positive), plus 300 bps of alpha. The remaining scenarios make no mention of market returns, which means they could occur under any or all market outcomes, including those previously defined. Scenario 5 mentions only the fund's future returns in isolation so we know nothing about any of the variables on which the fund's returns are dependent. Scenario 6 anticipates volatile markets and positive alpha leading to a 24.1% return. Scenario 7 expects a strong economy and market returns, resulting in a 33.7% return for the fund. Even reading through the reasons one at a time, it's difficult to see that there is a problem with the analysis, but there is a flaw, and it's significant.

Table 14.3 shows a summary of the information provided so far.

Table 14.3   Seven scenarios: probability

	Market Returns	Alpha	Market Volatility	US Economy	Fund Returns
Scenario 1	Very Negative				−5%
Scenario 2	Slightly Negative	None			−2.5%
Scenario 3	Flat	Positive			6.0%
Scenario 4	Slightly Positive	Positive			8.4%
Scenario 5					13.1%
Scenario 6		Positive	High		24.1%
Scenario 7				Strong	33.7%

Even seeing it in this table format doesn't really help us see the problem. To make it leap off the page, rather than using a matrix, let's review the information one scenario at a time using decision trees (Figure 14.12–14.17).

If done correctly, every branch should be represented by one, and only one, mutually exclusive scenario. When added together, they will total 100%. As you can see in the Figure 14.18, quite a few branches are part of more than one scenario, and we haven't even included Scenario 5, because it isn't defined according to the variables chosen by the analyst.

The point I'm attempting to make here is that based upon the way these scenarios have been defined they are neither mutually exclusive nor are they likely exhaustive. That's important, because it means the +12.5% expected return spit out at the end of his analysis is incomplete, incorrect, and essentially useless.

The correct way to carry out such a complex expected return analysis begins by laying out the relevant variables (Figure 14.19). The analyst must then set his expectations for each and every branch segment (Figure 14.20). You'll notice that each choice node (represented by circles) has a set of branches that add up to 100%.

The only things left to do then are set return expectations for each scenario and multiply each of them by the relevant probability. It requires time, effort, and cognitive strain to produce this analysis which is why so few do it, and so many struggle with trade management decisions during an investment's lifecycle.

The decision tree is not only an excellent tool for unearthing mistakes in an analysis, it may be the most valuable tool available for those looking to shift from a reactive decision making process to a proactive one.

Valuing Liquidity

Let's explore one final situation in which investors could benefit from the use of decision trees. This one helps us to truly appreciate one of the great advantages of liquidity.

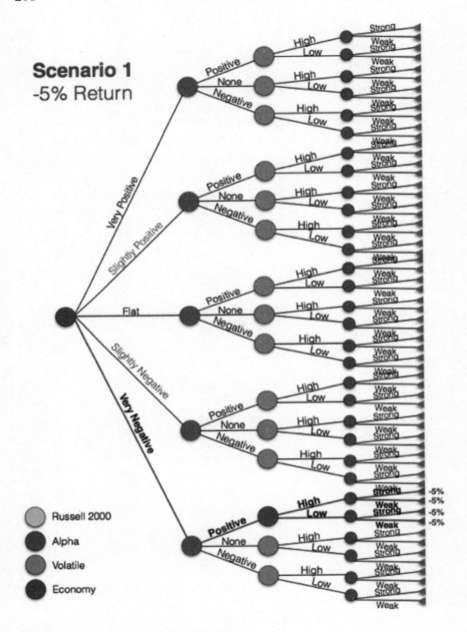

Scenario 1
-5% Return

Russell 2000
Alpha
Volatile
Economy

Figure 14.12   Scenario 1 decision tree

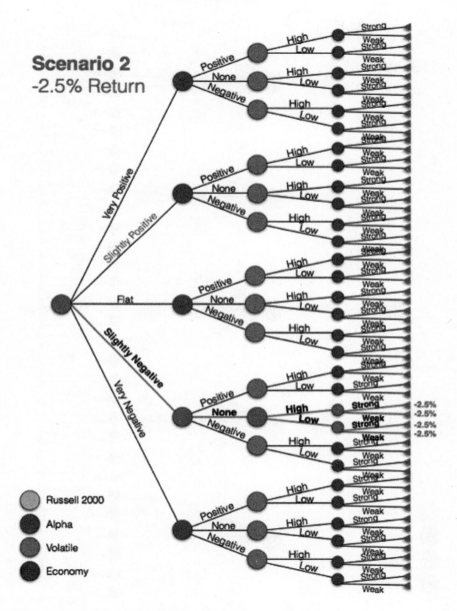

Figure 14.13 Scenario 2 decision tree

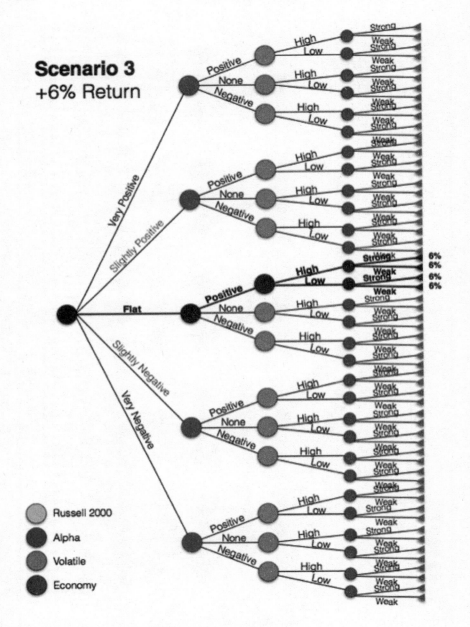

Figure 14.14   Scenario 3 decision tree

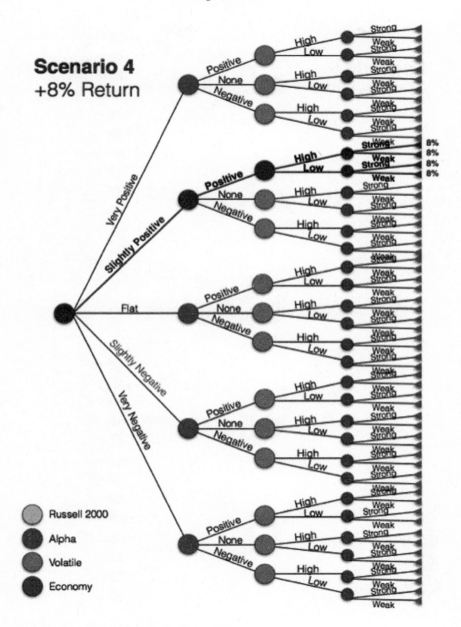

Figure 14.15   Scenario 4 decision tree

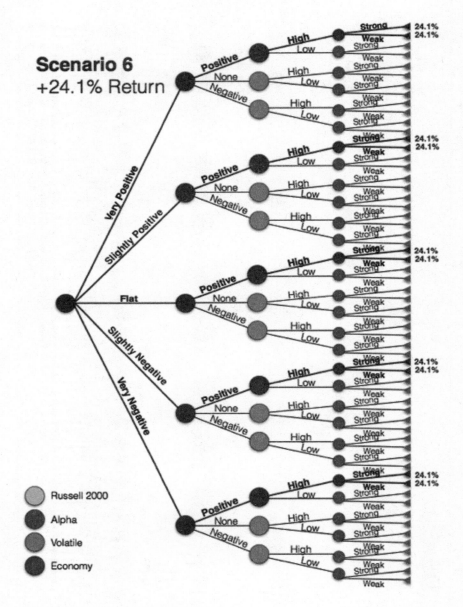

Figure 14.16   Scenario 6 decision tree

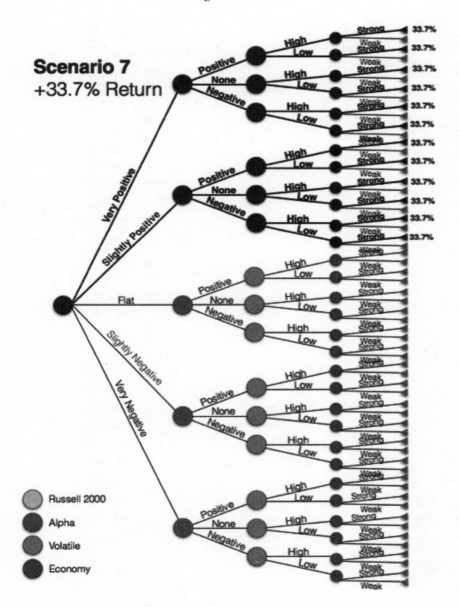

Figure 14.17   Scenario 7 decision tree

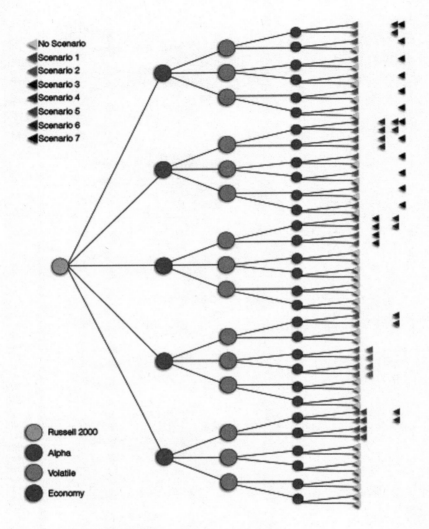

Figure 14.18   Decision tree for Scenarios 1–7

Assume you are choosing between a private equity deal
(Figure 14.21) in which you are locked in for three years versus
an allocation to a global macro hedge fund that allows for monthly
liquidity. You've done a significant amount of analysis on the history of
returns on your allocation decisions and it turns out that the two funds

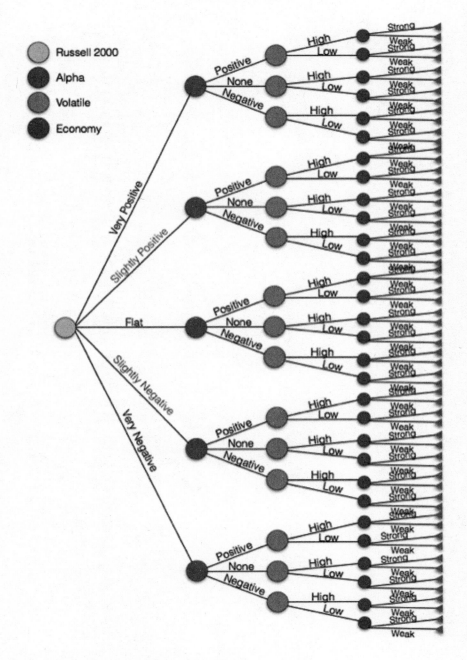

Figure 14.19 Relevant variables only

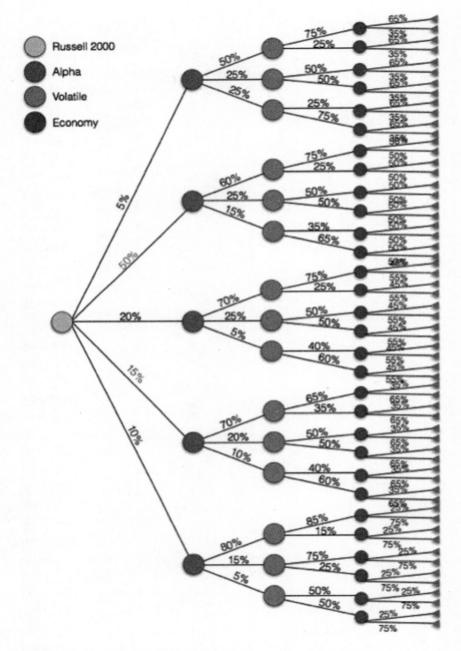

Figure 14.20   Expectations for each branch segment

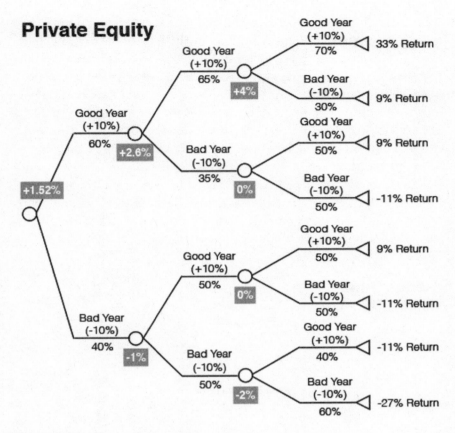

Figure 14.21   Private equity deal

you are considering for an allocation share the same three year expected return profile as the average investment in your "Moderately Aggressive" risk bucket. Therefore, the decision tree for both investments should look identical, right? Of course, you recognize that there is a tangible benefit to the hedge fund's liquidity terms, but how can you quantify that benefit so that it is appropriately and consistently assessed?

Just because the expected return profiles for both investments are identical doesn't mean that the decision trees will be the same. They will differ for this investor for two reasons. First, she has recognized a trend in the investments she makes. Year 1 returns provide predictive value regarding year 2 returns, and the combo of year 1 plus year 2 returns offers valuable information about the likelihood of profitability in year 3. Although this is true for both the private equity fund and the hedge fund, liquidity terms only allow the investor to capitalize on it in the hedge fund allocation. The ability to potentially act on that new information is the second reason the decisions trees will differ.

Let's look at the decision facing the investor in the hedge fund at the end of a bad 1st year (Figure 14.22). The choice she faces is whether to redeem from the current hedge fund and invest the proceeds in something else or stick with the current hedge fund manager. Based on the investor's data, the rational choice is to redeem and invest elsewhere. (After a good year 1, the rational choice is to stay with the current manager.) The same analysis should be done after a bad year 2 (Figure 14.23).

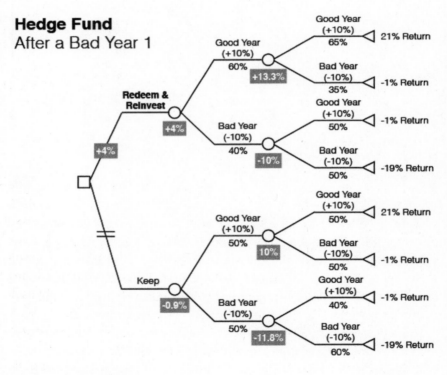

Figure 14.22 Bad year 1

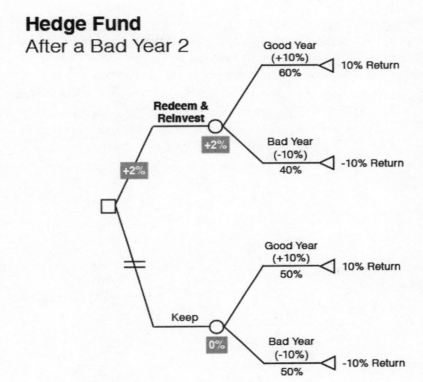

Figure 14.23   Bad year 2

Based on her data, she decides ahead of time that she will redeem and invest elsewhere whenever a hedge fund manager has a bad year. Given that information, we can create the full decision tree, and expected return, for an investment in the hedge fund (Figure 14.24).

Turns out the expected return for the hedge fund is +2.6% versus +1.52% for the private equity investment with the only difference being the ability to make an adjustment to the investment as more information becomes available.

(Notice, again, the decision is made ahead of time. Only the execution occurs in the moment the new information becomes available.)

In the first section of this chapter, "What Makes Trading So Difficult," I made a seemingly controversial claim that your maximum

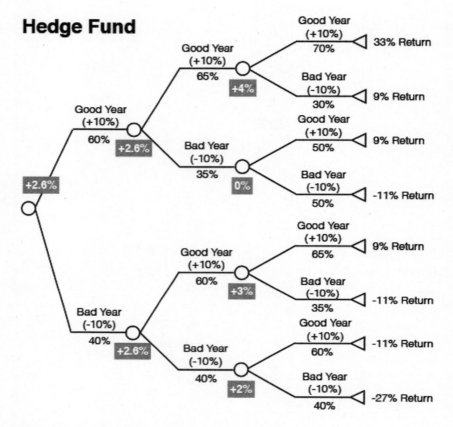

Figure 14.24   Full expected returns in year 1

position size should be at the bottom of an upward sloping trend channel while gradually reducing the position until there is nothing left just below the top of it. The alternative is the approach most investors take. Wait until it bounces back up to $20, thereby "confirming" your view, which gives you confidence to size up the position, but at a far less attractive level.

Now I know many of you will argue that you should move the stop-loss up along the way to reduce the potential maximum downside. And yes, it does reduce the maximum potential downside, allowing you to size up the position, but when you do that, you must also

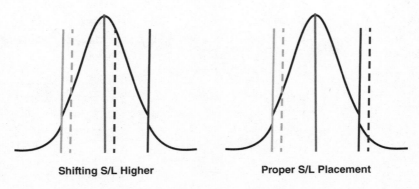

Shifting S/L Higher   **Proper S/L Placement**

Figure 14.25 Shifting stop-loss higher (left) compared with proper stop-loss placement (right)

shift the probability of triggering that stop-loss significantly higher (Figure 14.25). Because in this trade we have binary expectations, meaning that these probabilities are a function of hitting the take-profit level *prior to* the stop-loss level and vice-versa, if we raise the probability of triggering the stop-loss, we must also reduce the probability of triggering the take-profit by a commensurate amount, the combination of which will have a negative impact on your expected return. So, although moving the stop-loss up will reduce the likelihood of a maximum drawdown, it doesn't make it a more attractive investment, and certainly nowhere near as attractive as it is near the bottom of the range.

There is a way to make it a more attractive investment opportunity, though. Given that technical support (i.e. the bottom of the range) represents a discrete moment where the odds of spot trading below that point drop disproportionately, moving the stop-loss to a level just below the support line will have a disproportionate impact on the attractiveness of the trade.

Now let's assume the court ruling came out as you expected. Does it change anything? Do we need to make any adjustments? Absolutely. The expected returns change, even if the maximum potential drawdown doesn't. Table 14.4 reflects the updated expectations. As you can see, your take-profit should be raised to $26.

As I stated at the beginning I have purposely kept this example simple. However, the approach can be expanded to accommodate all of

Table 14.4   After court ruling

Stock Price	Expected Return	Prob of Upper Tgt	Rtn at Upper Tgt	Prob of Lower Expec	Rtn at Lower Expec	Max Downside	Notional
30	−13.33%	80%	0.0%	20%	−66.7%	−1,000,000	1,500,000
29	−10.00%	80%	3.3%	20%	−63.3%	−1,000,000	1,578,947
28	−6.67%	80%	6.7%	20%	−60.0%	−1,000,000	1,666,667
27	−3.33%	80%	10.0%	20%	−56.7%	−1,000,000	1,764,706
26	0.00%	80%	13.3%	20%	−53.3%	−1,000,000	1,875,000
25	3.33%	80%	16.7%	20%	−50.0%	−1,000,000	2,000,000
24	6.67%	80%	20.0%	20%	−46.7%	−1,000,000	2,142,857
23	10.00%	80%	23.3%	20%	−43.3%	−1,000,000	2,307,692
22	13.33%	80%	26.7%	20%	−40.0%	−1,000,000	2,500,000
21	16.67%	80%	30.0%	20%	−36.7%	−1,000,000	2,727,273
20	20.00%	80%	33.3%	20%	−33.3%	−1,000,000	3,000,000
19	23.33%	80%	36.7%	20%	−30.0%	−1,000,000	3,333,333
18	26.67%	80%	40.0%	20%	−26.7%	−1,000,000	3,750,000
17	30.00%	80%	43.3%	20%	−23.3%	−1,000,000	4,285,714
16	33.33%	80%	46.7%	20%	−20.0%	−1,000,000	5,000,000
15	36.67%	80%	50.0%	20%	−16.7%	−1,000,000	6,000,000
14	40.00%	80%	53.3%	20%	−13.3%	−1,000,000	7,500,000
13	43.33%	80%	56.7%	20%	−10.0%	−1,000,000	10,000,000
12	46.67%	80%	60.0%	20%	−6.7%	−1,000,000	15,000,000
11	50.00%	80%	63.3%	20%	−3.3%	−1,000,000	30,000,000
10	53.33%	80%	66.7%	20%	0.0%	−1,000,000	0

your expectations no matter how detailed they may be. In order for any of this to work you must properly define all of your expectations ahead of time. I believe you will be impressed with the benefits of shifting from the standard reactive approach to decision making to a proactive one. Yes, it requires a significant amount of work and cognitive strain to be invested up front, but it dramatically reduces the number of decisions that need to be made throughout the life of the trade. Most importantly, it reduces the number of decisions that will need to be made under emotional distress and time constraints, thereby improving the odds of more rational choices being made throughout. In the end, that is the key to better returns.

Chapter 15

How to Stop Losing Money

How to Stop Losing Money on the Right View

In the global macro community it's fairly common to express a general view on commodities, or even a specific one, by positioning via a highly correlated instrument. Let's say you are bullish on oil, for example, you might get long one of the traditional commodity currencies such as the Canadian Dollar (CAD), Mexican Peso (MXN), or Russian Ruble (RUB). Looking at the charts in Figure 15.1, it would seem that really any of these would make an excellent proxy.

These are the kinds of charts that salespeople and analysts like to include when making trade suggestions for good reason. By appealing to our inherent desire to simplify what is a rather complex world with a nice, neat, coherent story, in which A leads to B and B leads to C, they get us to take action. Unfortunately, neither the world, nor our investment mandates work so linearly, and that creates some real problems. It is what often leads to us getting our view right while simultaneously experiencing losses.

Figure 15.1   Commodity currency charts
SOURCE: Bija Advisors.

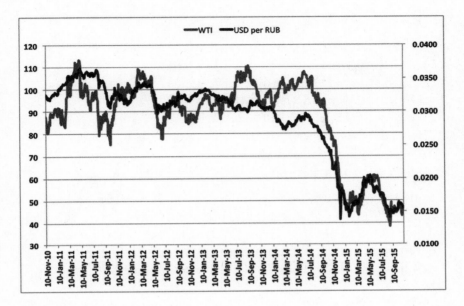

Figure 15.1   (*Continued*)

There are a couple of key issues we are dealing with here. First, you have to not only get your view on oil right, but you also have to do so both in the long run and the short. Second, the commodity currency must also be highly correlated not just in the long run but in the short run as well. That last aspect is made all the more significant when markets become more volatile as they have been recently.

Before I detail how difficult a task this is, and particularly just how much more difficult you have made it for yourself by using what is essentially a derivative instrument, let's take a look at a classic study from cognitive psychology published by Kahneman and Tversky in 1983 that can provide some perspective. It's called The Linda Problem.

Linda is 31 years old, single, outspoken, and very bright. She majored in philosophy. As a student, she was deeply concerned with issues of discrimination and social injustice, and also participated in antinuclear demonstrations.

Rank the following from most to least likely to be true:

A. Linda is a teacher in elementary school.
B. Linda works in a bookstore and takes yoga classes.
C. Linda is active in the feminist movement.
D. Linda is a psychiatric social worker.
E. Linda is a member of the League of Women Voters.
F. Linda is a bank teller.
G. Linda is an insurance salesperson.
H. Linda is a bank teller and is active in the feminist movement.

Eighty-five percent of respondents ranked H as more likely than F which is statistically impossible. At best, they could be equally likely, but that would mean that every single female bank teller is active in the feminist movement.

What Kahneman and Tversky were attempting to exhibit is an inherent flaw in our judgment called Representative Conjunction Fallacy. It combines the representative heuristic (a fancy term for mental shortcut), wherein we note some key characteristic of someone or something, and elevate its importance well beyond its statistical significance. In Linda's case, most of us see the feminist label as highly representative of who she is, whereas the bank teller label is far less certain. Therefore, it's easier to see her as a feminist who happens to be a bank teller than simply being a bank teller.

It's a very similar leap that we make when we develop a bullish view on oil. Let's consider a few possible (and fictitious) reasons for our optimism on oil. Perhaps OPEC has made some comments reflecting their displeasure with the current low price level, consumption numbers have unexpectedly increased recently, or a pipeline project has been shutdown for fear that war is growing in one of the major oil production countries. (Note: This list is fictitious, created purely for the purpose of a hypothetical analysis.) These are all excellent reasons to tilt the odds in favor of higher rather than lower oil prices.

Given this information, rank the following from most to least likely to occur:

A. Oil goes up.
B. Oil and commodity currencies go up.
C. Commodity currencies go up.

When you imagine oil going higher it's difficult to imagine that Russia's economy and its currency not benefiting as well. Intuitively it makes sense, and when combined with the charts in Figure 15.1, it only serves to solidify that intuition. Still, let's dig a bit into the data just to confirm what we feel in our gut.

On a quarterly basis over a recent five-year period WTI crude oil has a 0.78 correlation to the Russian currency against the Dollar (RUB/USD) confirming what appeared obvious in the chart. So you might put on a short USD/long RUB position in anticipation of higher oil prices. Maybe we diversify a bit, going long CAD and MXN as well. In that moment, when we have a clear view and thoughtfully establish a position to express it, it's difficult to imagine how many different ways our P&L can diverge from the path of that vision. It seems almost unfathomable that oil could trade 20% stronger six months from now, yet we somehow lost money not just on these three positions, but on "hedges" that were established along the way. Unfortunately it happens all the time.

Very few investors have the investment time horizon and tolerance for pain they believe they do, and therein lies the real issue. You see, although the correlation between WTI and RUB is 0.78 on a quarterly basis, it is 0.65 on a monthly, 0.46 on a weekly and a mere 0.29 on a daily basis. Its R-Squared is 0.60 on a quarterly basis, but daily it's a minuscule 0.09.

Over the same five years WTI has gone up just 50% of the time on a daily, weekly, monthly, and quarterly horizon, but let's assume your timing is impeccable and you nail oil perfectly. Even when oil went up, RUB strengthened just 60% of the time, and yes, that includes quarterly snapshots. So, if we pretend that the data in Figure 15.1 represents roughly 1200 balls in a jar, with each of them painted one of four colors representing WTI up/RUB up, WTI up/RUB down, WTI down/RUB up, and WTI down/RUB down, the probability of you drawing one that represents your perfect scenario is just 30%.

Perhaps you're thinking, "that's not bad." Fair enough. Now consider that so far we have only been concerned with the matching of direction. How *far* they diverge when going in opposite directions is also significant, both to your P&L and your emotions, especially when markets become more volatile. Let's say they suddenly diverge by

5%, 10%, or even 20% in a given week, which they have done several times. All these positions that are "highly correlated" suddenly don't feel that way. So you improvise. With commodity currencies down 15% and a big event on the horizon for oil, perhaps you buy some short-term oil puts to protect against things getting even worse for your portfolio. After all, if oil rallies your currency positions are likely to reverse more than making up for the loss of premium. Then, oil rallies, you take a deep sigh of relief, write off the premium, and look forward to better days ahead. The option expires and the currencies sink again. Finally, exhausted from the markets not making sense, you call it quits and stop out of all the related positions. That's when the currencies play catch up and in the end, as Figure 15.1 appear to show, it all winds up exactly as you had anticipated, only without the profits to show for it.

Consider one more data point for this highly correlated pair. On a quarterly basis, the beta of RUB to WTI is 0.56. When WTI goes up, the beta is 0.44, and when WTI goes down, it is 0.87, or roughly two times greater, making it a tricky play for relative value enthusiasts.

It's difficult when you're focusing on one driver, like oil in this case, to recognize that there are other significant factors to consider at the same time. For instance, while Mexico is a major player in the oil industry, roughly 80% of its economy is tied to the United States. So, if you were instead focused on the US economy and predicting a sizable decline in economic activity, you might short MXN as a high beta play on that view, while ignoring other factors like oil. Yes, cognitive science has a name for that too called availability bias.

The reason I bring this up is that many long/short equity managers are struggling for this exact reason. Correlations that continue to hold up over a quarterly or annual basis are either breaking down in the short run, or even when reflecting the same short-term correlations, because of the spike in volatility, those low correlations have become much more painful, often too painful to ride out. *That* is how you can get your view right while losing money. The best defense is a more proactive, evidence-based approach to position structuring, portfolio construction, and risk management.

I Knew It!

I unwound a trade called JPY1. As I described it to my clients:

> With US & Japanese policy and economic expectations at opposite extremes, this trade is a way to express a different opinion. If our view is correct, either US expectations will be dampened or Japan's picture seen as improving relative to expectations, either of which has the potential to break technical support around 116.00. If it gets through, there is little between it and 100. We are looking to play that break and compound the returns through the development of a long vega position with downside skew, all of which is currently trading near the long-term lows. A combination of spot, skew, and implied vols all moving in favor of this trade provides great potential for leveraging the underlying idea. It's this combination of inputs at relatively attractive levels that makes the position particularly compelling. If all factors come together in an optimistic fashion, this trade has the potential for a 10-to-1 return. That potential, along with numerous other very attractive outcomes (based on a far more mundane repricing of implied vols, skew, and/or spot), is what drew our attention.

So far, it hadn't hit any reassessment triggers and everything was going according to plan. Volatility, skew, and spot were all moving in the right direction and all for the reasons I had laid out in the trade write-up. For the unwind this was my thinking:

> I decided to err on the conservative side. Having had an opportunity to add to the position at 120 as planned. Everything had very rapidly moved in all components (risk reversal, volatility, and spot FX) and with the key 116 level having broken faster than expected. After only 25 days in the trade risking 150bp, the return is now 145bp. Will look to re-enter on a pullback.

Clients sent emails congratulating and thanking me for the idea.

In the minutes that followed the unwind and hitting send on the email, spot ticked higher, leading one subscriber to remark on my "uncanny timing." I, however, wasn't so sure and it showed in my response. "Only time will tell." I'll admit, it was a relief to see it go higher, for I had gone against my plan and taken profit early. I wanted to be vindicated for that decision. I wanted to be right.

Between coaching sessions, my eyes would glance over at the Bloomberg monitors. As the close approached, spot began the next leg of its descent and didn't look back. Regret kicked in. "I knew it!" shouted my inner voice. Not only had spot continued to move toward my initial target, but so too did implied volatility and skew. Rather than being up 145 bps on the trade I'd be showing a 228 bps profit, and every reason for entering the trade remained intact. "I knew it!"

Truth is, I didn't *know* it. If I did I'd still be in the trade. Yes, I believed the odds were in favor of doing this trade when I initiated it. At that moment, particularly when I doubled up after the BoJ policy decision, I received plenty of push back. It was a clear case of WYSIATI (What You See Is All There Is), which, at that time, were negative rates for Japan.

Well, it's a similar phenomenon that occurs now, only in this case it's called hindsight bias. It's difficult to see how the past 24 hours could have played out any other way, especially given my original write-up. It's all right there. Clearly, I *knew* this would happen. However, what's also there is my postmortem, the explanation for why I unwound it when I did.

Simply by writing that postmortem, I have helped myself overcome the regret I would likely feel in this moment. Thanks to an understanding of how our brains work I really did know that if things played out as they have that I would be experiencing regret in this moment. That postmortem was really a note to Steve of the future, letting him know that he *didn't* know this would happen. The reason that's so important is that it allows me to move on. It reminds me that this is but one trade of many that are available. Yes, I missed out on 83 bps, but this isn't the only trade out there. Literally billions of opportunities exist to make the next 83 basis points. I can either expend the limited mental effort I have available to me laser focused on the one that got away, or I can search for more bait, put it on my line, and drop it back in the water.

Want to know how money is made and lost in this business? It's right here, in these moments. You either prepare for them ahead of time or suffer their consequences.

Stop-Loss Trade Entry

On June 12, 2015, I wrote the following:

> I remain bullish 30 year US Treasuries, but am of the opinion that they should be treated as a trading instrument until one to two months after the Fed raises rates, or it becomes apparent it is off the table. Use the taper tantrum period, when we saw rates ebb and flow around Fed meeting dates, but with an upward trend bias, as your guide.

Ideas like this are easier said than done. When stocks are rallying, we often hear people say, "If the S&P goes down to (insert level here), I will get very long." Then, when it gets to that level, the plan goes right out the window. Why? Because something will have happened to push it down to that level, something clearly negative for stocks. That's the part we rarely consider when devising the plan. The same lack of foresight also tends to occur when we reach our take-profit levels (what I call a *reassessment trigger*).

Here is an actual response from a very experienced portfolio manager I coached a few years back when I inquired about his lack of action when a trade hit his predefined take-profit.

> Portfolio manager: "1336 reassesment trigger is here, but given weakness in Asia, sovereign spreads in Europe, political uncertainty in Europe, monetary policy paralysis in US (as it currently looks), I'm not really inclined to take trade off, more tempted to add to position on break, looking for 1300 initially. I'll update sheet if needed when in office (going to see a show)."

Me: "No opinion re: the 1336 level being right or wrong, but I will say its unlikely you would have hit your reassessment trigger on a bearish S&P trade without some bearish news getting you there."

What I'm trying to explain to the portfolio manager is when you were nonemotional, not impacted by your P&L and confirmations around you, you planned this level for a reason. Listing the facts that got us to this point is only explaining the move to here. This is what you were looking for, for the reasons you were expecting. You didn't expect the S&P to fall to this level for no reason. Why change your plan because you were right?

He ended up unwinding at 1367, his new stop-loss reassessment trigger. Still think this job is all about having the right view?

Easy Money

Make the hard trade, not the easy trade.

— Paul Tudor Jones

I have a confession to make. I like the easy trades, the obvious stuff. My trades are structured to provide a wide range of profitability and an extended period of time to be right. It's very rare for me to ride a move all the way to the very end. Instead, I prefer to play the meaty part, and then move on. Many times, after presenting a new trade to colleagues in an investment committee meeting, I've heard, "Well that's not rocket science," in response. That's when I know I'm on to something. It's always baffled me why so many professional investors constantly try to thread the needle, both on the way in and on the way out. You see, my ego isn't tied up in being perceived as the smartest guy in the room. It's more concerned with the returns generated. I don't get attached to trades regardless of how compelling they might be. It's the investment process that is paramount to me.

Case in point, when USD/JPY reached the original targets identified in the trade called JPY1 back at the end of January 2016 (101.20 spot, −2.5 risk reversal, as shown in Figure 15.2), quite a few asked what

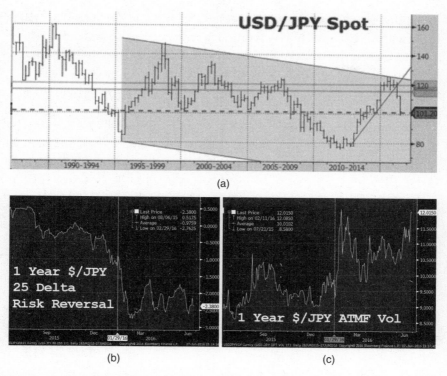

Figure 15.2 USD/JPY spot
SOURCE: Bija Advisors.

I thought about the currency pair. The simple answer was not much. Opportunity exists at the extremes, not in the middle. All the factors that made it a compelling trade at the end of January had been resolved. Spot was at the top of the range. By June, when the question was being asked, it was in the middle. When the trade was established risk reversals (skew) had been very low relative to the norm, especially given where spot was trading. By June, they were back up. Implied vols had been trading near the lows at trade initiation, but not in June. It was the combination of heavily skewed expectations based on what I believed to be a flawed analysis of the macro picture, particularly as it related to the United States versus Japan, along with market prices that underweighted the possibility that the prevailing view could be wrong, which created the opportunity. In other words, the fact that so few thought USD/JPY lower was even a remote possibility was reflected in the price. The trade was attractive given that I believed a big move lower in USD/JPY was a high probability. None of what made it attractive to me back then was in play when everyone was inquiring about my opinion in June.

Here's the thing about big contrarian calls like this one, people tend to become attached to them. For many, it's difficult to walk away, to stop talking and thinking about it, because it is the narrative to which they become attached. Narratives can morph if they aren't prescripted, making it difficult to know when they end. However, if you treat it as simply another expression of a view, one with gradually diminishing risk/reward attractiveness, with specific and finite expectations, it is easy to leave it behind when they are triggered.

Positive Expectancy

For quite some time I was very vocal about my oil view. I believed it would take a tremendous spike in demand for it to stay above $50 for any length of time, and given how every country in the world had been struggling to stimulate demand of any kind for years, I just didn't see that happening anytime soon. Some read that and draw the conclusion that I thought oil was going down. That's how our brains work. We tend to think in terms of binary outcomes. Yes or no. Black or white. Up or down. Spike or collapse. We spend far more time talking about the extremes all while muddling through gray "maybes" right in the middle.

One of my clients shared my oil view but for weeks was having trouble putting on a trade to express it. In considering different possibilities, he would inevitably begin with a put on oil and then explore different ways to offset, or at least reduce, the cost. He kept coming to the conclusion that implied volatility was too high.

For nonoption traders, volatility is the key determinant of options pricing. Essentially, implied volatility is the market expectation of how much the market will move or the uncertainty. Realized volatility is how much it actually did move. What the client is saying here is that the market is pricing oil to move too much to be able to buy an option on oil falling. An option is buying for a set price (or selling) the right, not the obligation, to buy or sell something (in this case oil) at a set price in the future.

For example, oil is at 60, you can buy the option giving you the right to sell oil at 50 for a price (based on the implied volatility). If oil is below 50, you can sell at 50 and hold that short or cover it at the current market rate. Your profit is 50 minus the current price of oil. Also minus the cost you paid for that option. If oil is above 50, you lose what you paid. You cannot lose more. When buying options this means your worst-case outcome is known going in. If you sell an option, you are paid upfront and someone has the right, in this case to sell you oil at 50 dollars, regardless of the current price.

If this approach sounds rational, it's because that's how we are programmed to think about markets and positioning. I mean, when was the last time you heard an analyst come to your office or a talking head on TV say, "I think Company XYZ will just sit right here." Maybe once, because they'd never be invited back. Consider a probability distribution (Figure 15.3). You'd be hard pressed to find one that isn't heavily weighted toward the center, anticipating no change. Yet, because of the way information is presented to us and because most investment instruments require movement in order to generate returns, our first instinct is to position for a directional shift. Even in the case where the trader's view was that oil would not go higher, the first thought was to position for it to go lower. They are not synonymous. It was a mistake, but not the only one.

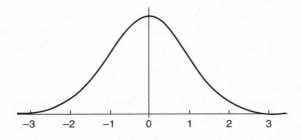

Figure 15.3   Probability distribution

Given that the trader believed that implied vols were too high, spot was trading at $50, and the trader thought it unlikely that it could stay above there for very long, the best expression of the trader's view would involve selling volatility and betting that it wouldn't go much above $50 for any length of time. The simplest expression of that would be the sale of a European digital call. To review, a European digital call option is an exotic, but relatively simple, option. It involves a fixed payout of 100% of notional if the price is above the strike on the day of expiration. The seller would receive a proportion of the notional amount up front as a premium. If spot finishes below the strike, they keep that premium and the option expires worthless. Typically, the premium is roughly equivalent to the delta of a plain vanilla option with the same strike. If the seller were to sell a European digital call option struck at $50, it would likely be priced around 50% of payout, reflecting the 50/50 odds of it being above versus below $50 at expiration. However, selling that wouldn't take advantage of what he believed to be high implied vols. To do that, he could either look to sell a 35-delta strike or a simple call spread, say, selling a $50 call versus buying a $55 call. Both trades have predefined, limited downside, and both are short volatility and profit if spot doesn't rise above $50 for an extended period of time. There's one problem with both of them though, they don't adhere to the misguided, yet generally accepted principle regarding risk/reward, similar to that proposed by Paul Tudor Jones.

My client immediately rejected the idea to sell the 35 delta equivalent European digital call (struck at 55). Why? Well, it would mean risking 65% in the hope of making just 35%, and who in their right mind would do that? Not many investors, but why not? Knowing the payoff is only part of the equation. If the payoff was all that mattered we should just have Powerball tickets in the portfolio. In order to judge whether it's a good investment we need to know the investor's expectations. In other words, the probabilities he or she assigns to the different outcomes. In this case, the investor believed there was just a 25% chance that oil would rise above $55 and an even lower probability it would remain there until expiration. The expected return on the trade is therefore $(0.75 \times 35) + (0.25 \times -65) = +10$. Given the investor's expectations, that's a trade that should be done.

Three Key Reasons Investors Should Use Options but Rarely Do

I began trading options early in my career, and they have been an integral part of my DNA ever since. Whether as a market maker, prop trader, portfolio manager or CIO, I have always expressed every view through options, with a particular penchant for exotics. When it comes down to it, I believe there are three separate and distinct reasons to intelligently employ options. First, they are an excellent tool for helping us to overcome cognitive biases, including inertia and emotional attachment, by forcing a level of discipline we can rarely attain on our own. Second, they enable investors to express a view while protecting against the black swan event. Finally, they offer a way to isolate very specific expectations, both individually and in combination, creating a leveraged means by which to capitalize on or protect against them. If you do it right, you can combine all three benefits in one beautifully crafted position. Let's explore all three in some detail, with specific examples.

1. A Tool for Avoiding Cognitive Bias

Recently, one of my coaching clients was grappling with whether he should unwind a long equity position after it had experienced a far bigger drop than anticipated. Like many portfolio managers, he doesn't typically employ hard stops but rather gathers information as a trade progresses and depends on his experience to dictate when to exit. It's a very common approach, but one that leaves you vulnerable to a number of powerful, and potentially debilitating, cognitive biases. In this case, he was concerned that he'd be selling at the lows, effectively getting out when he should be doubling up. He feared the potential for regret.

Over the coming weeks he continued to take a beating on the position. Every step of the way, the potential opportunity cost weighed on his psyche far more than the accumulation of real losses. Each call ended with him acknowledging that the right decision was to unwind the position and to move on to finding more predictable opportunities, only to begin the next session with, "I should have listened to you."

Two weeks in to the trade a narrative developed concerning the company's earnings announcement which were due to be announced in one week. My solution was to convert the long into a call position representing the same number of shares using options that would expire in two months. I didn't make the suggestion because implied vols were cheap, but because it was the only way to help him overcome his inertia bias. In essence, I was weening him off the position. The rationale went like this: if the stock continued to collapse, the loss for the strategy would be finite, so the bleeding would end and he could move on to opportunities that presented better odds of success going forward. If the stock jumped back up on the back of the earnings announcement he could capitalize on it thereby resolving his fear of potential regret. If the announcement turned out to be a non-event, he could sell out the options before decay became an issue. (In effect, the pending time decay would serve as the "unbalanced force" needed to break the inertia.) As it happened the stock continued to plummet, and although the option was quickly worthless, it saved him millions in P&L, putting the emotional trauma to rest and allowing him to move on to better opportunities.

Postscript: A month later, largely as a matter of luck, a positive announcement came out that pushed the stock back up to where he'd first swapped into the options, allowing him to recoup half his premium. I say *largely* because this potentiality was a factor in choosing the two-month expiration rather than a shorter horizon.

2. Black Swan Protection

No matter how much research we do, how many possible scenarios we explore, we simply cannot anticipate every possibility, nor can we fathom just how ferocious a move can be ahead of time. By positioning with options, we can express almost any view while limiting the maximum possible downside to a predefined limit. By employing exotic options, you could go so far as to sell volatility in a currency and still limit your loss to the same amount whether it winds up moving 5% or 150%. In fact, Nassim Taleb concluded from the research that went into his book, *The Black Swan*, that you should build a portfolio exclusively betting on black swan events. Taleb concluded that black swan events were underpriced and you should buy options that express them. Instead, I take his lesson as never sell black swan options, but relying on buying them is not part of my process. You can't predict black swans so never be short them.

As an example, in July 2012, corn had exploded on the back of the 50-year drought. I saw this as an opportunity to express my bearish view on commodities. To simply go short corn at a time when it was in uncharted territory was too risky for my taste. Instead, I went short via put options. By fixing my risk to the premium paid, while allowing me to position for what I believed was a very likely event, I could effectively ride the train without getting run over (i.e., without exposing my portfolio to great risk). As someone who has traded emerging markets for more than 20 years, this approach has served me well during more than a few crises.

There is a huge benefit to this strategy, particularly in this situation, which often goes unnoticed. You see, if I had simply gone short and spot jumped, it is likely that I, like so many others, would have been spooked by the move. In response, I would have been "disciplined" enough to stop out quickly. When it started to come back off, I'd likely have been tempted to reenter, only to be taken out again with another "disciplined" tight stop. By the time it made its big move lower, yes, I probably could have participated, but I'd first have to make up for all the previous little losses before showing a profit. Just as importantly, by using options, I avoided the emotional trauma along the way which allowed me to participate in other opportunities as they presented themselves in the meantime.

3. Expressing Views with Pinpoint Accuracy for Maximum Leverage

Purchasing and selling plain vanilla puts and calls to express a directional view in the underlying is one way to use options, but it isn't where their true power exists. Options are merely an instrument for expressing a view. The simpler your view, the fewer the benefits options offer, and vice versa. Let's say, for instance, you believe EUR/USD is headed lower, but you haven't developed any specific expectations for how much lower, how long it will take for the move to begin, how rapidly it will happen, what will happen to implied volatility if it does, what role interest rates will play, what alternative outcomes might look like, or what the odds of the different scenarios playing out might be. In this case you have a fairly undeveloped view which can be expressed with any number of unsophisticated instruments. However, if you have taken the extra time and effort to fully develop your expectations, options can be a phenomenal tool to help you maximize your return on that investment of time and effort.

Let's take the example of USD/SAR (US dollar versus Saudi Arabian riyal) from back in June 2015. At the time, I put out SAR1, a trade I structured to express my view on the currency pair. I wasn't alone when I got involved, but the structure I chose was very different from those selected by most other market participants. USD/SAR is a pegged currency which explains why it typically trades at a very low implied volatility of roughly 1.0%. Anytime tensions flair up in the region or oil takes a beating, market participants who don't normally play in the currency take notice of the low vol and see it as a "cheap punt," just in case they were to let the peg go. These are the moments guys like me live for, when the uninitiated come to play in our sandbox.

Having seen this happen numerous times over the last 20 years or so I began setting my expectations. First, I was looking to capitalize on what I call the "meaty" part of the trade while ignoring the aspect that would likely become the focus of blogs and research reports catering to the speculators. In other words, I wasn't looking to benefit from the peg breaking, but rather from a modest repricing of that potential event. At the same time, if I could position in such a way that I could also benefit if it didn't break – and even if it broke in the opposite direction of the expectations – then I could put far more capital behind the idea. This last aspect is where my structure differed. Most were playing for the expectation that the Saudi authorities would be forced to let the Riyal devalue. What made the bet particularly appealing was that the implied vols were so low. So, even if the probability of the peg breaking was low, the potential payoff from an explosive move made the position interesting for them. Understanding this point is important, for it lies at the heart of the difference between how I chose to position and how most others did.

If you are betting on an event that has little chance of occurring, you will wisely risk a relatively small amount on the position. Since you are betting a small amount, the only way the trade is worth having is if the potential payoff relative to that bet is very large. Therefore, traders were looking for options that were heavily biased directionally, so they could cheapen the premium as much as possible, thereby creating a highly leveraged position. In order for it to pay off commensurately they needed an explosive move in spot, forwards and/or implied vols. A combination of all three would provide the mother lode. Understandably, most opted for the low delta USD call/SAR put.

Instead of betting a small amount in the hopes of an explosive, low probability event, I sought out a structure where I would be willing to apply a significant amount of capital, but with a high probability of benefitting from a modest repricing of risk and even in the absence of that, at least recouping my premium. I chose to purchase a one-year at-the-money forward straddle. The reason is that the forwards had already increased in price, but the implied vols were still near their lows. That is what made the USD puts an essential part of the trade.

By purchasing the combination of calls and puts, if nothing happened, i.e. the peg remained in place, the carry earned on the USD put was so great, it actually paid for the full straddle premium. Since I was primarily interested in benefiting from an increase in implied volatility (vega), it didn't really matter whether I owned calls or puts. Finally, it was helpful to know that in a previous episode when the Saudi authorities were pressured to devalue, they actually surprised all the speculators by first revaluing, before finally allowing it to devalue. If that were to happen again, it would have proven to be of huge benefit to me, while everyone else would have suffered. By structuring to benefit from the three most likely outcomes, while losing in only the most extremely unlikely event, I could invest a significant amount of capital in the idea. As a result, I only needed a mild repricing to benefit greatly, which is what happened.

In effect, I had combined all three of these reasons to use options into one simple yet elegant solution. The result was a 540 basis point return to the portfolio after just four days in the trade, while avoiding any sleepless nights.

Chapter 16

The Danger of Shortcuts

Blinded by Myopia

Myopia can mean either nearsightedness or a failure of imagination: both definitions apply here. We are blinded by self-enforced closeness to noise and narrative, and an inability to see past it, or outside the prevailing narrative. We look at what is right in front of us and extrapolate. Furthermore, there are many people in the investment industry who encourage us to react to the noise and narrative because that's how they get paid.

Volatility Is in the Eye of the Beholder

I was recently one of seven speakers at a volatility conference. As I prepared, I worried there wouldn't be much to say and figured the other speakers were likely struggling as well. I was wrong. One by one, chief strategists, heads of structuring and risk takers from the sell and buy sides expressed concern over the "structural shift higher in volatility" and provided compelling reasons for the move. The impact of algorithms (algos), poor liquidity, and great uncertainty surrounding central bank policy, not to mention the insatiable and seemingly irrational appetite for risk from the investment community, were chief among them. The charts used to illustrate long-term structural shifts rarely included data prior to two years earlier, and the evidence of the damaging effects of algos showed 20 tick moves in pairs like US Dollar versus Norwegian Kronor in the seconds leading up to the release of non-farm payrolls.

The moderator then asked me about my apparently contentious argument that we are experiencing a moment of extreme risk aversion, especially in light of the points every other panelist had made. I described what it must feel like to be in the Twilight Zone, that perhaps it is a function of my being located in Santa Barbara, where I am not engulfed by the minute-by-minute deluge of news flow, scrolling headlines, and endless array of central bank prognostications that has provided me with a very different take on the current environment.

I did my best to show that besides an impressive multiyear run for equities and evidence of spread compression which has accompanied the collapse in risk-free rates, there was little to support the belief that market participants were exhibiting great risk tolerance. In fact, I argued just about every decision maker of consequence is exhibiting risk-averse behavior. Politicians' willingness to vote against party lines had hit record lows. Rather than investing profits in R&D, infrastructure, and their employees, CEOs were sitting in short-term risk-free assets and returning capital to investors. Although some may have seen the rise in corporate borrowing as evidence of risk tolerance, the fact that the proceeds weren't being invested in the underlying business told me it was still more risk aversion. Hedge fund allocations were up, and some saw that as a sign of risk seeking behavior, but the fact that 93% of those dollars were being invested in funds with AUM over $1 billion, in spite of their relatively poor return profiles, reeked of career-risk aversion among allocators. Finally, the historically low VaR levels among many of those large hedge funds confirmed my view as well.

One of the other panelists respectfully disagreed with my assessment and proceeded to enlighten me. Perhaps I am at a disadvantage being located so far from the action, away from the hustle and bustle of the big trading floor where flow provides significant insight. He noted the increased foreign exchange activity his bank was seeing among multinational corporate clients as evidence that market participants were more risk tolerant. I thanked him for reminding me. You see, when more corporates are hedging foreign exchange exposure, it is proof that risk averse behavior is expanding, not receding. After all, hedging is what you do when you are attempting to reduce risk exposure.

I wrapped up by making the case that much of the perceived volatility of the previous four years had been a function of relatively minor differences between expectations for a particular data point and the actual result, which was then extrapolated out well into the future and typically accompanied by a beautifully woven narrative to explain the discrepancy. So, a disappointing Network Financial Printing (NFP) print became evidence of a failing recovery and incompetent Fed, while a slightly better number proved just how behind the curve the Fed was and the inevitability of wage pressure. Similar disconnects were being witnessed in politics, where relatively minor events were being portrayed as outliers of historic proportions and with global ramifications for generations to come. Take your pick from among the coverage of the Ebola panic to the "socialist" president who had presided over the biggest jump in wealth disparity since the 1920s. What gets lost in a world that has an insatiable appetite for rapid fire content creation and the technology that makes it possible for just about anyone to satisfy that craving, is just how difficult it can be to distinguish between fact and fiction as rapidly as it is delivered to us.

Macro Myopia

In meetings with clients and subscribers when I returned I typically opened with what I had witnessed at the conference and how there seemed to be such a wide divide between the world we were experiencing and the one we were perceiving. I suggested it was likely due to an attempt to use very short-term indicators, many of which I would categorize as noise, in order to create a macro narrative that resonates for us. When the narrative turns out to be fallacious, we carefully select alternative indicators to quickly generate another version, repeating the cycle and thereby creating the sensation of higher volatility and heightened uncertainty.

Surprisingly, almost all portfolio managers very quickly recognized this in themselves. One said, point blank, "I think of myself as a macro trader with a six-month to one-year investment horizon, but if I'm honest, I know I have become something more like a day trader." Half the battle in getting better is admitting you have a problem that you want to solve. Unfortunately, without the other half of the strategy for improvement, knowing what you are doing wrong while continuing to repeat the error only serves to weigh more heavily on you psychologically, making the problem that much worse.

For those of you who can relate, here are my suggestions for getting back on track.

1. Get away from markets, news, screens, the office, and coworkers. Take a step back and think about the world with fresh eyes. Work hard to rid yourself of the bias that has been building for months, and possibly years.

2. See if you can identify the biggest trends since 2011 and what would make it possible for *all* of them to exist at the same time. See if you can figure out why they came to be and what could derail them. Begin by asking questions rather than seeking questions to match your answers. For example, if you can't explain why commodities broke multigenerational ranges early this millennium, you probably should not be participating in those markets today. By default, that should also exclude you from trading emerging markets.

3. Formalize your trading process with investment plans for every trade in your portfolio, something akin to a business plan, but for a trade. Identify the stumbling blocks, the supporting evidence, action items, as well as strengths and weaknesses. Then share that plan with someone you admire. I know of no greater way to avoid impulsive trading than to force this discipline upon yourself.

4. Take the time to analyze the value of every source of information you allow to infect your assessment of the world. Every newsletter, economist, and analyst, even the choice of newspapers, TV stations, and number of screens on your desk should be reviewed. Once they influence your thought process the odds of you overcoming the bias they inject goes down dramatically.

Twitter TV

During an interview I was asked five questions on very different topics, each of which was worthy of a 30-minute discussion (or even an entire book). Unfortunately, I had less than one minute to answer each. As I sat in the green room, I wondered, what value could I deliver in such a short amount of time? Better yet, why would anyone take even five minutes to watch something that provided so little substance? When I asked the host this he told me that traders are very busy, they don't have time to watch in-depth pieces. They will look up from their screens for a couple of minutes if the topic catches their attention, but then quickly return to their screens. "If they find what you have to say interesting, they'll seek you out independently."

In other words, financial market-related television is something akin to a commercial for me, and a teaser for the audience. In order for it to be effective, for me to truly capitalize on this opportunity, I really needed to say something dramatic, perhaps invoke hyperbole, or, better yet, pepper my answers with hashtag worthy terms like *Grexit, systemic,* or *collapse.* That's not really my style, and in fact, because I tend to focus on topics that are not the popular fodder of the moment, and I am often working hard to bring perspective back from the edge of lunacy, I worried that it was a mistake to participate at all.

In reality, much of what we think of as industry-related content is little more than an infomercial dressed up in formal attire. As an example, an investment conference organizer once contacted me about a speaking engagement. Included in the email, he told me how much they charge speakers to be included in the schedule. Did you catch that? Although the organizer pitches the conference as bringing together the best and brightest minds in the business, no thought whatsoever was put into the value of the content or who was delivering it. It is quite simply a pay-to-play scheme, an infomercial. For the record, I would never pay to speak at a conference, whether outright or surreptitiously by becoming an event sponsor. I equate it to purchasing followers on social media.

Postscript

If I'm correct in my assessment that the media, analysts and our own colleagues are driving the wedge between reality and our perception of it, we need to do more to build a defense, even if it's just a minimal hurdle. Perhaps it would be a good exercise to speculate what tomorrow's irrational concern might be today. If it will truly be worthy of our attention tomorrow, we should be able to at least identify it as a possible candidate today. If we can't, that will serve as a first indication that it should probably be treated more like noise than signal.

Odometer Readings and Negative Interest Rates

Back in 2011, researchers gathered data relating to 22 million wholesale used-car auction transactions.[1] Their goal was to see what affect mental heuristics (shortcuts) have on price. In particular, they were curious about whether there is evidence of a particular type of inattention known as "left-digit" bias. In other words, they wanted to know if a car's odometer ticking over to the next big round number had an inordinate impact on the selling price. For example, is there a disproportionate drop in sale prices at 10,000-mile thresholds? Does it matter significantly whether a car has 59,500 miles versus 60,000?

One look at Figure 16.1 and you have your answer. As irrational as it may be to value that one mile between 59,999 and 60,000 so radically different from the one that lies between 60,000 and 60,001, the evidence clearly shows that we do. The reason is that our brains' ability to process information is limited. There is only so much information we can retain in short-term memory for the comparison of data, a mental process that requires both ability and motivation to carry out.

So, in that moment when this information becomes available and we are forced to make a quick decision based upon it, we tend to employ heuristics. Often, the result is a suboptimal decision. In the case of these auto auctions, rational participants, the kind that seem to exist only in the imagination of economists, would purposely avoid purchasing the overpriced cars with odometers that read just below the major thresholds. In turn, that would erase the disproportional drops at those levels and

---

[1] Nicola Lacetera, Devin G. Pope, and Justin R. Sydnor, "Heuristic Thinking and Limited Attention in the Car Market," NBER Working Paper No. 17030, May 2011.

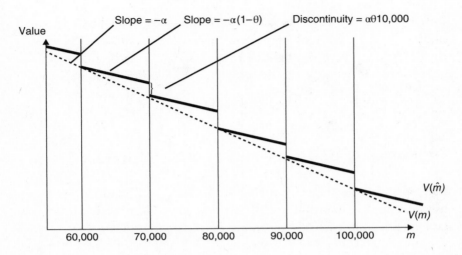

Figure 16.1   Auto odometer and value

you'd have a more efficient market. Alas, we don't, and that creates opportunity for those who can avoid the bias.

When this data is mapped as a value function (Figure 16.2), you can see that although these discontinuities occur, in general, across the full range of odometer readings, mileage has a somewhat linear relationship to value. So, a pattern consistent with rational expectations does emerge.

A similar phenomenon occurred in financial markets on January 29th, 2016. When the Bank of Japan moved policy rates below zero, our brains perceived it to be new territory, similar to the way it treats the turn of an odometer. However, along the continuum of interest paid by a borrower to a lender, the move from +10 basis points (bps) to 0 should be treated no differently than the one from 0 to −10 bps.

After all, the incentive to hold Yen denominated assets is not solely a function of the interest rate earned in Japan, but also of the relative return that can be earned on alternatives as well. A decision to hold one currency is, by default, a simultaneous decision to not own all others. When the Bank of Japan moves its policy rate into negative territory, nothing miraculous occurs as it crosses over that threshold. The interest

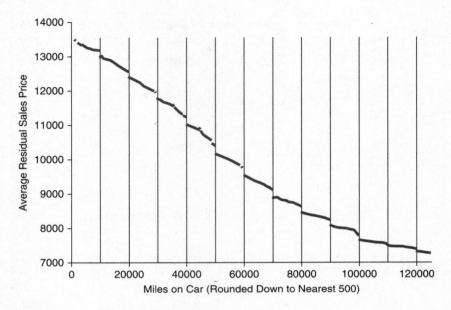

Figure 16.2   Data mapped as a function of value

earned is now 10 bps less than it was on January 28. It's really that simple. If expectations for the future trajectory of interest rates in the United States are simultaneously lowered as well, the net change in incentive to sell JPY and buy USD may be unchanged, or even possibly made less compelling.

Given the evidence produced by studies in behavioral psychology, like the one related to odometer readings, we shouldn't be surprised by the irrational reaction to the announcement of negative rates. The spike higher in USD/JPY was to be expected, and it is further evidence of cognitive bias. Bias, by definition is a systematic error in judgment, meaning it is predictable.

When I entered a trade in US Dollar versus Japanese Yen on January 15, 2016, one of the Reassessment Triggers stated that if USD/JPY were to trade up to 120.00, I would double the capital at risk on the trade through the addition of another one-year 10 delta USD put JPY call. In order for that to occur, JPY would need to weaken by 2.5% from where it was when I first wrote that plan. At the time, I had no idea what would drive it higher, but whatever it might be, I had to know it was unlikely to be supportive of the trade. In other words, at the time that I stated my plan to double up if USDJPY went higher, I was assuming that move would be accompanied by news that would have me questioning my view.

We are all susceptible to irrational behavior, particularly when we must make decisions under emotional duress and/or time constraints. Knowing this, in those moments of lucidity, when we are particularly objective, we should do what we can to help our future selves make better choices when we are most likely to be vulnerable.

Anchored to Missed Opportunities

As I've said repeatedly, we humans are prone to decision-making mistakes and it's those mistakes that make it possible for skill to exist in our industry. Remove all decisional mistakes made by market participants and your investment performance will be determined purely by chance. Ipso facto, the only way to generate true alpha is to capitalize on the mistakes of others.

To review, decision theory is the field of study that focuses on decision-making, and it is broken into two main categories, normative and descriptive. Normative decision theory is the study of how we *should* make decisions. It is objective, systematic, and unemotional. It relies heavily on statistical analysis and requires an understanding of probabilities. Descriptive decision theory, on the hand, is the study of how we *actually* make decisions.

There are times when a decision will fall under the domain of both, typically occurring when we are dealing with what is known as a "decision under certainty." For instance, when faced with the decision about whether we should touch a stove that is red hot, assuming we do not want to burn our hands, very often we will *actually* make the decision as we *should*. In our business, it is extremely rare to face a decision under certainty. Instead, we must make "decisions under risk," which means we have historical data from which to generate probabilities of future outcomes. This is the type of decision we face when forecasting weather, predicting demand for electricity, producing mpg estimates for new cars, and making investment decisions.

What separates a decision made descriptively from one made norma-
tively can only be described as a mistake. Cognitive scientists prefer the
term, *cognitive bias*, but whichever term you choose, they both reflect
systematic errors in judgment, and they tend to occur when we are
employing heuristics. Once again, heuristics are mental shortcuts, such
as intuition, gut feel, and rules of thumb. One of the more commonly
employed heuristics is known as *anchoring*.

Anchoring is a popular phenomenon among retailers and negotiators. For the retailer, it provides a simple, inexpensive way to manipulate
customers into spending more. As an example, they will create an
anchor by first showing something like an MSRP (manufacturer's
suggested retail price), and then emphasize how far below that price
they are willing to sell it to you. In reality, the MSRP is completely
arbitrary, created merely to set an anchor by which all transactions will
be compared. It is how some people can actually think of shopping in
terms of money saved as opposed to money spent. Good negotiators will
often present the first offer, knowing that all discussions from that point
forward will be anchored to it, and *we rarely adjust very much away from it.*

Anchoring can be powerful in far more subtle ways too. Tversky
and Kahneman first exposed the effect in a study 42 years ago, when
they asked people to estimate "how many African nations are part
of the United Nations?" To test the anchoring effect, they first had
participants spin a wheel with 100 numbers painted on it. Unbe-
knownst to participants, the wheel was rigged to land on either 10
or 65. Although you would think that the random number generated
by spinning a wheel would have no effect whatsoever on someone's
estimate regarding how many African nations are part of the United
Nations, you'd be wrong.

There is a simple formula to quantify the anchoring effect called
the *anchoring index*. To calculate it, you take the difference in the mean
response from each group and divide it by the difference between the
high and low anchors. In the case of Tversky and Kahneman's experiment, the average answer from those who had the low anchor of 10 was
25, whereas the average for those who were anchored to 65 was 45 – an
anchoring index of 36%.

The anchoring effect is evidence of a *systematic* error in judgment. Given that mistakes are required in order for skill to present itself in investing, we should be using the information gleaned from 60-plus years of research that effectively presents a roadmap of psychological vulnerability to predictably irrational decisions. What makes it difficult to create a competitive edge in this area is that we are all inherently vulnerable. No matter how intelligent, experienced, or even educated we may be specifically in this area, we are all susceptible to both making the mistakes, and even more importantly, being oblivious to the error as it's occurring. The only real defense against it is a willingness to accept just how powerful the effect can be and an openness to allow the evidence to override even the most deeply seated belief.

The reason I mention this right now is because I believe there is a bias being exhibited by even the smartest, most highly educated, experienced, and respected people in the investment and policymaking communities today (This section was written when the Fed maintained its policy of zero interest rates and quantitative easing). It is a mistake caused by the anchoring effect, and true to form, no one seems to be acknowledging its existence or even contemplating the possibility that something could be amiss. The mistake occurs in the belief that *zero* means something as it relates to interest rates, that it is, in effect, a *floor*, below which it should never go, and if it does, it should go for only a very short time and by a very tiny amount.

This belief is equivalent to an MSRP of markets, unsupported by economic fundamentals or market principles. Yet, so much of what is happening in monetary policy and investment management is being affected by it. If you believe the risk/reward of holding US Treasuries is unattractive here, there's a good chance you're experiencing the anchoring effect. If you believe interest rates are too low, you might be experiencing the anchoring effect. If you believe *low* interest rates didn't work so we might as well raise them, you are probably experiencing the anchoring effect. If you believe there isn't plenty of powder left in monetary policy, you might be exhibiting the anchoring effect. If it makes you feel any better, nearly every central banker and economist is making the same mistake.

What gets lost in conversations about Fed policy is the fact that the Federal Reserve, for all intents and purposes, is in the business of behavior modification. Every tool, from open market operations to the discount rate and even quantitative easing, is meant to alter the behavior patterns of its target audience. Although their mandate is tied to inflation and growth, how they achieve it depends on their ability to alter behaviors. Effectively, they stand as the floodgate between financial assets and the real economy. If too much capital is being invested in the real economy, threatening to push inflation higher than their goal, they will raise the interest rate offered on risk-free investments, effectively saying, "why take risk when you can earn attractive returns without it?" On the other hand, when not enough capital is finding its way into the real economy, threatening growth and/or inflation below the lower end of the targeted range, they will lower the incentive offered to sit in risk-free assets. In essence, saying, "you will have to take some risk if you are going to achieve the returns you seek."

If they aren't getting the responses they want, they just go lower, and lower, and lower. Why should zero be the floor? Why can't the risk-free rate go as deep into negative territory as it does into positive?

When it is deep in positive territory, it serves to shift capital from the public sector to the private. If owners of capital are deep in risk-seeking mode, it will require very high rates to draw them away from the riskier alternatives. On the other hand, if investors are exhibiting extremely risk-averse behavior, as we are currently witnessing, then it will require very low rates to push them to take risk. If it requires rates so low that they enter very negative territory to force that action, it will also begin shifting capital from the private to the public sector, thereby rebalancing the imbalance created by the massive bailouts. That too would serve to move policymakers closer to where they want to be, wouldn't it?

You see, the fundamental issue is that capital continues to flow out of the hands of spenders and into those of the savers. Thanks to income and wealth disparity, every transaction that occurs in the real economy lowers the probability of a future transaction (see the trajectory of the velocity of money, Figure 16.3), while simultaneously increasing the demand for financial assets. Those who control the overwhelming majority of the world's wealth are exhibiting extreme levels of risk aversion – yes, even at

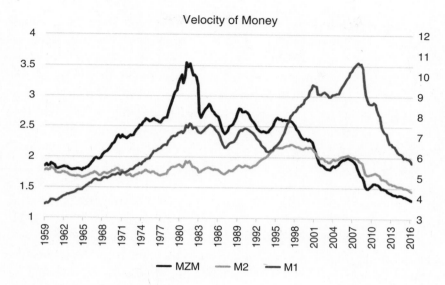

Figure 16.3 Velocity of money

zero or negative rates. If they won't start spending more of their income, and it's highly unlikely they will (or even can), then policymakers need to push them in that direction. They have two tools to do so. Either they can raise taxes and redistribute that capital through fiscal spending, or they move interest rates deep into negative territory. In so doing, savers will transfer capital to the government, and then the government can redistribute it through fiscal spending into the hands of spenders.

The old argument that negative interest rates are "unsustainable" is true. Eventually, if the owners of capital don't shift out of financial assets and into the real economy, either by spending or investing in R&D, equipment, and/or people, they will run out of capital. But let's be logical about that. At −50 bps, assuming 100% of the private sector's funds were invested, it would take 200 years for that to occur. At −5%, it would take 20 years. Of course, by that time, we wouldn't be talking about onerous government debt overhang anymore.

Getting back to the specific issue of zero as an anchor, rather than a valid discrete moment, consider the marginal impact on an investment portfolio. If interest rates shift down 100 bps, from +250 bps to +150 bps, the annual return on a $100 million portfolio will be $1,000,000 less.

If interest rates shift down 100 bps, from +50 bps to −50 bps, the annual return on a $100 million portfolio will be $1,000,000 less. Yes, the marginal change is exactly the same.

On a related note, someone once mentioned that one of the major stock market indices had been on a multiyear run that has never occurred before. As a result, he was considering going short the index. This is a cognitive mistake that should be easily refuted with a simple statistical analysis. However, the argument rarely changes anyone's mind. Nonetheless, I felt compelled to make the case.

At the time of the analysis, since October 1959, the DAX index had experienced 671 rolling 12-month periods, of which 62% had been positive. The DAX index had been positive for the previous four calendar years. Throughout its history we've only seen the DAX up five years straight 8% of the time. One might leap to the conclusion that based on historical results there was a 92% chance that the DAX index would be negative that year. However, they'd be wrong.

You see, the hard part of a five-year run had already occurred. The DAX had only had four straight up years 13% of the time. In this case though, the odds of the DAX being up four years straight was 100%. I can say that because it had actually happened. Now you might think that it makes the odds of it continuing to extend another year a long shot, but statistically speaking that is incorrect. You see, historically speaking, the odds of the DAX index ending a 12-month period higher than it began was 62%, even after four straight positive years. The consistency of the return profile is quite remarkable. See Table 16.1 for a comparison between the actual percentage of times the index had experienced different winning streaks versus what the expectations would be if every single year was a constant 62%.

What I'm saying is, based on historical data, the odds of the DAX index being up that year, given that it had been up the past four straight calendar years, remained 62%. That's what a machine would tell you. The question is, would you listen?

Table 16.1   Actual versus predicted percentages of DAX winning streak

	1 Year	2 Years	3 Years	4 Years	5 Years
Actual	62%	39%	22%	13%	8%
Predicted	62%	39%	24%	15%	9%

Chapter 17

The Power of the Unexpected

Unconscious Influence

Over the years I must have given well over a hundred talks touching on the subject of cognitive bias in some way. The residual effect is that anytime something comes up in the news where it appears that someone has fallen prey to it, but doesn't realize it, an article will be forwarded on to me along with the caption, "Thought you'd enjoy this one." What makes this topic so fascinating to me is the "but doesn't realize it" aspect. A subscriber once remarked to me, "I understand most of what you write about. *For me,* it's intuitive."

This belief that "it doesn't apply to me," is a fundamental aspect of the phenomenon. It's right there in the very definition of cognitive bias. An *unconscious influence* that produces systematic errors in judgment.

Here's an example of cognitive bias at work. On October 25, 2016, a conference organizer sent me a link to an article about a man who had developed a model for predicting the winner of the US presidential elections, along with the following commentary: "gotta love his quote!

=> 'The model predicted a Trump win in February and nothing has changed since then. **Whatever happens in the real world doesn't affect the model**,' he said." (Emphasis is the sender's.)

At the time he sent the email it appeared to most that Clinton's victory was all but guaranteed. To the person who sent it to me it seemed ludicrous that the prognosticator mentioned in the article that he wasn't updating his model as new information was being gathered. He shared it with me because he felt it served as a prime example of someone exhibiting flawed decision-making.

The question is this: For what reason should the model have been updated? This same model had been covered by the press ad nauseam when Trump first won the GOP nomination. At that time it was crystal clear that the model had accurately predicted the winner in all but one presidential election going back to 1912, and it had done so without gathering additional data after the primaries. If there was a flaw in ignoring postprimary data, it should have been pointed out back then, but it wasn't. However, because his model had predicted a Trump victory, and the latest polls had swung so far in the opposite direction, his model suddenly appeared deficient and his defense of it categorized as absurd.

Changing his model to reflect the latest polls or anything else simply because someone, even everyone, deems it worthy of inclusion, would be a mistake. However, this is what is done all the time in our industry. We develop a process and then adjust, amend and contort it in the moment to accommodate the latest unemployment data, the most recent central banker quote selected by news sources and whatever else happens to make its way into our line of sight. Without even recognizing it, we undermine the process, converting it into an inconsistent mess, all while rationalizing our irrational behavior. That is what happened to the conference organizer. He was swayed by the latest polls, and mocked the prognosticator who had done his research and developed a model backed by data-driven evidence. Without even realizing it, it was the conference organizer who was exhibiting cognitive bias, *he* was making the mistake, but most importantly, he had no idea it was happening.

My response at the time was, "I have some real sympathy for his argument. His model is based on certain factors, what he defines as 'signal.'

Everything after the primaries is effectively 'noise,' according to his model. There is no reason for him to make adjustments, regardless of how wrong it may *feel* in the moment. The historical returns on the model, which is designed to ignore this updated data, are very good. If the model doesn't make sense now, then it didn't make sense when everyone was first quoting it. If they didn't call it out as nonsense back then, they shouldn't be calling questioning it now. Those who are, are the ones exhibiting cognitive bias."

Ready, Fire, Aim

On LinkedIn, I posted the Monty Hall Problem. The post reads:

> The host begins by unveiling 3 numbered doors & explains that behind one of the doors is a brand new car, while the other 2 each contain a goat. The contestant selects a door gets to keep whatever is behind it. After the initial selection is made, the host opens 1 of the remaining doors to reveal 1 of the goats. The contestant may then change their selection.
> Q: Should the contestant switch to the other unopened door?
> A: Although most people intuitively and confidently answer, "it doesn't make a difference," the only rational answer is, YES!

This response came from a Harvard MBA with more than 30 years of experience in finance:

> This "analysis" is total BS. The host knows where the two goats and the car are. No matter which door the contestant picks, the host will reveal a goat behind an unpicked door. At this point – which is when the contestant makes the switch/no switch decision – one unopened door has a car and one a goat. There is an equal probability of the car being behind either door and the contestant has a 50% chance of winning by staying with his original pick and a 50% chance of winning by changing. There is no advantage (or disadvantage) to changing picks. This isn't foolish intuition, it's REAL decision science. You should refund your fees if you are charging clients for the nonsense presented here.

In other words, a smart, highly educated, experienced and successful person had not only made a mistake, he was absolutely certain his logic was correct. His intuition was so powerful, not only didn't he hesitate to correct me, he chose to publicly chastise me as well.

I shared his response with my students because it serves as powerful evidence of the "unconscious" aspect of cognitive bias. We just don't know it's happening to us. My students seemed more excited to read my response, though. "Oh I bet you ripped him to shreds, didn't you?" one student said out loud. I did not. The reason is, every one of us makes mistakes like this all the time, and we are equally unaware and equally confident in our intuition. (As you recall, it's a lesson my mother-in-law taught me years earlier.)

I responded:

You're not the first to vehemently oppose the solution. When the problem and solution were first published (back in 1975 not by me) it created quite the stir among some of the best minds in mathematics. In the end, those who initially argued your conclusion came around when they realized the flaw in their argument. I understand your frustration. It's the nature of dealing with cognitive bias. It's almost impossible to see it in ourselves, particularly when our intuition is so incredibly convinced it is correct, which is clearly the case for you here. And understandably so.

To which he responded:

I looked into this further and I am wrong. It was NOT my intuition; it was an error in my analysis. What I missed is that there is POSSIBLE new information in the door selected by the host. When the host selects a goat door to reveal, it may be the case that he must select that door because the car is behind the other door. Switching improves your chances of being right because you leverage this possible new information. Not to shoot the messenger, but I think if you explained the problem the way I just did it would persuade more non-STEM types that you are correct!

I give him credit for taking a moment to look into it further (even if it did come *after* his initial comment). However, he missed the point. It is not my job to properly frame the information for him. In the real world, *you* are responsible for taking in data, commentary, and every other form of information, and then processing that information in a way that delivers an accurate representation of the world. Unfortunately, that information is often framed in a manner that is purposely designed to trigger cognitive bias. It is actually meant to trigger an emotional response or to lower your defenses. In the preceding case, I provided all the information necessary to properly solve the problem. To blame me for his error is like blaming the newscaster or the analyst for our inability to properly assess the macro environment.

Another person chimed in as well:

It can be made clear even to the intuition if you increase the number of doors (and hence the information gained from the host's choice).

So if there are 100 doors and you pick door 23, then the host opens all other doors except 23 and 96, it should be clear intuitively that it is more likely to be behind door 96 than 23.

He too may be correct, but it's important to understand that what appeals to one person's intuition doesn't necessarily appeal to everyone's. The better we understand how we intuitively approach problems based on our history and education, and the more we challenge that intuition to see beyond what automatically comes to our mind, the further we can expand the "box" within which we make all decisions. My goal in sharing the problem was not to teach someone how to solve this one problem, but to show that we are all vulnerable to decision-making mistakes, even smart, educated people and even on relatively simple problems. In order to improve our decision-making skills, this must not only be understood conceptually but also experienced first hand. Only then can a decision-maker experience a leap forward in the evolution of their decision making. In other words, only after you realize that it doesn't matter how many books you read on cognitive bias or how many biases and heuristics you can name off the top of your head, you will still be vulnerable to these types of mistakes. Only then can real progress be achieved.

The Importance of Identifying What Is Beyond Your Control

In normative decision-making, after the outcome is properly defined, the decision-maker must identify the factors that influence the outcome, but which they do not control. In decision theory, these factors are known as *states,* but in the business of investing, we call them *signals.* Regardless of what term we use to describe them, this step may be the most important part of the decision-making process for investors. It also happens to be the step that is most often glossed over. The combination of it being so vital to the investment process while being so commonly overlooked or summarily dealt with by investors is why the machines are targeting it, and if you want to create a distinct competitive edge, so should you.

Problems most often occur when the distinction between noise and signal is made on gut feel and intuition rather than on data and evidence. When noise is mischaracterized as signal it increases the probability that we will not dig deep enough to find the factors that actually matter, and by that I mean, the ones that offer predictive value. When we are watching the wrong factors, the ones that don't offer predictive value, it creates confusion and uncertainty. Things feel like they don't make sense. More often than not though, the world does makes sense, it's just that we haven't properly framed it. The narrative is flawed. Let's explore this concept with a few examples from the real world.

The Real Reason Commodities Collapsed

> *The key to good decision making is not knowledge. It is understanding. We are swimming in the former. We are desperately lacking in the latter.*
> —*Malcolm Gladwell,* Blink

Since 2011, I have been writing and trading my view that the trigger behind the spike in commodity prices that began early this millennium had reversed, and would result not just in a return to the old ranges, but also likely to the lower end of them, and probably for an extended period.

Let's begin by looking at the selection of long-term charts shown in Figure 17.1.

No matter which commodity chart you choose, they all look very similar. Each exhibits extended periods in which a clearly defined range held, until something happened around the millennium. If we are going to discuss where commodities are headed from here it would be absurd to do so without first addressing what it was that caused them all to *simultaneously* break out to the upside. In other words, we must identify the key factor(s) that caused the explosive outcome. If we can define those states, and they remain in place, then the odds of reverting to the old, long-run mean are small. However, if those states have reverted back, then it's very likely prices will too.

Back in 2002, China was *suddenly* becoming the most talked about topic among investors, pundits, and politicians. What I couldn't figure out was why. So I asked. Almost unanimously, the answer I heard was, "They have two billion people." Not only was the response factually incorrect (it was closer to 1.2 billion), it also didn't make sense. With a population growth rate of just 0.65% per year, in 2002, China's population represented 19% of the world total. That was down 14% since the institution of the One-Child Policy. Based solely on overall population, China actually mattered less than it had at any other time in modern history, so that could not explain why everyone was suddenly talking about it. If I could understand what factors caused us to talk about it, it might shed some light on why it might affect supply, demand, and market pricing, not to mention future growth and policy action.

What Happened and Why It Was So Powerful

In 1996, without any warning or global policy debate, and certainly void of any fanfare, China began orchestrating the biggest urbanization project in the history of mankind. In 1996, they moved 22 million people from rural to urban areas. To put that in perspective, 22 million is more

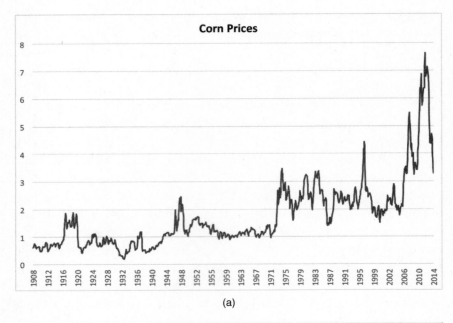

(a)

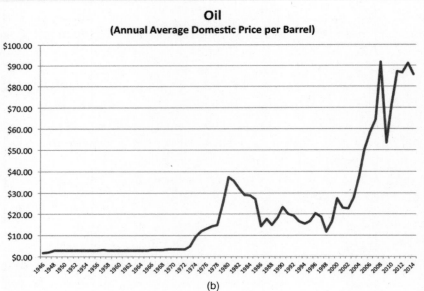

(b)

Figure 17.1 Long-term commodity charts

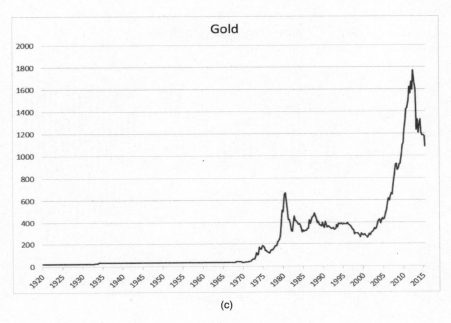

(c)

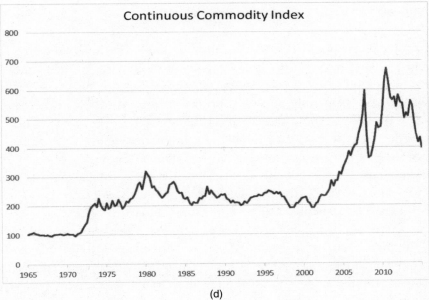

(d)

Figure 17.1   (*Continued*)

Figure 17.2   China's urbanization project

than the entire population of Manhattan, London, Paris, Sydney, Berlin, and Stockholm *combined*. Now, imagine all those cities being empty at the beginning of a year, then completely full by the end. That's essentially what began happening in 1996, and has continued unabated *every year* since (Figure 17.2). How is it comparable? Well, the urbanization of a country like China is like population growth on steroids. In essence, people go from being economically invisible to the rest of the world, to suddenly competing for jobs, raw materials, and food on a global scale. The fact is, city dwellers live dramatically different than their rural counterparts, particularly those from rural China.

They live in smaller groups, use four times more electricity, earn more money, and have greater expenses. They even eat differently, consuming far more sugary foods, more meat, and, importantly, they no longer produce it themselves (Figure 17.3). (Fun Fact: Cows are seven times less efficient at converting corn into calories than people are. That means when someone stops eating corn and instead chooses to consume beef, they actually create seven times more demand for corn.) Urban Chinese also have far more disposable income (Figure 17.4).

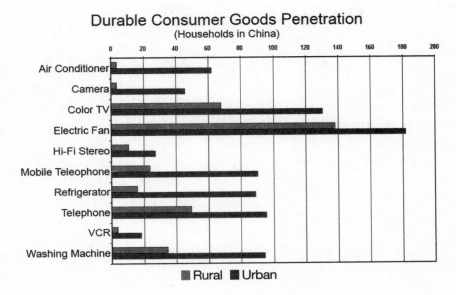

Figure 17.3   Durable consumer goods penetration in China

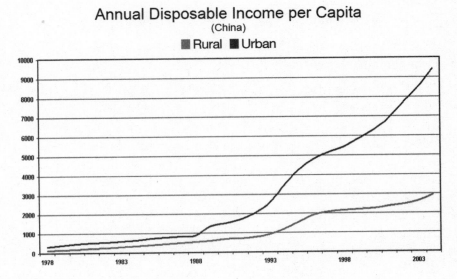

Figure 17.4   Annual disposable income per capita in China

Urbanization of this magnitude, and the industrialization that accompanies it, leads to a spike in demand for raw materials and food. It always has. Think America, England, Rome, Greece, Egypt. The difference this time around is that the demand wasn't satisfied through colonization and theft. This time, those who produce what was in demand – namely the tropical emerging markets, were paid fair value for what the world needed. As a direct result, it was the first time in history they had the opportunity to become as wealthy as their temperate counterparts. (The temperate emerging markets were simultaneously hampered because their competitive edge, primarily cheap labor, was facing serious competition from China's outsized supply of the same.)

However, even when talking about a country as massive as China, urbanization has a finite life. In 1996, 30% of China's 1.2 billion citizens were urbanites. Meanwhile, almost every developed nation was and is 85% urbanized. When economists finally picked up on what was happening, China had reached as high as 50%, which means another 540 million people would still need to come online before they too hit that magic 85% level. Therefore, these economists and analysts came to the conclusion that commodity prices would not only remain high, they would probably continue rising.

They Were Wrong for Two Reasons

The first flaw in their assessment is that in order to bring people online, someone has to pay for it. The incredible expansion of credit fueled by the combination of low interest rates, financial innovation, and irrational exuberance funded it for many years, but it couldn't go on forever.

The second fly in the ointment was, well, math. When you consistently increase the denominator (total urban population) by adding 22 million to it each year, each additional 22 million will have a gradually declining effect on the year-on-year growth rate (Figure 17.5b). Figure 17.5a, however, shows that although the Chinese authorities did what they could to prop things up during the crisis, the notional increase has also begun slowing from the steady pace of 22 million per year to 18 million in 2014. So, in this case, the numerator has also been getting

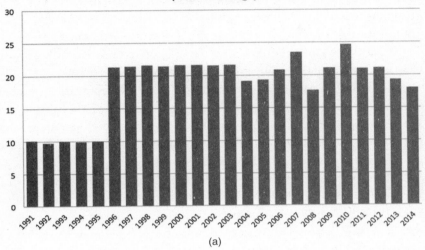

(a)

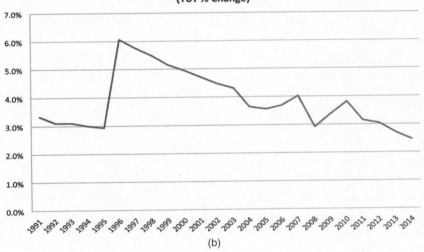

(b)

Figure 17.5   China's urban population

smaller, and the result is that the growth rate fell to pre-orchestration levels just as the crisis hit (by pure coincidence), and after the brief propping up by the powers that be, is now well below it, and going lower.

Who cares, right? I mean, they're still urbanizing 18 million every year and another 500 million plus are waiting in the wings.

Well, as it is with almost everything, it isn't the notional increase in population that matters, it's the year-on-year growth rate. Take a look at Figure 17.6, charts from England in the 1800s showing the relationship between notional population growth and prices, and the population growth rate and prices, to see what I mean.

That's why it doesn't really matter that China is only 50% urbanized and that another 540 million are waiting in the wings to come online. Both flaws have become exposed.

That's the bad news for commodities, but it is actually far, far worse than demand growth simply receding back to long-run averages.

Although everyone knows demand can affect commodity prices, the power of the demand side is almost always discounted, particularly

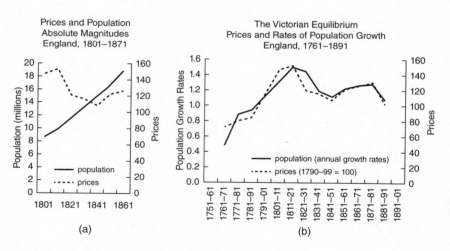

Figure 17.6   Price and population in Victorian England

by the commodity experts. There's good reason for that too. Demand shocks don't tend to last very long, which is why producers were so slow to respond to the spike in demand this time around. However, when it became clear that higher prices were here to stay (or at least it seemed that way), the supply side kicked into high gear on a number of very impactful fronts.

It began by drawing down on stock. Then the spigots were opened, which sparked concern that demand would soon overwhelm even potential supply. (Remember all those peak oil papers?) Well, although many think tanks and even practitioners think these things occur in a vacuum, they do not. When projections of radical shortfalls gain traction, opportunists rush in to capitalize on the void that is predicted to develop. With oil over $60, then $80, and even $100, the money for exploration poured in and the peak oil theory quickly petered out, even if its proponents still aren't willing to admit it (Figure 17.7).

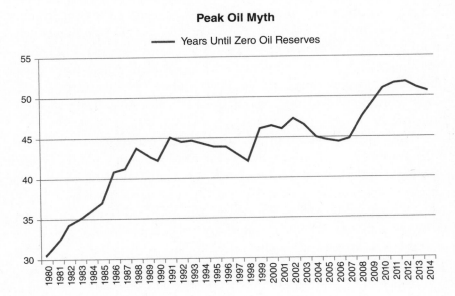

Figure 17.7   Peak oil

Investment also went toward devising ways to reduce future demand. As the price of gasoline spiked, consumers shifted away from their SUV monstrosities toward more fuel-efficient alternatives like the Prius and Tesla. Manufacturers responded and fuel efficiency has spiked over this period.

However, the real impact has yet to be truly realized. What Figure 17.8 shows is the average miles per gallon achieved by models released in a given year. It ignores the fact that not every car on the road is brand new. In the United States, the average lightweight vehicle is 11 years old. So, the average mpg for cars on American roads is something more akin to the chart on the right. Meaning, demand is only now about to show the true impact of the efficiency gains we've achieved over the past decade.

Fuel efficiency of the cars on our roads hardly scratches the surface of what has been gained since the commodity boom began. GMOs, mining technologies, newly discovered oil reserves, and the technology that made it possible – wind, solar, and Tesla's new batteries – are but a few of the many improvements already made on the supply side, with many more sure to follow, which will continue putting downward pressure on commodity prices. Add to that concerns over global warming and other environmental drivers pushing for greater efficiency, recycling and upcycling, and you have additional downward pressure coming from the demand side of the equation, possibly for generations to come.

The bottom line is this. Without the orchestration of the biggest urbanization project in the history of mankind, commodities would not have exploded out of their long run ranges. With the impact of that event having run its course, you could argue that we should simply go back to the well-worn ranges that preceded the boom. However, even though the direct impact of urbanization is now over, the aftershock of its secondary effects will remain with us for a long time to come.

As a result, I expect commodity markets to continue performing similarly to how they did in previous periods of urbanization of this magnitude. In other words, lower for longer.

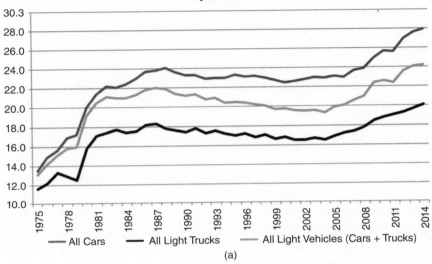

(a)

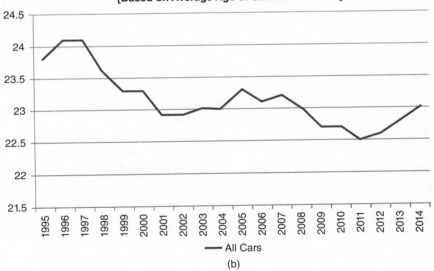

(b)

Figure 17.8   Production–weighted average miles per gallon

Slower Is Faster

Every once in a while someone will question whether my investment process isn't too confining. There is no doubt that limiting us to trades that have a self-liquidating feature (i.e. defined downside), requiring that we adhere to predefined take profits, having to take the time to pre-script trades, and sticking strictly to only the most liquid markets and instruments, curtails our opportunity set. The question is whether it is too restrictive.

If you distill the job of an investor down to its essence, it is to predict the future. No matter how artificial our intelligence or learned our machines become, predicting the future will always involve uncertainty. Our objective then is to improve our predictive abilities, to nudge the odds of a successful prediction in our favor. As it relates to the restrictive decision-making process prescribed in this book, the idea is rather simple. The opportunity set that remains when these restrictions are in place is somewhat positively skewed. That means, all else being equal, including the portfolio manager's skills and the market environment, the odds of putting on a winning trade are slightly better than that of a losing trade. Conversely, the odds, when selecting from outside the restricted zone, are negatively skewed. It's important to acknowledge up front then that there will be trades that make it through the barriers yet won't be profitable. Conversely, there will be some winning trades that won't pass muster. In other words, they will be *right* but not *rational*.

Try this analogy, from Mark Buchanan's *The Social Atom*:

> A crowd rushing to the exit piles up in a traffic jam, whereas people avoid the jam and get out if they move more slowly. As Helbing puts it, "Slower is faster." But now for a bigger surprise. A room might obviously have some tables in it. How would their placement and size affect the escape of a crowd? It seems obvious that obstacles have to make the situation even worse. Yet, counterintuitively, they can be quite beneficial. In particular, a table placed a few feet in front of the exit can help regulate the human flow. The table changes the pattern of self-organization, helping everyone get out more quickly.

The self-imposed restrictions embedded in the investment process prescribed in *AlphaBrain* are very similar in nature to the tables strategically placed in front of the exits in Buchanan's experiment. For those who are impulsively inclined, obstacles of any kind can feel confining, even dangerous at times. Once again, Phil Jackson (the highly successful long time NBA coach) offers some relevant words of wisdom. "Inevitably, paradoxically, the acceptance of boundaries and limits is the gateway to freedom."

Everyone is vulnerable to cognitive bias and heuristics. Some may be intuitively better at avoiding some forms or others, but no one is immune. There is no magic bullet to decision-making, no matter how badly people want one. The keys are incremental improvement and fewer mistakes — two skills that can be built with time, awareness, and practice. It sounds simple. In fact, it *is* simple. But it's also incredibly difficult. This is an individual process, and it takes real self-analysis, grounded in data. At its core improved decision-making comes from a normative decision-making process, one that is planned ahead of time with minimal influence from emotion and cognitive bias. The difficulty comes from the discipline required to follow through with that plan. The art of decision-making comes when you practice discipline but resist the urge to be dogmatic and inflexible.

This doesn't mean you should allow yourself to become reactionary. In order to thrive we create as beneficial an environment as possible, and then invite cognitive strain. This approach is diametrically opposed to reacting in the moment while experiencing cognitive stress.

Be clear in your goal and in what you cannot sensibly change. Accept your states; do not deny them or try to change them. Dig through noise, emotion, and distraction to focus on what matters and why. Consider that external forces can apply pressure as well. Many industry-wide standards of risk management are not helpful to good investing, and many firms are set up poorly. These, too, are states that you must manage and adjust to.

As investors, our task is clear-cut: Create a trading plan in advance and do not deviate from it, without very good cause. Write it down. Clearly include your rationale, states that impact your trading, your stop loss, your take profit, your size-up and size-down reassessment triggers. Write down other triggers that would challenge your rationale. Most important, write down what your exit was and do a postmortem on the reasons that led you there so you can apply what you learn to the next trade.

The world around us is set up to use our cognitive biases against us, but developing a decision-making process based on increased awareness can help us find our way to profitable trades or a clearer everyday experience.

Index

275

E

Earnings announcement, 106
Easy money, 231–233
Eat, Drink and Be Healthy (Willett), 99
Economics, problem, 113
Education, waste, 111–112
Efficiency, maximization, 61, 189
Efforts, minimization, 30–31
Elway, John, 186
Emerging market trading, local advantage, 72–73
Emotional triggers, 197
Emotion, factor, 59
Employee information, 60
Endowments, 105
Engaged reading, 78–79
Equities, pricing, 89
European digital call option, sale, 235
Europe, sovereign spreads, 230
Exotic options, usage, 237–238
Expected returns, maximization, 130
Eyedropper (Photoshop), usage, 29

F

Fair trial, occurrence, 26–27
"Fascinating Story Behind Why So Many Nail Technicians Are Vietnamese," 73–74
Fear, confrontation (power), 187–190
Fed meeting dates, 230
Fee income, expenses (ratio), 140
Ferentz, Kirk, 16, 17
Financial resources, usage, 93
FinTech, 107, 109–110, 178, 179
Floor, 241
Fooled by Randomness (Taleb), 70

Foreign exchange exposure, hedging, 243
Fox, John, 186
Fuel efficiency, 270
Full expected returns, decision tree, 218f
Full-text reports, substitute, 87
Function, value, 248f
Fund of funds, 105
Fungibility, law, 116

G

Gains, segregation, 120
"Garbage in, garbage out," 56, 77, 109
Gates, Bill (Gates Foundation), 81–82
Geeks, involvement, 22
Genius, 141–144
Gladwell, Malcolm, 260
Global macro hedge fund, allocation, 212, 215
Goldman Sachs, 45
Golf, 141–144
Gostkowski, Stephen, 17
Government debt overhang, 253
Gruden, Jon, 186
Guardiola, Pep, 17, 20
Guilt, probability, 27
Guilt threshold verdict, 26f

H

Halo effect, 77–78
Handicapping, 69–70
Headlines, functions, 86–87
Health, listicles (impact), 85–87
Hedge fund, 215
    bad years, decision tree, 216f–217f

correlation, determination, 79
expected return, 217
portfolio manager action,
153–156, 168
proliferation, 133–134
Hedge notional, 106–107
Hedge size, determination, 106
Hedonic framing, 119–120
Hero pose, 181–182
Heuer, Richards, 69–70
Heuristics, 48, 55–59, 61, 73, 76, 250
Hexadecimal code, 30f
Hindsight, 34–35
Hippocratic Oath, 152
Holmes, Holly, 175

I

Idiot America (Pierce), 87
Illusory invulnerability, 107–109
Implied volatility, 233
Inefficiencies, creation, 116
Information, 72–73, 76–77, 80–84,
87–90
collection, ability, 68
consumption, dieting (impact),
97–100
misinformation, source, 100
provision, 100
source, value (analysis), 244
Input paradox, 101
Interest rates, 246–249, 253–254
Investing, sports (contrast), 132
Investment, 129t, 137, 157–158,
200–201, 205
complexity, 53–54
funds, ranking, 36f
horizon, 244

management, 35, 37, 125
performance, systematic
adjustments (presence/absence),
168t
plan, usage, 244
return, maximization, 239
slowness, advantage, 272–274
time horizon, 225
Investors, options (usage), 236–240
Irrational behavior, 190, 256
Irrational decisions, 35, 116, 251

J

Japanese Yen (JPY), trade, 227–229
Jones, Paul Tudor, 231, 235
Judgment, systematic errors,
167–169, 251
"Judgment under Uncertainty"
(Tversky/Kahneman), 70–71

K

K-12 education, problems, 81
Kahneman, Daniel, 47, 70, 76, 83,
113, 223–224, 250
Kidney/ureter cancer, US death
rates, 93f
Kiffin, Lane, 174
Kim, Junyong, 5
King, Andrew, 144
Knapp, Greg, 39
Knowledge, limits, 77

L

Learning process, creation, 166
Left-digit bias, 246
Leverage, 236, 238–240
Licensing effect, 108